D1587204

REASON & INTUITION
AND OTHER ESSAYS

REASON & INTUITION

AND OTHER ESSAYS

BY

J. L. STOCKS

Late Vice-Chancellor of the
University of Liverpool

EDITED WITH

AN INTRODUCTION BY

DOROTHY M. EMMET

Lecturer in the Philosophy of Religion
in the University of Manchester

IOWA STATE AMES IA COLLEGE LIBRARY

OXFORD UNIVERSITY PRESS
LONDON NEW YORK TORONTO
1939

OXFORD UNIVERSITY PRESS
AMEN HOUSE, E.C. 4
London Edinburgh Glasgow New York
Toronto Melbourne Capetown Bombay
Calcutta Madras
HUMPHREY MILFORD
PUBLISHER TO THE UNIVERSITY

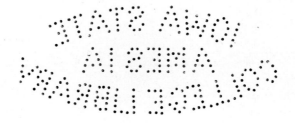

PRINTED IN GREAT BRITAIN

B1667
S28
R4
1939

ACKNOWLEDGEMENTS

ACKNOWLEDGEMENTS are due to the editors of *The Hibbert Journal, Philosophy*, the *Proceedings of the Aristotelian Society*, and the *Social Service Review* for permission to reprint certain of the papers in this volume; also to the Manchester University Press for *Jeremy Bentham*, originally given and published as the Sir Samuel Hall Oration for 1933; to Mr. Gilbert Ryle for *The Empiricism of J. S. Mill*, from the *Proceedings of the Seventh International Congress of Philosophy*; to the Senate and Court of the University of Durham for the three lectures *The Kinds of Belief, Religious Belief*, and *Conflicts of Belief*, originally given as the Riddell Memorial Lectures for 1934 under the general title of *On the Nature and Grounds of Religious Belief*; and to the trustees of the L. T. Hobhouse Memorial Trust for *Materialism in Politics*.

The note by Sir David Ross (pp. xix–xxii) and some parts of my introduction were originally contributed to the current number of the journal of the *Philosophia* Society (Belgrade). They appear here by kind permission of its editor, Dr. Liebert, and of Sir David.

I wish also to record my gratitude to Mrs. Stocks and to the late Professor S. Alexander for their advice and help.

D. M. E.

The University,
   Manchester.
October 16, 1938.

296453

CONTENTS

INTRODUCTION

By the Editor

THE sudden death of Professor J. L. Stocks in June 1937 deprived both the study of philosophy and the public life of the English universities of one of their most valued leaders. John Stocks was an Aristotelian in the technical sense of one who made his contribution to the study of Aristotle.[1] But he was also an Aristotelian in the broad sense, both in the practical wisdom expressed through his philosophical and public work, and in the extent to which, as the ensuing essays may show, his re-interpretation of Aristotle's Formal Cause may be said to be the unifying conception in his own thinking.

Stocks wrote no long book on philosophy. That he intended to do sustained writing if he had lived, and after his retirement from heavy administrative work, we may confidently conclude. As it is, his published work (in addition to his Aristotelian and Epicurean[2] studies) is to be found in a few short books,[3] a volume of collected papers published in 1932 under the title of *The Limits of Purpose*, and the subsequent essays and addresses which I have collected in the present volume.

But in spite of their brevity, the reader of these *opuscula* is left marvelling that so much has been said in so small a compass. For Stocks had a rare gift of conciseness and clarity of statement; the distinction of his style, in its

---

[1] See *infra*, p. xix, for a note contributed by Sir David Ross on Stocks's studies in Greek philosophy.

[2] He had been engaged on certain studies in Epicurus and Philodemus, based on Crönert's transcripts of Herculanean papyri, and also on an index of Epicurean words for the new Liddell and Scott. The collection of these manuscript notes is at present in the care of Dr. C. Bailey.

[3] *The Voice of the People* (an essay on representative democracy written at the end of the War), *Patriotism and the Super-State* (Swarthmore International Handbooks, 1918); *Aristotelianism* (Harrap's); *An Introduction to Philosophy* (Benn's Sixpenny Library); and *Time, Cause and Eternity* (Macmillan, 1935).

pointed simplicity, is in itself a perhaps unconscious testimony to his belief in the formative activity of Mind, sub-
duing material to an economy of intelligible order.

'Distinction' is a word which offers itself readily when
thinking of Stocks, whether as writing, lecturing, presiding
at a meeting, or playing games. He had, moreover, a
certain impersonal objectivity, which is of the essence of
justice, and which was among the qualities which made
him a good administrator. It may have been partly this
quality which drew him to the study of Aristotle, in whom
he appreciated something 'as impersonal and inevitable
as Shakespeare'.[1]

'He was ready to admit that Plato was the greater genius,
and plumbed depths that Aristotle scarcely knew to exist. Yet
the exactitude of thought, the precision of phrase, and the
minimizing tone of the pupil allured him more than the
spiritual fire and dramatic intensity of the master. . . . His
method was to choose a manageable field of inquiry and work
it with a careful analysis and precise correlation of its parts.
The result might be small, but it would be reliable. He had a
deep dislike of large and fluffy phrases.'[2]

But this choice of limited fields of inquiry meant no
narrowness of philosophical interests or sympathies. He
was strongly critical of those tendencies in the thought of
our times which would restrict philosophy to an analysis
of propositions. He looked on philosophy as the gradual
achievement of a synoptic insight into the nature of mind,
as expressed in the forms of human activity. Philosophy,
he held, must satisfy the legitimate demands of the scientist,
the historian, and the practical man. This meant that on the
one hand his method was phenomenological and empirical;
he was interested in studying how in fact men thought
and willed and acted in their intellectual, spiritual, and
political endeavours. To this extent philosophy was to
him a secondary activity, not dictating beliefs to the

---

[1] *Aristotelianism*, p. 150.
[2] From the Archbishop of York's Introduction to *Time, Cause and
Eternity*, p. x.

primary activities but clarifying them and exploring their implications, and thereby guiding and correcting movements which it did not itself originate. But, on the other hand, philosophy, though a secondary activity, is no mere description, but an operative criticism of principles at work in the characteristically human activities. Philosophy is receptive of ideas from other sources (such as science, history, or constructive political experiment), but its main concern is to discern the spiritual unity of which each of these activities is a facet, and thereby to try to discover what each contributes to the central philosophical problem—the formulation of the conscious attitude of an integrated human mind to the reality which confronts it.[1]

Since this final theoretic task depends on discerning intelligent informing principles in the primary activities, such as religion, science, or statesmanship, when these are in a state of transition philosophy also is likely to be disintegrated. This means that the constructive answers which philosophy can give to men's questionings are likely to be least articulate just when apparently they are most wanted. Such seems to be our fate at present; and Stocks's reply to so uncomfortable a situation was no reiteration of 'large and fluffy phrases', or premature construction of beliefs, but a vigorous defence of his faith in the formative activity of mind. Hence the central importance of his adaptation of the Aristotelian conception of Formal Cause. His real enemy, both in philosophy and among the assumptions of contemporary life, was Materialism, in the sense of an interpretation of the processes and complexities of history and society in terms of the rearrangement of already existent materials and forces. Such a materialism is a legitimate methodological assumption of science, since science restricts itself to the investigation of the material

[1] Stocks's view of the method of philosophy on its constructive side is indicated rather than fully described in his published work. In my opinion, the most valuable of these indications are in the essays on *The Unity of Thought* (in *The Limits of Purpose*), *Reason and Intuition* in the present volume, and the *Introduction to Philosophy* (Benn's Sixpenny Library).

and efficient cause (and he vigorously defended the right of the scientist to make this restriction[1]); but, as carried beyond science into the study of social and historical activities (and, indeed, into metaphysics), it is the denial of any formative contribution of mind. Here he would say, quoting Aristotle, 'What we seek is the cause, *that is the form*'. That is to say, explanation must include not only the analysis of an object into its parts and temporal antecedents, but also a judgement of the character of the object in its wholeness, which character is a constitutive principle guiding the arrangement of the parts. Such judgements of individual character are described as Total Judgements in the essay on *The Kinds of Belief*. They would appear ultimately to be based on intuition, as being responses of the mind to objects in their totality. The claim of such intuition to be a part of Reason in the wide sense, and its relation to the more restricted rational processes of analysis and ratiocination, will be found to be a recurrent theme in the essays in this volume. That such informing of a whole with significant structure can be an operative factor is evidenced, Stocks claims, by our characteristically human experience of thought and action. He saw the world after the Aristotelian fashion, as constituted by different levels of organization, each level providing the materials which are both the opportunity for the exercise of formative activity at a higher level, and the odds against which that activity must strive.

So his main interest in his study of logic, ethics, politics, or religion was to see the formative activity of mind which these exhibit. This did not mean a lack of interest in the social consequences of these activities, but that his main concern was to see them as *expressive*, testifying to mind's own standards. This comes out most clearly in his four papers on Ethics, printed at the beginning of *The Limits of Purpose*. The title is itself characteristic. Stocks is here concerned to show not the lower, but the upper limits of purpose; to ask whether ethical, aesthetic, or religious

---

[1] See, for instance, *infra*, p. 49.

activity can be adequately described in the category of purpose. 'Purpose' is defined as the concentration of effort needed to bring about a certain result; so that a view of ethical action as primarily purposive evaluates such action in terms of its anticipated results. Stocks here turns his criticism not only on the more obvious forms of utilitarianism, but also on the whole assumption (albeit an Aristotelian one) that the *differentia* of rational action is that it is primarily purposive.

'Purpose', whether special or generalized (as is a purpose to promote the general good), is concerned, he holds, with an economy of means to bring about an end. But there is no purpose, however laudable, which morality may not demand that we forgo, if the means to its attainment be such that they cannot be judged to be a fitting expression of the human will. Such scruples may seem strange to the practical man; but to the man who is committed not only to living, but to living as well as he can, the judgement of the mind on its own activity will be more exacting than any appeal to the beneficial results of that activity.

Stocks's limitation of 'purpose' to the taking of means to a desired end has been criticized, notably by Mr. Joseph.[1] Such a limitation lays him open to misrepresentation, as does also his summary statement[2] that 'morality is not, as such, a device to bring anything in particular into the world, that it has no distinctive ideal, that it is not a search among the possibilities of the present for the materials of a better world, that it involves no notion of improvement and no ideas on evolution'. For the wholesale rejection in every sense of the *dictum* that the end justifies the means may create as many problems for morality as its uncritical assumption. A complete exclusion of purpose from morality would make the moral act no more than a gesture— that is to say, an act which is designed to express a good will, but not necessarily to effect anything. This is not

---

[1] 'Purposive Action'—*Hibbert Journal*, vol. xxxii, nos. 2 and 3 (also included in his *Ancient and Modern Philosophy*).
[2] *The Limits of Purpose*, p. 16.

Stocks's intention, since he observes that an act which
served no purpose would be pointless, and what is pointless
cannot be right. Morality supervenes on purpose, in that
it takes the whole complex of means and end, and makes
of it a fit expression of a good will. Here, as against all
forms of utilitarianism, I should hold that Stocks has
placed his emphasis in the right place. But by his limitation of 'purpose' to means-taking activities, he has left
largely undetermined the problem of moral judgement
upon ends.[1] Here he might have followed Aristotle's suggestion of a wider interpretation of purpose, where moral
choice is directed not to ends which are last terms in a series
of acts, but to ends which are activities immanent in the
series as a whole. In such purposive activities, different
acts in the series are constituents in the line of action taken
as a whole, rather than means to an ulterior end, and so are
not morally indifferent. Such purposes, moreover, take
shape as the informing activity clarifies itself, and so are
not necessarily undertaken with clear prevision of the intended end.

This distinction, of activities undertaken with clear prevision of a desired end from those which seek to express an
individual form, Stocks takes as showing that in art as
well as in morality we have passed beyond the upper
limits of purpose. Art is 'parasitic upon purpose' in that
it introduces into purpose a conscious enjoyment of the
means whereby it is effected (for instance, enjoyment of
skill in riding a bicycle makes the riding an aesthetic and
not merely a practical activity); so that means and end
become an organic unity with an individual form. Since
the essence of art is to be expressive and to afford aesthetic
enjoyment through its expressiveness, the contention that
art transcends purpose is more fully satisfying than the
corresponding contention concerning morality. For morality must find its *content* in extra-regarding right acts, and
so, it would seem, in the pursuit of purposes whether
general or specific which commend themselves as good.

[1] This is clearly the case in Essays VII and VIII of this volume.

Nevertheless, I should agree with Stocks that the distinctively *moral* judgement rests upon the quality of will expressed in that pursuit.

A fitting application of Stocks's contention that morality transcends purpose is given in the essay on 'Desire and Affection'.[1] Desire, as informing purpose, is shown to be for a *specific* satisfaction, for *a* moving machine, or *a* Morris car, and finds its satisfaction in an instance of the kind. But another principle, which we may call 'affection', dwells not on the specific but on the individual qualities of its object, not on its uses, but on its being what it is. Such a principle is the real root of the philosophical justification of private property as an extension of a man's personality. Stocks quotes a delightful poem by his little girl, aged six, to her bicycle, and I cannot resist quoting it again here.

> O beautiful bike, I love you so:
> It is so nice to see you go.
> I will wash you and clean you and take you home—
> O beautiful bike, will you come?

'The prey has become the charge: desire has been domesticated by affection.'[2] Such a non-possessive love, if universalized, might be the pre-eminent characteristic of a Divine Mind. This possibility is indicated in the two Riddell Lectures, *Religious Belief* and *Conflicts of Belief*. Stocks's debt to Dr. Nygren's discussion of the distinction of *Agape* and *Eros* is here apparent. His faith is of the Hellenic Christian type, in a God who is *Actus Purus*, and who thus excludes purposive activity. How to express philosophically the cruder but more concrete Hebraic side of Christian faith, in which purposes worked out historically in the temporal world are taken up into the eternal world, is one of the most persistent and unsolved problems of religious philosophy. I am conscious here of a certain failure on Stocks's part to integrate his belief in the reality of significant purposive activities on their own level with his final religious view.

---

[1] *The Limits of Purpose*, p. 33.   [2] Ibid., p. 55.

b

Nevertheless, in view of the contrary tendency in many forms of modernistic religious philosophy, I should hold that Stocks has emphasized a side which needs stressing.

In the distinction between technical activities and desires which aim at perfection of specific form, and aesthetic and moral activities which issue in expression of individual form, we find again the central interest to be the nature of Formal Causation. We find that this is also the case in Stocks's discussions of Politics. Perhaps the most significant in this regard is the essay on *Representation*,[1] itself a revision in a shorter form of the views of an earlier book *The Voice of the People*. His interest here is in the interrelation between the formative activity of government and the demands and criticisms of public opinion. He sees the realistic necessity that a government should govern, and so the need to secure the legal freedom of representatives to be no mere delegates, in order that government, as the main formative power within the community, may preserve a reasonable adaptability, which will enable it to act in the light of a situation as it now is rather than as it was at the last election. (We should hasten to add that this adaptability should be distinct from opportunism in being that inner logic of constructive innovation which is part of what is meant by formal causation.) At the same time, democracy has set itself the problem of seeing how a community may order its own life, and therefore the directing activity of government must be responsive to an informed public opinion.

That this latter was no mere academic aspiration on Stocks's part, but a cause to which we might almost say he gave his life, may be judged from the active interest he took in educational and political life, both within and without the University, when Professor of Philosophy in Manchester. Philosophy is never a popular subject of study in a modern university in an industrial community. Stocks endeavoured to bring it into closer relation to the study of other subjects, and brought a philosophical influence to

---

[1] *The Limits of Purpose*, p. 96.

bear on the development of the new department of Public Administration.[1] He thereby excited in the mind of the University and of people outside it an increased interest in philosophy itself, but his lectures were never over-simple popularizations. He laboured for the Workers' Educational Association and for the social and educational interests of the Manchester University Settlement and of the populations on new housing estates. He was chairman of the council of Hillcroft College, a residential college for working women, and while an Oxford tutor was a staunch friend to women's education in Oxford during a critical period. He was adopted as Parliamentary Labour Candidate for Oxford University in 1934, but was not elected. He was actively concerned in the steps taken in Manchester to help Jewish academic refugees.

Indeed, here was a notable instance of a man in whom philosophy and practical gifts were combined. He had just begun to show his capacity and wide sympathies as Vice-Chancellor at Liverpool when he died. It is, of course, difficult to say how far these practical interests interfered with his productive work as a philosopher. It is not my intention to give here an epitome of that work, but to direct attention to some of its salient characteristics, and thereby to ask whether we may not discern in them, as in his multifarious practical activities, the expression of a singularly unified and disciplined mind. His thinking was grounded in a direct empirical study of the main activities of a characteristically human life;[2] but it went on to in-

[1] The conclusion of his Sir Samuel Hall lecture on Bentham is probably pointed at his hopes concerning the services this department might render. (See *infra*, p. 207.)

[2] Perhaps this is the clue to his great interest in John Stuart Mill. In Mill he welcomed one who saw philosophy as grounded on a broad basis of human experience, and integrally related to social and educational interests. Stocks considered that Mill's own philosophical position represented too narrow a view of reason and too great concessions to contemporary fashions in scientific thought. But he, an Aristotelian and idealist, approached Mill with an intellectual sympathy rare among his critics. It is to be lamented that he was unable to finish his book on Mill (in the 'Leaders of Philosophy' series); but there are good hopes that another scholar may do so.

dicate a philosophy which could be both the outcome of those activities and their critic and guide. No one can have devoted himself more conscientiously and whole-heartedly to the duties and purposes of social and political improvement in the community in which he lived; and yet his clear conviction of the limits of purpose gave him a detachment from stress and strain which enabled him to fight for causes without a trace of personal bitterness.

NOTE

By SIR DAVID ROSS

On Stocks's contributions to studies in Greek philosophy

ONE of the strongest interests of this man of many sides and many interests was his interest in Greek philosophy. I well remember the freshness and vigour with which, as a pupil of mine in his undergraduate days, he used to discuss the problems raised by Plato and Aristotle, and to these authors, with one addition to be mentioned presently, all his later work on Greek philosophy was devoted. Of the two books which he published on the subject, the translation of the *De Caelo* was published in 1921. I have always thought it to be one of the best parts of the Oxford translation of Aristotle. Not only was he an excellent Greek scholar, but he had, as all his published work shows, an admirable command of English style. Furthermore, he was always on the look-out for emendations which a close following of Aristotle's thought rendered necessary, and Mr. Allan in the preface to his edition of the *De Caelo* pays just tribute to what Stocks had done before him in this direction:

'Verborum interpunctionem assidue emendare studui, in qua quamquam perdifficile est omnibus satisfacere, id tamen adhortabatur quod me in hac via praecessisset vir singularis iudicii I. L. Stocks, qui libros *de Caelo* Anglice interpretatus multas huiusmodi coniecturas, multas ad ipsum textum pertinentes proposuit.'

The other book, *Aristotelianism*, was published in 1925. It is a brief, but very well informed and well balanced, sketch of Aristotle's philosophy, with some account of its origins in earlier Greek philosophy and of its influence on later thought.

So far as I have been able to discover, his shorter

contributions to the study of Greek philosophy are the following:

(A) Republished in *The Limits of Purpose*:

(1) The Divided Line of Plato, *Republic VI* (written in 1911).

(2) Plato and the Tripartite Soul (written in 1915).

(3) Courage (written in 1919).

(4) Epicurean Induction (written in 1925).

(5) The composition of Aristotle's *Politics* (written in 1927).

(6) The Golden Mean (written in 1931).

(B) Not republished:

(1) The Argument of Plato, Protagoras, 351b–356c (*Classical Quarterly*, 1913).

(2) *ΛΟΓΟΣ* and *ΜΕΣΟΤΗΣ* in the *De Anima* of Aristotle (*Journal of Philosophy*, 1914).

(3) On the Aristotelian Use of *ΛΟΓΟΣ*: A Reply (*Classical Quarterly*, 1914).

(4) Aristotle's Definition of the Human Good (Oxford, 1919).

(5) Philodemus, Polystratus, and Diogenes of Oenoanda (in *New Chapters in Greek Literature*, ed. J. U. Powell and E. A. Barber, 1921).

(6) The Composition of Aristotle's Logical Works (*Classical Quarterly*, 1933).

(7) *ΣΧΟΛΗ* (*Classical Quarterly*, 1936).

There is hardly one of these articles which does not throw valuable new light on the subject treated of; and this may be illustrated by one or two examples. In the short article on 'The Test of Experience' (called 'Courage' on republication) he drew upon his experience on active service to justify Aristotle's account of courage as a mean, as being not a mere commonplace recommendation of moderation, but as involving the recognition that there are two instincts that have to be controlled by the soldier, not merely that of fear, but also that of 'cheer'; in fact, his

essay contains in brief the same illuminating view of the
mean as a 'valuational synthesis' which is worked out at
great length by Nicolai Hartmann. His article on the
Divided Line was, as far as I know, the first to question
the view that the Line is meant to express the gradual and
continuous progress of the soul through four stages up
to the highest knowledge; it anticipated to an important
extent the view which has been worked out more fully by
Professor A. S. Ferguson.

Latterly there were two subjects in ancient philosophy
which occupied his attention more than any others. One
was the study of the development of Aristotle's thought,
and the dating of his works in such a way as to show a
natural development from the idealism of Plato to a more
empirical type of view. He accepted very fully most of
Professor Jaeger's contentions, and the articles numbered
A5, B6, and B7 above illustrate well the way in which his
mind worked on this subject. The other was Epicureanism.
This is represented rather slenderly among his published
work by the articles A4 and B5; but this account of his
work would not be complete without a reference to the
constant and unstinting help which he gave to the editor
of the new 'Liddell and Scott', by searching the Epicurean
literature for all interesting or unusual uses of words.
There is extant in his writing a most careful word-list of
the Epicurean writings, with illustrative passages. But his
work on Epicureanism went far farther than this. He did
a good deal of transcribing of unpublished papyri, and he
collected very substantial materials towards an edition of
Epicurus' Περὶ φύσεως. His early death is an unquestionable loss to the study of Epicureanism, and it is but small
consolation that he left behind him notes which may be
found very useful by future scholars working in that
region.

I cannot conclude this brief and imperfect account of
Stocks's work on Greek philosophy without saying something of him as a man. He was a singularly happy mixture
of what is best in Plato and in Aristotle—the insight and

idealism of the one, the sobriety and capacity for laborious research of the other. Behind his gay and gallant demeanour there was a great seriousness, which had two main aspects—a deep and abiding interest in exact scholarship, and a burning zeal for righteousness, for liberty, and for the welfare of his fellow citizens, and especially for the betterment of the condition of the working class. And in addition to all that he was one of the best of companions and friends. All in all, he was one of the best men of his generation, and I have never known a better.

I. REASON AND INTUITION[1]

ONE of the strangest of the many strange habits of philosophers, which mark them out as the Ishmaels of the scientific world, is their refusal to agree as to the precise meaning of the words they use. No philosopher, it seems, is bound by the definitions given by predecessors or contemporaries of even the most central terms: each has to define his terms for himself. The resulting situation certainly lends itself to ridicule and caricature, as in the legend of the theological disputants who arrived after long argument at the conclusion that when the one said 'God' he meant what the other meant when he said 'Devil'. Still it is probable that this idiosyncrasy of philosophers has some real ground in the special nature of the task on which they are engaged, and is not a mere exhibition of aimless malice or sheer incompetence. Whether that is so or not, one of the consequences of this situation is that the titles of philosophic discourses are apt to be singularly unilluminating: as an indication of the problem to be raised they are, to say the least, highly ambiguous. How the reader may understand the title of this paper I do not know; but the question which I had in mind in choosing it was this. There is at the present moment in European thought generally a quite evident current of opinion hostile to 'reason' and 'rationalism'. It is not altogether a new movement: it can easily be traced back for thirty years or more, and, in a more general sense, for more than a century; but it has increased noticeably in force and activity since the war. The movement is by no means purely theoretical; in fact, as often in such cases, it is easy to argue that the theoretical side of it is secondary, and that certain practical tendencies constitute the central fact. Political movements like Syndicalism and Fascism openly proclaim their enmity to reason, and in Germany the political orthodoxy

[1] *Philosophy*, July, 1936.

B

of to-day represents Liberalism and Marxism as closely connected variants of a root heresy called rationalism. It is not my purpose to discuss these political tendencies— nor the related ethical tendencies, which are equally obvious and familiar, though not so easy to define with precision. I wish to concern myself only with the theoretical revolt against reason, and with that particularly in the form in which it opposes to reason a supposedly superior form of cognition called intuition. I want to ask how this opposition is to be understood, whether it can be justified, and if so whether the superior status is rightly accorded to intuition.

My general purpose in this paper is to challenge the current opposition of reason and intuition. I propose to argue that in any plausible sense which can be given to these terms they must be regarded as complementary, not as rivals; and in particular that (*a*) reason depends on intuition and (*b*) intuition depends on reason.

I

Meaning of the Two Terms

In the absence of agreed definitions, to which reference has been made, it is necessary to begin with some preliminary determination of the sense or senses in which the terms will be used. Here previous usage is the safest guide. The word reason has a long and varied history, and by one line of tradition, which goes back to the Greeks, summarizes all that differentiates man from the lower animals. That sense is too wide for our purpose, for reason in that sense will express itself in the practical field and in other non-cognitive or not purely cognitive activities. It is reason, in that sense, that domesticates animals, tills the ground, and builds cities. Even if reason is restricted to the cognitive field, as covering all that is distinctively human, it must include the intuition which is said to be the rival of reason. A narrower sense of the word is evidently needed. The word must stand, *first*, for a cognitive act or power, and, *secondly*, for an act or power which is not coextensive with cognition: otherwise there would be nothing for it to oppose. The *Oxford Dictionary* recognizes only one use of the word which satisfies this requirement, and this it marks as obsolete. The definition given is 'the act of reasoning or argumentation'. Following this clue, I think we shall not be wrong in supposing that those who oppose reason to intuition, to the disadvantage of reason, mean to include in the sphere of reason whatever in the way of knowledge or belief can be secured by reasoning.

Intuition is a much more modern and less familiar term. Attempts have been made at times to give it technical precision; but here again the tradition is rather confusing. It is derived from a verb which means 'looking at', and its extended use must be presumed to have originated as a metaphor from sight. It would stand, presumably, for a mental inspection in which a direct revelation is made to the mind, comparable to the direct revelation which accompanies the exposure of a physical object to the eye. We find the word in use in the early days of modern philosophy, e.g. in the writings of Descartes and Locke, to designate the apprehension of general truths which are self-evident and need no proof. It was obvious that there must be such truths: otherwise how could demonstration start? And it was equally obvious that such truths could not be directly credited to sight or any other sense. A quasi-sight of the mind, a mental inspection is supplied to fill the gap. This was the normal use of the term in the eighteenth century, and when Richard Price gave it prominence for the first time in ethical theory, he was consciously basing himself on this tradition. He was asserting (in his own words) 'an immediate perception of morality without any deductions of reasoning'. The moral intuition was for him an intellectual act, containing its own evidence, and not requiring or admitting of direct substantiation from without. In this use intuition is opposed to demonstration, and it is in a sense regarded as superior to it: for it is a simple act, while the other is a laborious and complicated process of reasoning, and the act is the foundation and starting-point of the process. We thus obtain *principles*, which are all-important. 'This kind of knowledge', said Locke, 'is the clearest and most certain that human frailty is capable of. This part of knowledge is irresistible, and like bright sunshine forces itself immediately to be perceived, as soon as ever the mind turns its view that way . . . the mind is presently filled with the clear light of it' (*Essay*, IV. ii). Intuition, though opposed to demonstration and reasoning, is the necessary basis of these, and all their certainty is derived from it. Where they succeed, it is by spreading this bright light, weakening it perhaps a little in the process.

Price's extension of the term to ethics first complicated the tradition: for whatever the fundamental truths of ethics may be, clearly they are not self-evident principles which serve as the basis of demonstrative reasoning. A further complication was introduced when the term was adopted as the English equivalent for the Kantian *Anschauung*. The famous saying *Anschauungen ohne Begriffe sind blind* was rendered 'intuitions[1] without conceptions are blind'. Here intuition stands for what is given or forced on the mind from without, as opposed to the conceptual framework which is supplied by the mind from its own resources. Intuition now includes sensation or sense-intuition, and the opposition between what is given and what is taken or supplied replaces the opposition between what is self-evident and what receives or requires demonstration. Intuition is still underivative, immediate, irresistible, but it cannot now of itself give us any proposition at all. Judgement can only take place when the matter of intuition is given conceptual form. Intuition is no longer an act of mind: the typical act is judgement. It has become an abstraction—the name for one of two complementary factors which can be detected by analysis in that

---

[1] Not always. Some translators prefer the word 'perception'. Professor Prichard, for instance, in his book *Kant's Theory of Knowledge* always uses this equivalent. But the latest and best translation of the *Critique of Pure Reason*, by Professor Kemp Smith, uses 'intuition', and it is increasingly prevalent.

familiar act. Intuition thus regarded tends to become a power to seize and hold in mind the *appearance* of an object, primarily of an object with which we have direct contact through the senses, secondarily of any other object which can be said to be taken in in one mental view. In its secondary applications the object of intuition may be something like a mathematical series, the thinking self, or God, which is not a physical object at all and therefore not accessible to sensuous intuition.

The inadequacy of the word intuition as an equivalent for Kant's *Anschauung* lies precisely in the fact that in our use the non-sensuous or not-purely-sensuous application is primary, and the sensuous application is secondary or non-existent, while in his use the application to the sense field is primary and all other applications derivative from it. This can well be seen in a passage from a recent English work on Perception. In Mr. H. H. Price's admirable book published two years ago[1] under that title he spends a long time on a careful analysis of sense data and other factors in the perceptual situation, and then adds that he feels obliged further to credit the perceptual act with what he calls a 'pseudo-intuitive' character. He explains that for him 'genuine intuition' is rather the *result* of active thinking than its precondition. It is the function by which we build up and keep in mind subjects for our judgements. This is for him the primary meaning of the word. But he is prepared to extend it, with the reservation expressed in the prefix 'pseudo', to sensory apprehension. His reasons for this are given in a passage which I will quote in full, because it throws much light on the connotation which the word intuition has now come to possess. He opposes 'intuitive' to 'discursive' consciousness.[2]

'In discursive consciousness', he says, 'there is a passage of the mind from one item to another related item, for instance,

---

[1] In 1932. Methuen & Co.
[2] This opposition is of course very ancient, going back to the Aristotelian opposition of νοῦς and διάνοια, in which the latter term is approximately equivalent to reasoning or the capacity for it.

from a subject to a concept under which we classify it, or from premises to conclusion. . . . And when we have discursive consciousness of a whole or complex of any sort (as in counting), although the whole may be vaguely present to the mind from the first, yet definite consciousness of the whole comes *after* consciousness of the parts. In intuitive consciousness, on the other hand, consciousness of the whole comes *before* definite consciousness of the parts. And there is no passage of the mind; whatever we intuit is present all at once. We might say that intuitive consciousness is "totalistic", not "progressive" or "additive".'

He adds the further mark that intuition lacks the activity of 'seeking' or 'following' which is characteristic of its opposite. It is not passivity, but yet it also is not activity. 'The mind rests, as it were, on its object.' Here, it will be observed, the reversal of which I spoke is complete. A word which first had direct application to sense-perception and was applied by a metaphorical extension to thought, here applies directly to a function of thought and is extended metaphorically to cover an analogous feature of sense-perception.

I believe that any significant use of the term intuition must be in close relation to the description given by Mr. Price. Intuition in this sense has no obvious claim to be described as the source of self-evident propositions. This older use of the word seems in fact to be becoming obsolete, but it must not be forgotten, because it is apt to turn up unexpectedly and confuse the issue. Thus in Ethics intuitionist is still used as the name of a school, and the characteristic tenet of the school is often taken to be the belief in self-evident principles of action. This clearly depends on giving intuition its older sense. Dean Rashdall's analysis of ethical intuitionism in his *Theory of Good and Evil* (1907, I. iv) presupposes the older sense throughout; that is why he thinks of intuition with special reference to the end of action, for the end, as Aristotle observed, is the starting-point of the argument of which the act is the conclusion. It takes the position in the practical syllogism of that science. This shows that the older use still persists.

If now we may sum up the line of interpretation represented by Mr. Price in his own word 'totalistic', and refer to the other line of tradition by the word 'self-evident',[1] we may provisionally conclude that the use of the term should be governed by reference to one or both of these marks, at the same time noting that on present evidence it does not appear that either of these marks directly involves the other, or even that they can be significantly regarded as combined in one mental act.

II

The Dependence of Reason on Intuition

If reason stands for the power to produce certainty or probability by means of argument, it is evident that it will be responsible for everything that deserves the name science and a good deal that is not commonly given that name. Its sphere will include mathematics and the most purely theoretical sciences, those which have a predominantly deductive character; but it will also include the more empirical sciences, those which rest mainly on induction. Unless some further restriction of the term reason is found possible, it is not easy to exclude even history: for the historian also is occupied in weighing evidence and has to argue his conclusions. But those who depreciate reason do not appear to have history in mind; and it may reasonably be maintained that the aim of the historian is differentiated from that of the scientist by the fact that the historian is occupied in determining the individual character of a period or movement, while the scientist seeks general laws governing individual behaviour. If we qualify our description of reason accordingly, it becomes the power to produce general truths or probabilities

---

[1] But there are two kinds of self-evident: (a) general principles, e.g. axioms of geometry, (b) what is directly assured by observation, the evidence of sense.

by argument, and its sphere will then be coextensive with science and the possible applications of the scientific method.

Now clearly every argument must start somewhere. This argument may rest on a previous argument, but, if an infinite regress is to be avoided, there must be an ultimate starting-point, which does not need or is taken as not needing proof. Our tradition therefore represents reason as dependent on intuition in one or both of its two forms, either in the form of apprehension of self-evident principles, as in mathematics, or in the form of empirical perception. In the former case the whole process is guaranteed by the self-evidence of the starting-point and the rigour of the demonstration which follows: in the latter case a high degree of probability may be attained by the exhibition of precise conformity on a sufficient scale between the deductions from the hypothetical principles and the observed events. Also it has frequently been asserted that intuition is operative continuously throughout every process of reasoning, since each step in the reasoning, taken by itself, is an intuition, self-evident and needing no external justification.

The champion of intuition may well reply that all this, however true it may be, is beside the point and does not touch his case, because the intuition which he regards as superior to reason is neither assurance in regard to what is presented to sense nor apprehension of self-evident general principles. To him I would reply that if intuition is given some such sense as Mr. Price gives it—what we have called its totalistic sense—in this sense also it must be regarded as an indispensable ingredient in the judgement of reason. How does the thinker, I ask, hold together the successive moments of his thought? His argument is a process occupying, it may be, a considerable stretch of time. In a physical process one imagines that the past is simply dead and gone, that all that is real and effective is carried forward through the successive terms to a single definable issue in the last. But in the case of a mental reasoning process this simply will not do. There is certainly an issue, a conclusion; but it is not asserted in its own right; it is not a view or vision secured by the path which constitutes the process. It depends for its truth, even perhaps for its meaning, on what was revealed in the course of the process, and it is not adequately asserted unless it is asserted in its dependence on all that. How, I ask, does the thinker hold all this in view? I answer that to explain this we require intuition in its characteristic function of making possible the keeping of a whole in mind, i.e. in the totalistic sense. We cannot suppose that the thinker, as he proceeds to each new proposition, remembers all the propositions which he has previously asserted, and it is equally impossible to suppose that he has forgotten them: he has them, evidently, in some real sense in mind. As propositions, as assertions, they are dead and gone; but their work remains. Each proposition, as it is asserted, has its felt source and confirmation in an intuition of the relevant whole, and contributes something to the development of that intuition, so that, when the development is fruitful, other assertions are possible thereafter which were not possible before. When the aim of the connected statement is mere description, the control of the intuition is obvious: the successive sentences stand in external relation to one another, united only by the intuition which is their common ground and product. Where the aim is proof, the control of the intuition is, I submit, not less necessary, but it is masked by the logical relations which give the series an *asserted* bond of union.[1] My contention is that these logical relations, together with all else that is, or can be, genuinely asserted, have their ground in an intuition.

I am tempted to give this theorem a yet wider range. What is the essential advantage of ripeness and maturity in any science, in competition with adventurous youth? Not merely, surely, wider knowledge, greater experience, a richer store of precedents and parallels; still less, greater acuteness in making deductions and in devising hypotheses

---

[1] 'Since', 'because', 'therefore', 'nevertheless', are examples of what I call asserted bonds of union.

contend that we have here the characteristic delusion of
rationalistic science in the unquestioned belief that correct
analysis results in the knowledge of the analysed whole.
In their view the need and value of intuition depends on
this, that it gives a knowledge of wholes in their integrity
which the methods of reason can never give.

A criticism of reason similar to this and a similar conception of the kind of rectification necessary is implied in
Spinoza's description of the goal of thought as *scientia
intuitiva*, intuitive knowledge. The recovery of individuality, lost or submerged in the previous scientific stages
of thought, is in fact Spinoza's leading idea. Mr. Roth
describes *scientia intuitiva*[1] as 'intuitive insight into individual essence'.

'Abstract recognition', he writes, 'passes into concrete
appreciation. Man is then conscious of nature as a unity, but
not as before from the outside. He feels it in himself; he understands its wholeness in and from his own being. He thus not
only contemplates externally the ways of the universe in which,
like everything else, he is caught up. He not only sees himself
as one item in the detail controlled by an all-embracing cosmic
order. Nature for him is more than an abstract whole of general
laws. It is a concrete system of self-directing individualities.
He knows himself in it as an individual, and realizes his place
in it among other individuals. He grasps both himself and things,
not in their universal aspect only, but in their unique singular-
ity. He has absorbed the truths of the discursive reasoning of
science and passed beyond it to the intuitive apprehension of
philosophy.'

It is important to notice that Spinoza's intuition, as
described in these sentences, while undoubtedly conceived
as something higher than what we have been calling
reason, is yet in no rivalry with it, or opposition to it. It
represents a further goal, but one only to be reached by
the incorporation of all that reason can contribute. Thus
Spinoza may be said to endorse by implication the criticism outlined above that scientific analysis can never

[1] *Spinoza*, p. 233.

reach the knowledge of the whole which it seeks, but to reject the suggested inference that such knowledge requires a method independent of reason. What Spinoza sketches is an ideal completion of the work of science, and his difficulty in finding concrete examples of intuitive knowledge springs presumably from the fact that human thought on the lower scientific level is still so imperfectly developed.

It is not the process character, the discursiveness, of reason which is now in question, but the generality of the truths which it reveals, and intuition is offered in contrast or as supplement not for its immediacy but as achieving the apprehension and appreciation of the individual. This being so, it is pertinent to ask whether already in our imperfect state of development we have not some knowledge of the individual. For in that case we shall not need to wait till science has done its work to get some notion of the structure of a thought in which individuality is apprehended, and if such apprehension is rightly called intuitive, we may find some substantial basis for the alleged rivalry of reason and intuition.

To this question I should reply that we certainly possess and constantly achieve knowledge of the individual, that many of our most massive certainties and probabilities depend on it; and, in particular, that history and biography represent a systematization of such knowledge, that all practice and theory of art is another expression of it, and that without it human action would lose altogether its moral, though not perhaps its economic, character. The knowledge aimed at and to some extent achieved in these activities is certainly something that science, as such, cannot give and does not claim to give—i.e. the questions asked are not included among those which the scientist tries to answer. But it does not follow that the scientist is precluded from making any contribution to the answer of the questions that *are* asked, only that any contribution he makes must be subordinate. There are special difficulties in the case of art and aesthetic judge-

ment, which must be passed over here. I would only say
that the aesthetic judgement seems to me to be the product of abstraction, though of a different order from the
abstractions of science. Therefore I put it on one side.
The other two types of judgement mentioned, the historical and the practical, are in no sense abstract; and if they
represent the work of intuition, they represent, I submit,
an intuition which is in no rivalry or opposition to reason
but welcomes every contribution which reason can make
to the solution of their proper problems.

This is best seen in the practical judgement, i.e. in the
judgement of a man faced by a concrete situation in which
action is demanded and deciding on which of various possible lines it will be best to act. Best seen here, because
it is obvious that no side of the complex fact can safely be
ignored, because in short here it is most imperatively
brought home to us that (as Butler says) 'things are what
they are and their consequences will be what they will be'.
In such a situation the ultimate issue, which is being prepared throughout the process of deliberation, is an individual response to an individual (particular) situation. This
is the issue, and it is this after the event that forms the
subject of moral valuation when the act is judged good or
bad. But beforehand in the process of deliberation the
action may be seen in other lights. Viewed economically,
in reference to this and that satisfaction, the bearing of
any proposal can be pretty exactly calculated. On this
side values are commensurate, and the balance of loss and
gain is fairly easily struck. Here reason is supreme in the
sense that the knowledge applied and the methods used
are scientific in character, and an irrefutably demonstrated
conclusion is not out of the question. Thus if the action
involves, e.g. the provision of necessary food, the results
of scientific investigation as to the nutritive value of
various foods will naturally be taken into account. But
when all the calculations have been worked out, the real
decision remains to be taken. The agent has finally to
decide whether he will or will not act on the line shown

to involve such and such possibilities of gain or loss. He has eventually to reach the position where he says 'this is the thing to do'. No amount of reasoning will bring him to that point. Here, I suggest, intuition is needed to supplement and complete the work of reason, and it is needed because what is in question throughout is, as I said before, an individual response to a particular situation. But that intuition is dependent on the rational analysis and conditioned by it: it is not a certainty, arising from mere inspection, to which reason makes and can make no contribution. On the other hand, since analysis can never exhaust the individual, no logical relation can be established between the final intuition and the arguments which preceded it. The arguments lack final cogency: they are only (to borrow a phrase from Leibniz) inclining reasons. The final intuition remains unproven and unprovable.

This practical intuition I give as an example of Mr. Price's 'genuine' intuition, which is the *result* of active thinking. The name intuition is, I think, appropriate, but it is no enemy or rival of reason. Its function is different, but in the performance of that function it welcomes whatever light reason can give. Intuition in this sense, in short, once more is dependent on reason.

IV

Conclusion

The time has now come for a final judgement on the issues of this controversy. In the foregoing I have been chiefly occupied in showing the interdependence of reason and intuition. But the discussion has been hampered throughout by two factors—first, by the acceptance, for the sake of argument, of what I personally regard as an awkward and improper restriction of reason to the field of argument or express inference; secondly, by the difficulty of avoiding ambiguity in the word intuition. The first point I will reserve for the moment. As to the second, a critic would have some justification for objecting that the

intuition on which reason is said to be dependent is not
quite the same as the intuition which is said to be dependent on reason, so that the thesis of interdependence (he
might say) breaks down. This charge of equivocation
would not be very easy to meet. But after all it is not
very important that it should be met. Even if it is upheld,
the main point remains untouched, that whatever sense
is given to the word intuition, it is always found in intimate relation to the reasoning process, never in sheer
opposition to it. It will be remembered that we distinguished two main tendencies in the use of the word, to
which we gave the labels 'self-evident' and 'totalistic'.
Perhaps we may be allowed now to substitute the word
'immediate' for 'self-evident'. It is a rather more expressive term and applies more naturally to sensation which
has to come in. Making that substitution, we may, I think,
say that any general description of the activity of thought
(which is also, it must be remembered, the actuality of
knowledge)—that any such general description is false
which does not include, in addition to inference and
reasoning, *both* senses of intuition. Thought starts from
the immediate and ends in the totality, which is and must
be individual. Reason (as defined) falls between these two
poles and is incidental to the passage of thought from the
one to the other. It is therefore fundamentally conditioned
by both.

The totalistic intuition, then, it is asserted, is the goal,
and this intuition is superior to reason. Some correction
may be necessary for metaphysical differences, but in
principle Spinoza's ideal of a *scientia intuitiva* is accepted.
Is not this, it may be asked, an endorsement of the case
against reason and of the contemporary reaction against
rationalism? Well, if rationalism stands for the view that
the world can be known and life lived by something like
a set of geometrical theorems, it deserves summary rejection. If it supplements this *a priori* geometry only by
the more modest and tentative construction of empirical
science, it still deserves rejection. For general truths are

not enough. They do not give knowledge of the individual ; and the individual is real. But if rationalism stands for the conviction that whatever can be scientifically analysed and examined should be submitted to such examination, that the fear and distrust of reason is a major crime against humanity, that civilization consists in and depends on nothing so much as on the prevalence of such rational analysis and the assistance and protection of those who practise it, then rationalism stands for health and sanity and should have the support of every thinking man. An intuition which claims sacrosanctity and declines the test of reason is, as Locke and Mill both protested, a moral and social offence, a mere misnomer for blind prejudice and crass superstition.

Finally, I come back to Reason and the question what it stands for. Why do we regard rejection of reason as a crime ? The answer is simple and was well known to the Greeks of the fifth century before Christ. The λόγος of Heracleitus of Ephesus, first ancestor in the line of descent which culminates in the λόγος doctrine of the Fourth Gospel, was called by him the 'common' or 'universal'. 'Though the Word', he wrote, 'is common, most men live as if each had his private wisdom' (fr. 92). By it alone we are saved from confusion and anarchy, as a city by its laws (fr. 91). He calls it also eternal (fr. 2). Reason stands in truth for what men have in common, for the ability to transcend the limitations of time and space, to discount the effects of position and perspective. The intuition which is opposed to reason is the 'private wisdom' of Heracleitus, the wilful refusal to attempt the universality which reason aims at, the defiant assertion of personal and collective particularisms as necessities of life. Such rejection of reason is a crime, not merely an error, because the striving for community and universality is the foundation of all genuine morality. The situation of man is surely plain enough. By his senses and by the appetites which are correlated with them he is at the mercy of his physical environment. From this bondage, so far as he is reasonable, he seeks to deliver himself, so that he may 'look abroad into universality'. The escape is at times painful and difficult, and among his fellow sufferers there are not only many who are sceptical as to the possibility of escape, but also some who denounce the very attempt at escape as selfishness and treachery. They say his duty is to hug his chains till they are chains no longer. To such doubts and scruples the truly reasonable man is obstinately deaf. He persists in seeking the common ground, inspired by the faith that truth, independent of place and position, is attainable to man. Such faith is rightly called faith in reason: for reason in the narrower sense is the instrument by which deliverance is sought and in the wider sense it is the freedom which is the goal. In the narrower sense it may be opposed to intuition, but only in the way in which analysis and synthesis may be opposed as complementary processes within a developing whole of thought: in the wider sense it includes the intuition which is at once its product and its justification.

II. THE KINDS OF BELIEF

WE each of us believe a great many things; we have come to believe these things in a variety of ways. I am going to begin by trying to enumerate and discuss briefly the main classes of belief. As soon as we go into the matter of our own beliefs we find that we should be hard put to it to give any account of how we came by these beliefs or to justify the degree of confidence we place in them.

(1) *First*, and most obvious to most of us, is the realm of *Matter of Fact*. We reckon, for instance, confidently on the existence of a geographical and social complex called China. Of this great complex of fact, probably we have no direct evidence at all, unless contact with persons who are reported to have come from it can be so called; but cumulative evidence of all sorts from every quarter has long placed this article of belief beyond reasonable doubt and given it a respectable solidity. We could all say quite a lot about China without serious fear of contradiction even from an experienced traveller in that country. It constitutes a massive deposit in the permanent background of our thought and speech. No single item of the evidence, if we could disinter it, would turn out to be beyond criticism: yet the concurrence of so many independent indications begets a degree of confidence which leads us to claim for our opinions the status of indefeasible knowledge. The case is similar with regard to historical facts like the death of Charles I on the scaffold, or the capture of the Bastille —events so far removed from us in time that they fall beyond the limits of possible observation altogether. These are spatial and temporal extensions of experience.

The body of knowledge or belief which we refer to as *Science* is very varied in character. Astronomy, for instance, in its descriptive aspects is merely an extension of geography, and thus in certain respects our beliefs about the stars are on all fours with our beliefs about China.

Astronomy, on this side, thus gives spatial extension to the field of thought. To the map of the earth is added a map of the heavens. Science also contributes to the historical background of our thought. The geologist who tells us of the stages by which the earth has come to wear its present dress is presenting us with authority for assertions similar in kind to that of the death of Charles I on the scaffold. The historical element is also central in the biological theory of Evolution. This is a theory as to how the world has come to exhibit its present variety of living forms: it thus reconstitutes an historical process and discusses the forces at work in it, which is just what the historian of the Roman Empire, for example, does.

So far scientific beliefs do not seem to differ in kind from those already considered. Their scientific character does not necessarily imply a higher degree of certainty; but it does imply that they are based on the use of certain established methods of investigation, that they are formulated with the greatest care and circumspection, and that they are the common property of a body of investigators pledged to nothing but the discovery of truth and ready to throw aside or reformulate any article of belief at any moment if the evidence may seem to demand it. Science is in fact a co-operative effort at the systematic extension of the region which we have called Matter of Fact, from the centre formed by the absorptive power of the observing mind. It extends the view, as we have seen, both in space and time, and thus offers a justification for a belief in particular existences and events (planets, stars, and ice-ages) of which direct evidence is wholly or partly unattainable. But its main function as generally conceived is not this, but rather to give us general truths as to what things are made of and why they behave as they do behave. To put it otherwise, the typical scientific truth is a timeless statement about kinds of things, a statement which, being timeless and general, can be applied at any time or place to justify particular assertions or operations.

This view of science is in the main correct. The typical

scientific interest is in repeatable features of experience, and the typical scientific proposition concerns these. But according to the general belief, which the scientist shares, nature never repeats herself exactly. Every single existent thing, though it conforms in general character to a certain type, is subtly and indefinably differentiated from all other instances of the type: each is in short an irreplaceable unique individual. In this individuality, as such, science is not interested, only in types and sub-types, and examples of deviation from type; and the scientist's traditional mode of treatment of a complex is to break it up into its simpler components. Face a scientist with a particular individual, say Socrates. He will investigate Socrates and make a number of assertions about him; but his results, if any, will concern not Socrates but man. He will hope, as the result of his inquiries, to see Socrates as a man, conforming generally in structure and organization to the human pattern, but differentiated from the generality of men by the preponderance of certain elements in his make-up. Thus the scientific examination of Socrates would be expected to lead to some such result as this: that the presence of a given observable constituent in an unusual degree in a human being leads necessarily to certain consequences in character and action, i.e. to the discovery and definition of a new sub-type and variety of humanity.

What science gives us, then, in the main is still Matter of Fact, but it is generalized fact. It seeks to tell us how types of things do in fact behave, breaking up the complex into its simpler components and thus aiming at the reduction o fits primary laws (statements of the behaviour of the primary constituents) to the lowest possible number.

(2) *Mathematics* is an ancient ally of Science. But if we ask what is the nature and ground of conviction in the case of any simple mathematical truth we recognize at once a difference in kind from any belief we have hitherto considered. We do not believe that $2+2 = 4$ because the evidence of our eyes is inescapable or because we accept the authority of an organized system of research based

upon this as a principle or involving this as an essential ingredient, but because our own intelligence forces us so to judge. We find ourselves in the presence of a sheer intellectual necessity, self-contained and self-justifying, from which there is no escape. Our assent is not provisional, liable to indefinite modification in view of future discoveries: it is absolute and irrevocable. Here we have what the philosophers have called *a priori* truth, truth independent of experience, not in the sense that if we had no experience at all we could nevertheless attain it, but in the sense that there is no specifiable empirical evidence on which it rests and there is no conceivable empirical evidence which could overthrow it. Two further points may be noted about mathematical truth.

(*a*) There is no real room for dispute or difference of opinion. A complicated mathematical construction may be difficult to follow, but so far as you follow you agree. It takes time for a child to master the multiplication table, not because he has to throw off wrong ideas and faulty preconceptions about it, but only because his unpractised mind is unequal to more than a certain degree of complication. We may differ as to the number of people in a room, but as to the character of the number 100, so far as we have opinions at all, we are all agreed.

(*b*) However useful mathematics may be as an *instrument* of science, as a *means* of determining Matter of Fact, it has itself no direct contact with that realm. The extension of our knowledge of mathematical truth does not of itself affect at all what we call our knowledge of the world. At most it helps indirectly by increasing our power to obtain full and accurate knowledge of it. The fact that mathematics is independent of experience (*a priori*), as already explained, carries with it the consequence that there is not and cannot be any contradiction between mathematical truth and Matter of Fact. Mathematics can never prove that anything exists and the ascertained character of the existent can never affect or modify in any way the constructions of mathematics. The two realms are in definable relation (otherwise mathematics would be of no use to science), but the relation is one that excludes all possibility of conflict.

(3) So far in this review of beliefs I have confined myself to explicit assertions. But there is a very important order of beliefs which seldom rises to the level of explicit assertion at all. These are the most fundamental of beliefs and they are those with which philosophy is specially concerned—so much so that it may be reasonably argued that the whole business of philosophy consists in stating and canvassing the implied principles and presuppositions of human thought in its various departments. They are of various kinds. In the theoretical field (with which we are at present concerned) they fall into two main groups, giving rise to the two philosophical inquiries known as Logic and Metaphysics. The logician penetrates below the surface of thought, seeking out its organizing principles. The premisses of an argument are commonly stated; the principle is usually not stated. 'Things which are equal to the same thing are equal to one another' is a principle of quantitative reasoning, which does not need to be stated to make the reasoning complete and cogent. A more general principle of reasoning is formulated in the case of the syllogism. These principles govern thought not in the sense of determining its object, but as governing method and procedure in regard to any suitable object. Thus they are as exempt from any possible collision with the beliefs of the Matter of Fact kind as the truths of mathematics are, and, like the truths of mathematics, they accept the consequence that of themselves they add nothing to our knowledge of the world. They cannot successfully be questioned or disputed, because the thought which tried to question them would itself make use of them. A metaphysical presupposition, on the other hand, is an implicit assertion that the real is of such and such a general character. In this sense we speak, for instance, of the metaphysics of the plain man. It may be doubted whether there is any *a priori* truth—a certainty totally independent

of empirical verification—of the metaphysical order; but it cannot be doubted that such implicit assertions, unexamined by those who make them, are involved in every department of human thought. Metaphysical philosophy is the attempt to give them the examination which they require.

To resume, we have so far three main orders of belief, indicated compendiously by the three terms Matter of Fact (including history and science), Mathematics, and Philosophy. The last is in somewhat dubious relation to the other two, but since the philosopher has by tradition and general agreement the task of determining the general nature of reality, it seems highly improbable that philosophic truth can be wholly independent of experience and thus wholly exempt from collision with Matter of Fact. But that only says that philosophic truth cannot be wholly *a priori*—it still leaves a large number of alternatives open.

(4) Man, however, is no purely theoretic animal, and the human interest with which we are concerned in these lectures, the religious interest, is certainly no purely theoretical affair. It is necessary, therefore, to extend our view and take into account non-theoretical or not purely theoretical activities. Besides religion, which we shall discuss in detail presently, there are the two great regions indicated by the two terms Art and Conduct. Is there a characteristic artistic (aesthetic) belief, and, if so, how is it related to the forms of belief already reviewed? Are there practical propositions, and, if so, of what order are they? In both cases it is obvious—and that is what is meant by calling them non-theoretical or not purely theoretical activities—that these interests are not primarily forms of belief or knowledge. Neither the artist nor the man of action is essentially and characteristically occupied in trying to know or convince himself of something. The artist is making and the man of action is doing. Yet belief and knowledge play their part here too, and thinkers have often been tempted to deny the apparent distinction of aim. In the famous saying 'Beauty is Truth, Truth

Beauty' a poet assures us that ultimately the goal of theoretic and artistic endeavour is identical, and in the paradox 'Virtue is Wisdom: Vice is Ignorance' the Greek philosopher asserts a similar identity of aim between the fields of theory and practice. Whatever suggestion of truth they may contain, such identifications have an air of paradox. They raise provocatively the problem of the ultimate unity of human activity. That is too great a problem to be dealt with here. We must remain on a more pedestrian level and assume the *prima facie* distinctions. On that level there are some points that may be usefully noted.

First, with regard to Art. For convenience and to avoid complications let us confine our view to poetry as the representative of this region. Does poetry, we may ask, say something which cannot be said in prose? It seems clear that any truth, any belief of any of the orders already reviewed—even the multiplication table—may conceivably be conveyed in the poetical medium, and, further, that in so conveying a truth the poet would not express his characteristic gift by introducing other, specifically poetical, beliefs into the statement, side by side with the belief he was attempting to convey. There may be difficulty in reconciling a certain kind of statement with the poetic atmosphere. For instance, it would only be by a *tour de force* that any considerable portion of the multiplication table could be introduced into a poem. But whatever truth is appropriated to the poetic purpose retains its meaning and its theoretical value, unaffected by that appropriation and unadulterated by specifically poetic material. This means that the poet as such is not asserting anything whatever about the world: he has no characteristic belief which could come into collision with any other order of belief—only at most a characteristic attitude, predisposing him to the appropriation of one kind of truth rather than another. What is characteristic of the poet is not a belief that such and such is the case (inevitably raising the possibility of conflict with other beliefs), but the determination to make use of any and every kind of experience and belief for his own poetic ends. To this end truth, which in the theoretic activity rules supreme, is in poetry (and in art generally) subordinated. Hence the poet's selectivity. If it is asked what this end is, we can only answer, in deference to a long tradition, if we are to remain on relatively undebatable ground, with the single word Beauty. But in this answer Beauty must be taken to stand not for a distinction in the things of which the poet or artist makes use, a character possessed by them before he uses them and constituting the reason for his making use of them, but simply and solely for his success in appropriating them. It is not to be supposed that there are beautiful truths and ugly truths, and that the selectivity of the poet consists in appropriating the one and rejecting the other: there are just truths, all alike artistically indifferent, until the artist gets to work on them, which become constituents of artistic beauty so far as he is successful in his work.

Thus, though the poet has no characteristic belief in the sense in which we have been using the word, he may be said to have—or indeed to be possessed by—a belief in Beauty so defined. This devotion is characteristic of the artist generally, and it is paralleled in the field of theory not by any of the orders of belief which we have mentioned, but by the unqualified devotion to truth which inspires and maintains all pure theoretic activity. But when we read the poem and appreciate the work of art and when the creative artist judges his own creation, then assertions are made of which the work of art is itself the subject. 'This', we say, 'is a very beautiful picture, or poem'—a judgement, obviously, conveying an estimate of the degree of success which has been achieved, precisely parallel to the judgement in which we assess the truth of a scientific or philosophical theory. In both cases we estimate value, but in each a different kind of value.

(5) I turn to Action. For this review of belief the field of action makes a contribution similar in principle to that

of Art. The man of action as such has no distinctive creed or belief, but anything he believes may affect his line of action. An action is an attempt to change a situation, and in any justification of his action the agent will produce his grounds for thinking that the situation was of such and such a character, and that alteration of this or that kind would be likely to have this or that effect. Action, in short, is interference with fact, presupposing for its justification knowledge of fact and especially a knowledge of causal connexions such as science seeks to discover. In determining these connexions obviously mathematics (for instance) will be as important as it is in science. We may say, then, that in so far as the problem of action can be expressed as that of extracting a certain kind of result— say, a sufficient supply of food—out of a certain kind of situation, the beliefs on which it relies will be of the scientific type. But even on this side there is a characteristic element in the thought governing action which escapes final scientific analysis. This element is represented by the word good. Why of several courses shown by scientific analysis to be equally attainable at approximately the same cost of effort, &c., one should be eagerly adopted and the others rejected, is only explicable in the long run by the recognition of a scientific surd in the brute fact of the agent's preference or desire. It *seems good* to him to take this course rather than that. Thus belief that certain types of situation are good or better than others must be recognized as a form of belief characteristic of action, not derived from, however much it may be influenced by, the other forms of belief reviewed.

But there is another element in the practical judgement which complicates the matter considerably. In addition to the opposition of good and evil we recognize also the opposition of right and wrong, and the relation of these two oppositions to one another constitutes one of the most difficult problems of ethics. In my view the attempts which have often been made to derive one of these oppositions from the other must be judged to be failures: but

whatever their relations may be, it seems clear that a
statement of right and wrong is not a statement of mere
matter of fact. Historical and scientific truths influence
it, but cannot establish it. Thus we have here a second
type of belief, characteristic of the practical intelligence
and peculiar to it.

To these two forms of practical proposition I feel obliged
to add a third, as distinct from the other two. When we
speak of a good action or a good man, we do not mean
simply a right action or a man who does what is right;
still less do we mean an action or a man productive of good
either to himself or to the world generally. We are making
a direct qualitative assessment of the spirit of the act or
of the man. It is no doubt true that a good man tends to
do good; and it is an essential part of the goodness of man
that he should try to do what is right: but these concessions do not remove the distinction between the three
orders of judgement. They only show that the three are
connected, as they must be if the practical field is to be
capable of being grasped as a unity.

To the three orders of belief, Matter of Fact, Mathematics, and Philosophy, which may be generally designated
theoretical, we have now added two other orders, the
Aesthetic and the Practical (Ethical). In conclusion we
may turn to Religious Belief and consider in a brief and
introductory fashion its possible relation to any and all
of these.

We find that history records attempts to assimilate
Religious Belief partly or wholly to each of these types.
(a) Its essence has been thought at different times and by
different people to consist in a belief that certain alleged
historical incidents did actually occur: that is to place it
within the region of historical matter of fact. The historian
becomes at once the expert by whose judgement religion
stands or falls. (b) At other times and by other people
attempts have been made to show that the observed facts
of nature are inexplicable, except on the hypothesis of a
ruling benevolent intelligence of infinite power and know-

ledge. Such an argument claims for itself the status of
a scientific hypothesis. The scientist is entitled to reply,
as Laplace did to Napoleon, that it is a hypothesis which
he does not require. He may be wrong, but after all it is
for him to say what principles he requires for his work.
(c) Others again have tried to show on various lines that
at least the fundamentals of religion—the belief in a God
and the conception of the Divine Nature—have all *a priori*
certainty like that of mathematics, owing nothing to experience and in no conceivable conflict with Matter of
Fact. The appeal is, then, to human reason. A theorem
has to be expounded in an argument, the cogency of which
must be conceded by any one who is capable of following
it at all. Those who cannot follow it will accept the conclusion on authority from those who can, in the way that
most of us accept the results of higher mathematics.
(d) Still more often and indeed almost constantly, since
there was anything passing under the name of philosophy
in the world, philosophy has been regarded as the court
of appeal which must pronounce as to the soundness of
religious belief. And a court of appeal in some sense it
seems that philosophy must be. But the trouble here is
that there is no general agreement as to what philosophical
truth is—or would be if we had it—and on what sort of
evidence it rests; and consequently the way is open to the
confusion of philosophy and religion—the religious mind
claiming that it is already in possession of a philosophy
which only needs at most translation, as it were, into
philosophical terms, and philosophers for their part claiming that they have a religion or something better than a
religion, which includes whatever truth religion may hint
at and makes religion obsolete. The ancient quarrel to
which Plato refers between poetry and philosophy in
Greece was at bottom a quarrel between philosophy and
religion, and his exclusion of poetry from his Republic
was accompanied by a denial of all independent value to
the religious life. Philosophy was for him the means of
salvation: his religion, in other words, was philosophy.

(e) A purely aesthetic theology, so far as I know, has never been attempted, but aesthetic elements are prominent in some religious theories. (f) The connexion with ethics has always been much closer, and there have been periods, such as the English eighteenth century, for which the distinction between moral and religious truth wore very thin. But more significant than any such movement of opinion is the recent tendency to look for the substantiation of religious belief in the region, as it is commonly called, of value. This tendency is not free from a certain ambiguity of aim. Sometimes it seems that we are asked to recognize in religion the recognition of a principle which, translated into philosophical terms, gives security and objectivity to certain non-religious values which inspire human conduct but receive little or no support from other orders of belief. God—one might say, rather frivolously— is offered to us as the means of making the world safe for Beauty, Truth, and Goodness. At other times the contention appears to be that the religious experience or activity has its own autonomous existence, like the pursuit of Truth and Beauty and Goodness, and represents the assertion of a peculiar and characteristic value co-ordinate with these. But whichever line is taken, the significance of the movement is plain. It represents a surrender of the ground of Matter of Fact and of the purely theoretical ground in general, and the transference of the issue to another field, which may perhaps be called, in a generous sense of the word, practical. Not by the mere exploration of the object known or contemplated shall we find the verification of the religious vision, but by an examination of the principles which inspire that knowing and contemplation itself, and all other human activities. In the second form in which I stated it, it carries further the important implication that religion itself stands for an independent human activity, self-governing like other human activities, and finding its own path.

III. RELIGIOUS BELIEF

THE commonest formulation of the central affirmation of the religious consciousness—at least in modern times (I doubt if this is true of ancient times)—is the proposition 'God exists'. This has the form of a statement of fact. We are accustomed to find our evidence of the existence of anything in observation and in artificial extensions of observation (by argument, testimony, &c.), i.e. ultimately in the use of the senses. As we say, 'Seeing is believing'. Thus there are certain specifiable items of immediate sense experience on which any ordinary assertion of existence rests. But as soon as we seek to verify this proposition in the familiar way we are baffled. It is not possible to find any special feature of the perceived world which justifies the proposition 'God exists' in the fashion in which certain features of experience justify the proposition, for instance, 'Elephants exist'. As Empedocles said 400 years before the birth of Christ: 'It is not possible for us to set God before our eyes or to lay hold of him with our hands—which is the main high road of persuasion leading into the mind of man' (fr. 133).

Now it seems to be true that all other assertions of existence, without exception, rest upon the senses. Hence it is not surprising that the uncomfortable truth stated by Empedocles has not found ready acceptance among the champions of religion. In one way or another they have obstinately attempted to evade the implication. The demand for a sign[1] rebuked in the Gospels and the tendency to identify religious belief with a belief in miracles (conceived as exceptional events giving direct evidence of God's existence) are natural expressions of the 'seeing-

---

[1] It is interesting that the Greek word for sign in the New Testament (σημεῖον) is the word commonly used in later Greek logic of the basis in what is preconceived for inference to the unperceived: e.g. from perceived smoke we infer unperceived fire. The smoke is the 'sign' and the process of inference is called 'signification'.

is-believing' attitude. But as T. H. Green says, 'if faith were really belief in the occurrence of certain miraculous events upon transmitted evidence of the senses to other people, its certainty would after all be merely a weaker form of the certainty of sense'.[1] David Hume suggests that religious ceremonies owe their efficacy to this factor in human nature. He sought to show that belief generally depends on the establishment of a close connexion between the object of thought and the 'present impression' of immediate sense experience.

'The ceremonies of the Roman Catholic religion', he writes, 'may be considered as experiments [i.e. experiences] of the same nature. The devotees of that strange superstition usually plead in excuse for the mummeries with which they are up-braided, that they feel the good effect of these external motions and postures, and actions, in enlivening their devotion and quickening their fervour, which otherwise would decay away if directed entirely to distant and immaterial objects. We shadow out the objects of our faith, say they, in sensible types and images, and render them more present to us by the immediate presence of these types than it is possible for us to do, merely by an intellectual view and contemplation.'[2]

But symbolism is one thing and evidence another; so that this example has only partial relevance here.

If the field of experience fails to provide the necessary verification, it is natural to seek it in the *a priori* realm, of which the early successes of mathematical speculation gave such dazzling glimpses. This is not the place to discuss the claims to an *a priori* proof of God's existence. It is only to my purpose to note that these proofs and their discussion show clearly how completely without parallel among the articles of human belief this belief in the existence of God is. Mathematics does not seek to prove that anything whatever exists. Its figures and numbers might, for any assurance it gives us to the contrary, find no exemplification whatever in human experience. In the whole history of human thought I believe there has

---

[1] *The Witness of God and Faith*, p. 81.　　　[2] *Treatise*, I. iii. 8.

been no attempt to assert existence on *a priori* grounds
except in this one case.[1] The proofs themselves rest on
the uniqueness of their problem. In this one case, they
argue, and in this alone, existence *must* be predicated. All
other existence is from the *a priori* ground mere possibility,
contingent on this and that: here we have an existence
which can be seen to be a necessity. Now clearly the
Divine, whether treated as singular or as plural, is a
peculiar form of being in its very conception, and hence
not easily brought into relation with other forms of being.
Some degree of abnormality in the evidence might be
expected; but an argument so completely *sui generis* as
this can hardly fail to be deficient in general persuasive
power, and it is not surprising to find that the *a priori*
arguments have been rejected by many religious philosophers, while those who have accepted them have not
usually been content to rely on them alone.

This proposition, then, that God exists, which is traditionally taken to express the central affirmation of the
religious consciousness, seems at least something of an
anomaly, if not an unwarranted intruder, both in the
realm of fact and in that of *a priori* necessity. It may be
a fact, but it is not and cannot be on all fours with other
facts. It may be an *a priori* certainty, but it has no resem-
blance or relation to the other beliefs which are accorded
this status. Let us now briefly consider its prospects and
relations in the third sphere—that of value.

However disparate the standards of Art and Conduct
may be, it is not difficult to see that they have something
in common. In saying that each applies standards we
have already indicated the point of agreement. Each involves the making of qualitative differentiations essential
to itself and non-existent from any other point of view.
Each has to meet scepticism and opposition, partly external, as to the general importance of these differences which

[1] A certain reservation is necessary for some philosophies. Spinoza
seems to consider such deduction ideally possible, but only from God
as a starting-point.

D

it detects, partly internal, as to the reliability of some of its discriminations. The search for truth may be interpreted with rather more difficulty on parallel lines. But whatever difficulty there may be with Truth, there is much more with Religion. None of these other activities is commonly interpreted as involving the assertion that anything exists which other persons might deny to exist. There are probably people in the world who are almost, if not quite, insensible to moral distinctions, and there are certainly some persons who see nothing in poetry. But these persons are debarred from putting their views into the form 'morality (poetry) does not exist', because the actions and compositions to which moral or poetical merit is attributed are undoubted features of the public world. Their difference of opinion is represented as a difference as to the correct interpretation of these things; and most commonly they would not even push the matter to a difference of opinion; they would leave it on the level of a difference of taste, concerning which proverbially there is no dispute. The believer, of course, in either region, will indignantly deny that it is a mere question of taste, because he is concerned to vindicate the reality and objectivity of the distinctions he makes. He wishes his judgement to be binding on all reasonable people, like a statement of indisputable fact or of transparent intellectual necessity.

In this sense the pretensions of art and morality require them to force an entry into the common world, to insist on qualifying men's view of reality. But it is a long way from this to the claim made on behalf of the religious consciousness, that in its name men must revise their whole conception of the origin and governance of the world. The difference is not one of degree merely: it is one of kind. Further, the detail of the activity behind this demand (covered by the term 'religious consciousness') shows no close family likeness to those already cited. There are religious practices, no doubt, public and private, but it is difficult to reduce the religious affirmation to the mere assertion of the value of these practices. Religion

does not surely stand or fall by these, as art stands or falls
by poetry and its other works. These are the aids and
instruments of religion, not its fruit and characteristic
product. Further, in the case of these other forms of
activity we have generally accepted names for the ends
to which they are directed, the supreme consideration to
which all else within the scope of their operations is subordinated, the distinctive character which marks their
products and successes. Goodness, Truth, and Beauty is
the conventional trinity, representing the directing principles in the three spheres of Art, Theory, and Conduct
respectively. What is there in the religious field to take a
corresponding place? There are certainly two (very likely
more) terms which are or have been of great and central
importance to religious thought and practice, the terms
'pure' and 'holy'. But it would surely involve a most
artificial exaggeration of their importance to attempt to
interpret religion as consisting essentially in devotion to
purity or holiness, unless that purity and holiness is objecti-
fied in a supreme ruler of the world. And *if* that condition
is granted, the parallel with the other activities at once
disappears. I will not labour this matter further. I have
said enough, I hope, to make good my point that it is not
obviously easier to introduce the affirmation of religion
into the sphere of values than into any of the other regions
we have considered. If religion is the assertion of a value,
its value is of a very peculiar kind.[1]

Whatever incidental enlightenment we may have secured
on the way, our discussion so far, viewed generally, yields
only the negative result that the demands made in the
name of religion are not easily accommodated in any
quarter of the intellectual field. In each sphere they refuse
to conform to the required pattern. In this sort of question
we rely largely on analogy for our protection and for

---

[1] I would ask the reader to note that the foregoing comments apply
to theories which rest on the assertion of a specific religious value, not
to theories which look to religion for security for values generally: they
apply, in short, only to the second of the two forms of value-theory
distinguished at the end of the previous lecture (*supra*, p. 30).

plausibility, and a satisfactory analogy is here wanting. If this is right, it suggests that the difficulty lies precisely in the fact that the religious affirmation is unprecedented and *sui generis*, and it may be that when one has said this, one has said in principle all that there is to say on these lines. But before going further it seems advisable to attempt to look the religious affirmation rather more closely in the face, with the hope of finding out in greater detail what it is and wherein its uniqueness consists.

It is a commonplace that religion involves a distinctive attitude to life generally and to the world as a whole. Religion is omnivorous—not in the sense that it suppresses or suspends what is non-religious in the life of the believer, but in the sense that it tends to give to all of this, without possible exception, a new colour and significance. Subjectively, then, it claims sovereignty, and this is equally true on the objective side. It involves a distinctive view of the world; a *Weltanschauung*, as the Germans expressively say—not of certain elements in the world which are its special interest, preferentially emphasized, as an engineer sees things with special emphasis on construction or a pictorial artist with special emphasis on colour and line, but of the world as a whole and in every part. 'All things declare the Glory of God.' Religion demands, then, we may say, nothing less than the special orientation of a man's whole life in all its departments to the world generally, in whatever shape it may manifest itself to him. Those who accept in any degree this demand are of course profoundly convinced of the value of this orientation: they value it for itself, they find their happiness in it: but they are not content to justify it merely in these terms. They are deeply concerned to assert also its truth; i.e. they feel obliged to claim that the intuition on which the religious experience centres is no mere function of the creative imagination, no mere making of something for men's delight, but a veridical vision of reality capable of being expanded and expounded in a set of true propositions. There are, therefore, and have been at all times, accredited expositors of religious truth, whose business it is to give unexceptionable expansion to this vision and so complete the structure of religious belief. And the completion of the structure of religious belief will be at the same time, in virtue of the demands we have already formulated, the completion of the structure of human belief generally.

To put this quite bluntly and briefly: religion involves for the believer the assertion of certain things about the world generally and as a whole. If these assertions can be shown to be false, religion must be admitted to be a delusion and superstition.

If this description of the religious attitude is correct, religious belief is brought into peculiarly intimate connexion with philosophical belief. For it means that religion, so far as it succeeds in expressing its own implications, must find itself making a philosophical assertion. What degree of assurance is attainable with regard to statements about the world generally and as a whole may be doubted: many are sceptical as to the value of any discussions of this metaphysical order altogether: but it can hardly be doubted that this is the province of philosophy. If such assurance is to be attained by any intellectual discipline it is for philosophy to attain it. The relation thus established with philosophy is peculiarly intimate, because, while each order of belief has no doubt its own characteristic presuppositions and implications, which it is the duty of the philosopher to disentangle, there is no other which issues similarly in a direct challenge to the philosopher. It is a challenge which the philosopher cannot ignore. Just because religion, so far as it is fully conscious of itself, issues in a philosophical assertion, a philosophy, if it is to claim any completeness, must take account of religion. A religion is necessarily always tending to issue in a philosophy and a philosophy must necessarily be either religious or anti-religious in character.

In considering this challenge I do not wish to confine myself to the bare and abstract proposition 'God exists'. With all proper apologies I should select as the

fundamental assertions of the religious consciousness these
two propositions:

(1) Mind orders all things.

(2) The all-ruling mind is essentially all-embracing Love.

The first of these propositions is some centuries older
than Christianity; the second, so far as I know, originates
in Christian thought. You may well think that a better
selection might have been made, but you will probably
agree with me in preferring these two to the other. They
seem to have more substance in them, more capacity for
arousing passion and thus inflaming that conflict of beliefs
which is an essential part of our subject.

Further on I will try to expand these propositions a
little, to explain what I take them to assert, and incidentally I shall perhaps indicate, by the way, why I have
selected them. But first I want to look at them from outside, as it were, and at a distance, to discuss what kind
of proposition they are and their general relation to other
kinds. We have already implied that they are of the type
known as philosophical, but we have said nothing so far
as to the relations of philosophical to unphilosophical
beliefs and assertions. The distinction I now introduce
to you is brought in with the object of elucidating this
side of the question.

I ask you to let me make a general distinction between
Partial and *Total Assertion*—an absolute dichotomy, providing two very capacious boxes into which any assertion
that ever has been or can be made must necessarily fall.
An assertion is to be called Total, which has reference to
the whole of the being indicated in its subject: an assertion is Partial which has reference only to a part of it.
Much the same then, you will perhaps think, as the distinction, familiar in formal logic, between Universal and
Particular Propositions—'all men are animals' on the one
hand, 'some animals are men' on the other. But please
put that aside and forget it. My distinction has nothing
to do with the frequency with which a character is found
within a kind. The answer to the question 'Is this assertion

Total or Partial?' will therefore not be found by asking
whether it is or ought to be asserted without restriction
or with limitations. It depends solely on the relation of
the predicate to the subject—and that means in the long
run that it depends on the relation of this assertion to the
other assertions that one is in a position to make about this
given subject.

Let me give you some examples:

(1) Consider a poem, say *Paradise Lost*. It is quite
evidently a Partial assertion to say of it that it is written
in blank verse or divided into twelve books. On the other
hand, it is quite evidently a Total assertion in my sense
to say that it is a fine (good, beautiful) poem. There are
other possible lines of estimate which leave room for some
doubt, e.g. the attempt to place it in reference to the conventional opposition of romanticism and classicism. As
to that I should say that so far as these terms represent
an attitude capable of permeating a whole work of art,
their ascription would be a Total assertion; but that they
are not always so understood.

(2) Take the example next of a person, an individual
human being. To say that he is six feet high, the father
of two children, or works in the docks, is clearly to make
a Partial assertion about him. To ascribe any virtue to
him, and more generally to call him a good man, is to make
a Total assertion. For in these former cases we have statements that can be established separately and independently by themselves, and can be relied on to hold good
whatever else is discovered. But in the latter set of cases
anything and everything in the man's life is potentially
at least relevant: further knowledge may at any time force
a reconsideration and a qualification of the judgement.

(3) Take thirdly the example of an action, not a *kind*
of action (e.g. murder, suicide) but the actual concrete
interference of an actual person with the course of events.
It may be Partially described in an infinity of ways: it is,
for instance, the writing of a letter. Each of these descriptions can be established separately and securely. But as

soon as we ask whether the action is good or bad, we are on different ground. We require to know everything about it, including the inner life of the agent, before we can pass that judgement. Hence it is a judgement that we are (or should be) very reluctant to pass. To ask whether the act was right or wrong is to ask a question which, though difficult, is not nearly so difficult. Probably ascriptions of right and wrong should be regarded as Partial judgements on actions. But, if so, we shall find that actions may be right and bad, and equally wrong and good—a conclusion which may strike you as paradoxical.

(4) The world generally, the universe, may also be the subject of both kinds of assertion. That it is extended in space and time is a Partial assertion, and all metaphysical systems are attempts to get beyond such partialities to a view of the world in its fullness—to achieve in short a *Weltanschauung*. I hope these instances are sufficient to explain my dichotomy.

Now you may well object that it is not much of a dichotomy after all, because nearly everything we can say falls on one side of it. That is only too true. In fact everything that we can *prove* falls on one side of it. For Partial assertions can usually be proved if you are willing to go to the necessary trouble, but Total assertions never can be. Science therefore progresses and has progressed by discarding Total assertions altogether and confining itself to the Partiality. Botany knows no flower, Zoology no animal: they know only the laws of certain functions and processes of which these terms represent the familiar theatre. But these Total propositions, which, as I have said, are excluded from science and are incapable of proof, are yet of fundamental importance for the conduct of life and are rightly regarded, I believe, as the goal of knowledge. Or, if you resent the ascription of knowledge where proof and finality are absent, you may say alternatively that knowledge, which is of the Partialities, is insufficient, insufficient even to itself. It is not what we are really seeking. It points beyond itself to an ideal of wisdom and judgement, and is of value only so far as it contributes to the progressive realization of this ideal.

I will develop this point by considering briefly the part played by these two orders of assertion or belief in the practical life. There is an aspect of intelligent conduct, as I have argued elsewhere,[1] in which it is ordered under the notion of purpose as the alteration of a situation in a certain sense (direction), i.e. as the effort to bring about a certain result. This is a universal aspect of action; for all action is necessarily the alteration of a situation; and obviously, if it is to be intelligent, if it is to be fully conscious of its own nature, as morality demands that it shall be, action must include awareness of the sense (direction) of the alteration introduced. A man's interference with events will have its effects, and these effects must be adopted in advance by the agent, so far as possible, as his intention, if he is to be a conscious agent. The conception of means and end is the familiar device by which we rationalize conduct from this point of view. The relation of means and end is, otherwise viewed, a necessary causal relation. The means, become fact, generate the end, as effect and result, by causal necessity. Thus all calculations of this kind involve necessary causal laws and connexions; and these hold, of course, only and always between universals. Such laws are precisely what science is always occupied in establishing. Hence action viewed as purpose, rationalized by means of the notion of means and end, can hope in the favourable case to prove its reasonableness. It can demonstrate its way, or if it cannot, that is only because the requisite information is not available or science is not sufficiently advanced, and something has to be done at once. But it can prove and demonstrate only because it excludes the Total judgement and is content to dwell in Partialities.

I have argued elsewhere[2] that purpose is the expression

---

[1] See my essay, *The Limits of Purpose*, in the volume published under that title (1932).

[2] See *Desire and Affection*, the second essay in *The Limits of Purpose*.

of desire or appetite, a feature of our natural endowment
which gives things an interest to us so far as they exhibit
certain general characters. Hunger, for instance, gives
things an interest for a man so far as they are food or in
proportion to their eatability. On these lines nothing has
value in itself, and anything in which value is transiently
recognized (e.g. a loaf to a hungry man) is liable at any
moment to be scrapped and superseded (thus becoming
relatively valueless) because something possessing this
same value in a higher degree becomes available (e.g. a
bigger and better loaf). Desire and purpose thus work
in general terms, their value-judgements are always relative: no absolute of satisfaction is or can be within sight.
Life, if this were the whole of it, would be much as
Hobbes describes it—'a perpetual and restless desire of
power after power, which ceaseth only in Death'. But
there is also in man, I have suggested, another principle,
of precisely opposite tendency, to which I took the liberty
of giving the name *Affection*, using the term in its familiar
conversational sense, as when we say a man is an affectionate father. In so far as we are fond of things and persons, in so far as we love them, these things and persons
are for us irreplaceable, uniquely significant, endowed each
with a value that is all its own, a value incapable of being
measured, except in the most vague inaccurate scale of
intensity of absorption, against any other object in the
world.

Now just as purpose, which is organized desire, is the
practical embodiment of the Partial judgement, owing
to that its eminent rationality (i.e. its perpetual willingness to drop the bone, if and when a bigger and better
bone can be found) and its unexceptionable balance-
sheets of profit and loss—so love, which is fully developed
affection, is the practical embodiment of the Total judgement; and Love, in its effort to embrace the totality of
the being of its object, necessarily excludes that kind of
rationality (for it will under no circumstances drop its
bone at all) and can therefore produce no intelligible

balance-sheet. Its judgements are absolute, not relative, consisting only in endorsement of and delight in the various features of the being of the object of its love, as progressive study reveals them. If Love were preference it could explain itself, but it would have become purpose. There is no reason for loving. Yet it is wrong to say that Love is blind. The lover in fact sees many times as well as others when he looks on what he loves. If we could all have such knowledge of the world as the lover has of his beloved, we should have left science far behind and feel no need of it, for we should be in the process of realizing the higher ideal of the Total judgement.

To bring this discussion together I will end with a brief and dogmatic statement of the nature of religious belief as I understand it:

(1) It is a Total assertion which has for the subject the whole world order.

(2) It asserts this world order to be the expression of infinite Wisdom and Love.

(3) This Love and Wisdom is conceived as the endorsement equally of every feature of the world process, of what seems to us bad as well as of what we think good (God is the cause not of all things, but only of the good, said Plato, but wrongly: his God was not a God of Love).

(4) The religious life is the attempt to realize this divine and all-embracing Love in the person of the believer.

IV. CONFLICTS OF BELIEF

THE subject of this discussion is the Conflict of Beliefs. By that I do not mean primarily such differences of opinion as give rise to private and public discussions between different people, but conflicts which arise, as Plato would say, in the conversation of the Soul with itself. I want to consider the possibilities and actualities of conflict, in your mind or mine, between the different beliefs which you or I in good faith hold, with a view to throwing light on the situation in which religious belief finds itself among enlightened people to-day.

(1) *Contradiction.* Generally it seems true to say that Contradiction can only occur between assertions of the same order. Two would-be statements of fact, of mathematical truth, of aesthetic or ethical value, may be in contradiction with one another; but there can be no contradiction between a statement belonging to one of these regions and a statement belonging to one of the other. Each sphere is self-contained: in each the investigator can go his way secure from disturbance from without. And in fact truth is cut up in many regions into very small pieces indeed. Within the sphere of value the artistic judgement seems to take no account of the ethical, nor the ethical of the artistic. Within the sphere of art each work of art seems to constitute a little world in itself, capable of being judged in complete separation from any other work of art; and even in the world of fact, with all its far-reaching causal connexions and chains of influence, it is often surprising how little information as to what is or was going on elsewhere is needed to enable one to define with sufficient accuracy what is going on in the restricted field under observation. It is as though we men had set ourselves with unconscious cunning and remarkable success to ask questions of the world, which could be answered in complete independence of every other.

It seems true, further, to say that between Partial and Total assertions, as I have defined them in the last lecture, there is and can be no direct conflict and contradiction. The two kinds of assertion use different predicates, or, if they appear to use the same, use them in different senses. Therefore, contradiction between them is impossible. But, if I am right in saying that science makes only Partial assertions, while the characteristic affirmations of religion are Total assertions, it follows at once that there can be no direct conflict between science and religion. You may well object, however, that there must be something wrong with this conclusion, for the conflict of science and religion is a notorious and familiar feature of the modern world. The answer to the objection is this. If the phenomenon of conflict is strictly limited to oppositions which can finally be reduced to directly contradictory assertions, then there is and can be no conflict between science and religion, for the reasons already given. The conflicts which are a familiar feature of all civilizations owe their bitterness and their longevity precisely to the fact that they are not reducible to direct contradictions and thus are not open to simple logical treatment. They are too fundamental to be formulated so neatly or settled so simply. This suggests, what I believe to be the truth, that all such conflicts fall within the philosophical field and involve on both sides the Total (not the Partial) judgement. The human mind in such a conflict is divided against itself, being simultaneously pressed from different directions to form divergent and irreconcilable estimates of the structure of reality.

(2) *Religion and Science.* The opposed tendencies which underlie the conflict of science and religion were first clearly formulated, as far as we know, by Plato and Aristotle in the fourth century B.C. In principle their diagnosis still holds. All the intellectual labour of the intervening centuries has only complicated the issue and induced certain changes of emphasis. The original simple statements are still worth recalling. In the *Phaedo,* Plato's Socrates

complained of those whom we may call the scientists of his
day, that they claimed to be able to explain such phenomena as his presence in prison awaiting execution, after
he had been offered and had rejected a way of escape, by
an analysis in purely physical and mechanical terms, in
terms which took no account whatever of mind, or, more
particularly, of that judgement of good and bad, of right
and wrong, which in Socrates' own interpretation of the
matter was fundamental. It was this exclusion of mind
and will as operative agencies that he found so unsatisfactory; and it was on this account that the quotation he
chanced to hear as a young man from Anaxagoras, 'mind
rules all things', seemed so immensely significant and
roused such extravagant hopes in his mind. These hopes
in actual fact, as he goes on to tell us, when he finally got
hold of the book and read the rest of it, he found to be
totally unwarranted. Anaxagoras turned out to be as
much of a materialist as the rest of them.

Aristotle makes precisely the same point when he says,
in the review of his predecessors with which he opens his
Metaphysics, that earth and air, and fire and water, the
supposed elementary substances of which all bodies were
composed, whatever else they might account for, were
plainly incapable of accounting for the rightness and goodness of the various things and situations that emerged
from their interaction and composition: and of this rightness and goodness some account, he says, is surely required:
so great a matter could not be left to chance. Hence, he
continues, when one came forward and said that there
must be a mind at work in all this, as there is in animals,
determining the order and arrangement of the whole, he
stood out from the rest, like a sober man among drunkards
incapable of controlling their tongues. The sober man in
this reference is, of course, Anaxagoras, and of Anaxagoras'
general theory as it finally worked out, Aristotle's judgement is in principle the same as Plato's. In the striking
saying which Plato had quoted and which Aristotle had
in mind, Anaxagoras had merely caught a fleeting glimpse

of the promised land which it was left for Plato and Aristotle afterwards to occupy. In some sense mind had to be established as the director of nature, if natural history and human life were to be made intelligible: for the only kind of necessity which the materialist could recognize was one which made of any whole a mere chance resultant. This holds equally of the great totality, nature, the universe, reality, and of the microcosm, the human or animal organism. Intention alone can exclude chance in this reference, and intention belongs only to mind.

There can be no doubt that here the real conflict is between two Total judgements—two interpretations of reality—two philosophies. The one, the materialist view of the world, has its basis in the success of the scientist's analytic method in elucidating certain types of natural process, a method which owes its success, as we have argued, to the fact that it confines itself rigidly to the Partial judgement. It can, I believe, be shown that on these lines finality, totality, is unattainable, since the field of exploration is infinite and inexhaustible. But the dream of finality still haunts the human mind; the rapid advance of scientific frontiers engenders in the scientific mind the ambition of world-empire, and with this he challenges the philosopher. He is tempted to think that his is the only way to truth and knowledge. He is aware that at present, with the existing resources of science, there are whole realms of being which defy his analysis. But science, he reflects, is still young, and its methods are in their infancy; its successes are at least capable by general admission of progressive and indefinite extension, and in this extension lies the only path to a vision of the whole open to man. For the present (he concludes) if we are wise, we shall frame our provisional estimate of the structure of reality on the basis that science is the truth and the whole truth. In the passage from 'the truth' to 'the whole truth' you pass from the partial to the total judgement. What might have been mere agnosticism becomes philosophical dogmatism. Thus this is, I say, a philosophical view to which the scientific mind is tempted, suggested, but in no way necessitated, by the advances of science. Those who maintain it usually know quite well that it is not proved—not proved even to the extent to which the doctrines of science are proved—that it is a conjectural extension of belief beyond the frontiers of science proper—and of course many scientists for a variety of reasons roundly refuse to subscribe to any such interpretation of the world.

On the one hand, then, there is an interpretation of reality suggested and recommended by the successes of science, built on the basis of the Partial judgement, springing as has been said from that half-conscious cunning by which man asks of the world questions that can be answered separately, without reference to one another. In the ancient controversy, to which Plato and Aristotle were cited as witnesses, this interpretation is opposed to another interpretation which has its roots and unfailing nourishment in the regions of the Total judgement, wherever spirit and its achievements are judged and valued, in the field of artistic and moral judgement, and in the aspirations of religion. To these must be added history, so far as it passes beyond the mere delineation of external sequences, and passes judgement upon agents and their motives; and even the scientist himself is inevitably a traitor to the scientific metaphysics and is drawn into the opposed camp, so far as he becomes conscious of his own scientific activity and affirms its independent value and significance. At this point his analytic method is bound to suspend itself at the risk of suicide; for the protons and electrons into which he dissolves the world offer no hint of a principle equal to explaining this thirst for knowledge.

This rival interpretation in terms of mind is in opposition strictly, as I have already indicated, not to science but to a conjectural prolongation of science into the metaphysical field. The conflict arises because the scientist transgresses his self-imposed limits. In reaction against the aggression of the scientist the partisans of mind are tempted to commit counter-aggression in their turn. They have at times tried to show, sometimes assisted by traitors within the camp of science itself, that science is not equal to the solution of its own problems; that the further postulate of some spiritual principle is necessary if the problems (for instance) of biology are to be satisfactorily resolved. Now some such postulate may turn out one day to be a scientific necessity or expediency; and if so the scientist will accept the necessity and make the postulate; but he will make it in his own fashion and on his own terms. If he accepts any such hypothesis it will be with reference to a particular set of phenomena, for the accurate analysis of which this additional factor needs to be posited.

Suppose the biologist did come to some such conclusion as this, the development would no doubt create something of a sensation, and we should be asked to note how scientific materialism is forced in the end to make concessions to spiritualism. But the concession would in fact do nothing to reconcile the two points of view. For the scientist would only have found, what he has long been seeking, the place of mind in nature, as one factor operating along with others to make the world what it is. The spiritualist on the other hand would still be unable to abate by one jot his demand that mind shall be shown to rule *all things*. The counter-attack of the spiritualist when he invades the territory of science is on a far wider front than this. He aims at constructing a spiritualist science, based on the Total instead of the Partial judgement, a botany which really knows plants and a zoology which really knows animals. Of the brilliant failure of a science so misconceived we have a record in the work of Aristotle, and the grain of truth in the traditional view that the authority of Aristotle was an obstacle to the development of modern science lies in the fact that in his reaction against materialism he gave countenance to this misconception, trying to recast the sciences on the basis of a spiritual metaphysics.

Thus there is or has been aggression on both sides. Aggression for aggression, the invasion of the scientific

E

sphere by the spiritualist is undoubtedly the more unwarranted and the more harmful in its results. On the
other hand, it is much the less common in these modern
days. The armaments of science have become so over-
whelming that such aggression is no longer a tempting
adventure. Armed neutrality perhaps best describes the
normal relation of the two camps to-day; but that is a
condition of tension, from which actual warfare may at
any moment arise. Such a situation is uncomfortable
between nations when one's loyalty is pledged commonly
only to one side. It is doubly uncomfortable when it ob-
tains between two lines of thought, each of which has the
strongest claim on the loyalty of us all.

(3) *Religion and Progress.* But there is another conflict
of beliefs, less well defined than this and less ancient, but
perhaps even more persistent and troublesome to the
modern mind, in which religion finds itself involved. For
convenience I will call the conflict the opposition of religion and progress. Any danger of misunderstanding arising
from this name will, I hope, be obviated in the explanations
which follow; but let me say at once that we have to deal
here, in my opinion, once more with a genuine conflict of
beliefs, in which our sympathies should be engaged to some
extent on both sides, not with an opposition which is
fundamentally false nor with an issue between plain black
and white, in which the whole truth lies on one side. But
the conflict is of a much more popular and general character
than the one we have been discussing and therefore the
real issue is more apt to be overlaid by confusions and
false antitheses.

My first task is to give some examples of the conflict.
In the middle of the nineteenth century Karl Marx de-
nounced religion as the opium of the people. The movement which he founded for the revolutionary reform of
economic organization, with a view to the raising of the
general level of life, has ever since been fairly definitely
anti-religious in character. England constitutes a partial
exception in this matter, but the socialist parties of the

continent have shown a strong and uniform tendency to regard religion as not the least important of their enemies. Their programmes may content themselves with negatives—such as the separation of state and church, the secularization of education—but in actual practice the temper of these parties has been so hostile to religion that it has been almost impossible for a genuine believer to belong to them. Some years ago there was a crisis in the French Socialist party when it became known that Jean Jaurès, its leader, had allowed his young daughter to make her first Communion. Jaurès had to defend himself before the party: the passionate plea for freedom of action with which he won his case was voted one of the greatest speeches of his life. The general tendency of course is older than Marxism and is not confined to Socialists. In France, as M. Siegfried has recently reminded us in his acute analysis of French parties, it is an essential part of the seemingly indestructible tradition of the Revolution that all radicalism shall be definitely anti-clerical; and the boundary between anti-clericalism and hostility to religion is hard to draw.

In this connexion the example of Mazzini is full of interest. He lived and worked side by side with those who forged the modern Socialist movement and he had much in common with them; but in his teaching to Young Italy this Quixote of revolutionaries sought to bridge both of the two gulfs he saw threatening; first, the gulf between nationalism and internationalism, secondly, the gulf between religion and progress; and on both counts he must be said to have lost his case in the court of contemporary opinion. To him the religious basis was indispensable, if the fight against Machiavellism and Materialism—twin evils that threatened the working-class movement—was to be sustained. Without the spirit of God there was no liberty, no morality. This spirit of God he conceived as a progressive spirit, resident in the general body of believers. Humanity for him was 'the successive incarnation of God', discovering the Law of God 'article by article, line by line', by the power of accumulated experience and the growing efficacy of association. 'I believe in Humanity, *sole* interpreter of the Law of God on earth.' In this sense he revived and adapted for his own use the Hussite cry 'the Cup for the People'.

Why is it, we may ask, that Mazzini's conception of a religion of progress has an undeniable air of paradox? To answer that question let us go back once more to the pre-Christian atmosphere of Platonic thought. We shall find there a part—perhaps the main part—of the answer. In the *Republic*, Plato, constructing his ideal city, finds himself carried forward on successive waves of paradox. He recommends that his ruling class shall live on terms of absolute community of goods, shall never buy or sell; that men and women shall enjoy equal rights and privileges; that permanent marriages shall be abolished; that wives and children shall be held in common. But shocking as these proposals are, his most outrageous proposal yet remains: it is that philosophers shall be kings. This in his view is the crowning paradox. Why? To be a philosopher for Plato is to be skilled in the art of dying, that is, in the capacity to separate soul from body. To separate soul from body is to throw off the senses and the appetites, to intermit all mental functions in which the body is a partner. Thus to put rule in the hands of a philosopher is to put rule in the hands of a man who is by profession, as it were, blind and deaf. He is a man, as Plato tells us in the *Theaetetus*, who does not know his way to the courts or the assembly, who does not listen to the laws of the city when they are read out, who does not care how things are going for his city, who is ignorant of what he is doing and wholly unacquainted with his next-door neighbour.[1] The positive qualification, which redeems and explains these negatives, is that he has knowledge of the eternal and changeless reality, and in virtue of that is incapable of wrong. For it is Plato's view that in contact with the eternal alone is security for men or for cities

---

[1] *Tht.* 173–4.

to be found. But in the light of that contact human affairs necessarily become trivial and insignificant. 'Human affairs', he writes in his last work,[1] 'are not worth serious attention; and yet we take them seriously, we cannot help it. . . . Man is made to be the plaything of God, and this, truly considered, is the best of him.'

These are the words of a man who, being a Greek, had no belief in progress. He represents religion (I think we may fairly say 'religion' in many places where Plato says 'philosophy') as scandalous to the vulgar only by reason of its contempt of the body and its conviction of the triviality of the temporal. Even so, there is a tension in the mind of the philosopher himself, as the quotation from the *Laws* plainly recognizes. This difficult art of dying is severely restricted in its exercise by the pressure of surrounding fact. But transfer this same religious spirit to a nineteenth century for which progress is the law of life, and the tension is enormously increased: the attitude of indifference becomes an unforgivable crime. The Greek sage who does not care to know who won yesterday's battle was likely no doubt to make himself unpopular in his city; but the modern religious leader who in face of great plans of national reform, on which for their passionate advocates the whole future of the human race depends —in face of these calls for a change of heart and a truce to partisan controversy, has to meet the full fury of all the organized righteousness of his day.

The greatest plans of national reform deal necessarily with externals, and religion is a preoccupation with the things of the spirit. It is because the belief in progress is essentially a modern belief that the conflict of religion and progress is essentially a modern conflict.

I think we shall see a little further into the nature of this conflict if we see it as an expression of the tension in human nature between the opposed and complementary principles of desire and affection. Desire is the principle of change: we must want what we seek to get. These

[1] *Laws*, 803.

great schemes of reform are, or seek to be, national purposes based on a widespread desire for something that
men have not got or want more of. All effort, constructive and destructive, all struggle and warfare, is actuated
by desire and purpose. But no desire and no purpose,
not even the highest and most selfless ambition, has any
direct endorsement from religion. They may be limited,
prohibited, regulated in its name, but never initiated or
directly encouraged. For religion seeks rather, as I have
said, to waken an all-embracing love in the believer. But
affection is a conservative principle which attaches men
to things as they are. Its fulfilment is the love or charity
of St. Paul, which 'taketh not account of evil'; which
'beareth all things, believeth all things, hopeth all things'.[1]
Its faith is not a faith in a project of human improvement,
for the realization of which it commands every sacrifice, but
a faith in a divine order, actual though but dimly apprehended, to which it enjoins absolute surrender.

It is not fanciful to see the conflict of these principles
in the Gospel record of the life and actions of Jesus of
Nazareth. The organized righteousness of His day stood
for the maintenance of the Jewish religion in all its strict-
ness, and aimed at the recovery of Jewish independence
under a Jewish deliverer. Jesus offered Himself as the
Deliverer, the Messiah: but He took little account of those
who felt themselves the natural allies of any such deliverer
and gave no support to their plans. Instead He preferred
to consort with tax-gatherers and evil-livers, and pro-
claimed that His message was for them rather than for
the righteous. He condoned and even encouraged laxity
in the interpretation of the Law. In many parables such
as those of the Prodigal Son, the Labourers in the Vine-
yard, the Unmerciful Servant, His teaching encouraged a
similar laxity in the moral sphere, since it tended to weaken
belief, so strongly inculcated in the Old Testament, that
the Divine judgement will reward men strictly according
to their deserts. For all this, as for the precepts of non-

[1] 1 Cor. xiii. 7.

resistance to evil and of love to one's enemies, the justification offered is the universality of the Love of God who
'maketh His sun to rise on the evil and on the good, and
sendeth rain on the just and on the unjust'.[1] It is not so
much that the Pharisees are condemned (though in certain
respects they may be) or that their plans are judged un-
sound, as that they and their plans are ignored. Their
plans concern temporalities in which Jesus has no interest;
and the Divine Love is not a preference for the deserving or
a reward for merit.

What I am suggesting is that we have here in a heigh-
tened form a conflict which is at least latent in every individual and in all societies, between the spirit of reform,
the man of purpose and action, on the one hand, and the
spirit of religion, the contemplative spirit, the loyalties
of affectionate acceptance, on the other. Each one of us
is in healthy revolt against circumstance, eager to re-
fashion the world nearer to his heart's desire, and in this
spirit he finds his other self at times a drag and a handicap:
he rebels against the ties of affection and the complaisance
of Christian charity: 'he who is not with me' he feels 'is
against me'. With his other self each of us reacts similarly
against the practical effort, against the exaggeration of
immediate issues, against the ill will and fractious divi-
sions which they generate. 'A plague on both your houses'
he cries in this mood; for he sees how unimportant by any
absolute standard the issue is, and is disposed to embrace
in a large tolerance all the contending sects.

(4) *Reason.* I am afraid I cannot now offer you, what
perhaps you expect of me, a final reconciliation of the
two conflicts of belief which I have been discussing. In
the case of the second it may be doubted whether a
theoretical reconciliation is possible. Instead of attempting that, by way of conclusion, I want to say something
about Reason and Unreason in these matters. Long
tradition requires of any belief that it shall show itself
to be reasonable. But there are periods when men

[1] Matt. v. 45.

uneasily revolt against this demand. They complain that
Reason never has given and never will give satisfaction to
the human heart, and seek to enthrone in its place some
irrational or super-rational principle. This tendency is
very active at the present day; and since I believe it to
be potent for mischief, I wish to make my protest against
it, and to explain that what I am saying, as I understand
it, gives no support whatever to any such tendency.

I have put religious belief in the region of what I have
called the Total judgement, and I have emphasized the
point that such a judgement cannot be proved. Further,
I have almost excluded the possibility of direct conflict
between this belief and any other, unless it be one of the
same kind, viz. another statement of religious belief. If
all this is accepted, it may be said, religious belief becomes entirely arbitrary and subjective: the believer is
left free to belief what he pleases. To such an objection
I should reply, first, that I do not say these things of religion alone. Every one of them I am prepared to assert
equally of philosophy. It also is incapable of demonstration and of coming into direct conflict with any except
another philosophical belief. Secondly, I should say that
the regions of Total judgement are the regions of intuition,
and that the opposition of Reason and Intuition is false
and misleading. On the first of these points I need not
say anything further, but the second needs some development, particularly because a good deal of use has been
made of this opposition recently by defenders of religious
belief.

We must begin by deciding what Reason stands for.
Those who oppose Reason and Intuition seem to confine
it to, or confuse it with, reasoning, the giving of reasons.
There is an older tradition which makes it the differentia
of the human species, the root therefore of all that distinguishes man among the animals, of cities and theatres,
of art and poetry, as well as of science and mathematics.
Perhaps this latter interpretation is inconveniently wide,
but the former is preposterously narrow; for no intellec-

tual act can possibly consist solely in the giving of reasons. All judgement and therefore all reasoning rests on a basis of intuition. Thus even in the fields in which reasoning is prominent, intuition is not excluded. Reason includes intuition.

But consider the matter more generally. It is in thought that reason is primarily manifested. Thought starts from sensation, in which man is a creature of his immediate environment, and, starting from this basis, reveals itself as a persistent effort to throw off these limitations. Out of the spectator of a few changing miles of the earth's surface it aims at making a spectator of all time and all existence. The thinker is required to discount his position, his partialities, his interests, and all passions except the passion for truth, and achieve a selfless objectivity which will allow the whole realm of being to reveal itself in its true proportions. The degree of man's success in achieving this aim is the degree of man's rationality and of his freedom; but it is a curious freedom, for, as Bacon said, *natura non nisi parendo vincitur*, 'we conquer only by submission'; and the ideal of thought is that it shall be wholly determined by its object. In this persistent struggle of thought the starting-point and the goal are equally intuitive, at one end the unstable kaleidoscope of the senses, at the other end, in idea at least, the final and total revelation: and the intuition which is the goal—or rather such distant approximations to it as we can compass—is built up, not without reasoning, out of the intuition which is the starting-point. Reason consists, I suggest, essentially, in the transcendence of the spatial and temporal position, the suppression of self, and the surrender of thought to its object.

It is only necessary to say further that such objectivity is as peremptorily required of one who would judge truly the moral value of an action, the aesthetic value of a poem or a picture, the theoretic value of a philosophy, as of one who would work out a theorem of geometry or determine the composition of the Milky Way. It may be more difficult to sustain, but it is equally essential to success. It is also worth while remarking that though an intuitive judgement cannot be proved, it can make some sort of a justification of itself. But the justification always comes in the last resort to a request, addressed to one who disagrees, that he shall look at the object again more carefully, with special attention to this and that feature of it, and see whether after such reinspection he is not disposed to modify his verdict. Such discussion we should often call argument, and the parties to it might call their points reasons; but they are different in logical character equally from the irresistible demonstrations of the mathematician and from the massive probabilities of natural science.

But man, whatever he is, is not merely a thinking animal, and religion is not a mere matter of thinking certain things. The religious spirit, if the brief analysis of it which I have given has any truth, may claim in another way to be the most powerful of all allies of reason in human affairs. The ideal of Christian charity, as expressed in such commands as that of loving one's enemies, aims at a universalization of man's affections precisely parallel to the liberation of the thinking mind from the initial limitations of sense, to which the cognitive effort is directed. Man's affections are limited at the start in the same way, mainly by the accident of spatial and temporal position; it is not that he prefers his home and his family, it is that they and no others are his. But these are to be for him merely a point of departure. He is to aim at widening the basis of his life until his action is as free from partiality as that of the sun which shines freely and indifferently on all creatures. This, if it could be achieved, would surely be reasonableness in action; and the attempt to conceive it suggests that the two sides of human nature cannot be kept divorced, since love, the fulfilment of affection, is seen to be a previous condition of the fulfilment of thought in reason.

V. THE ECLIPSE OF CAUSE[1]

I

WHAT has happened, is happening, and is going to happen to the notion of Cause? That is the question I wish to discuss in this paper. In the history of European thought from its obscure origins to the present day, few notions, if any, have maintained a more central position. The very existence of knowledge, apart from its bare rudiments, has been commonly thought to depend on the discovery of causal connexions. 'We suppose ourselves', said Aristotle, 'to possess unqualified scientific knowledge of a thing . . . when we think that we know the cause on which the fact depends'.[2] In the nineteenth century J. S. Mill described the notion of Cause as 'the root of the whole theory of induction'[3] and law of causation as 'the main pillar of inductive science'.[4] He was saying something which he took to be hardly open to question; and in his day, as far as I know, it was not in fact seriously questioned. But before the end of that century James Ward (in his famous Gifford lectures, *Naturalism and Agnosticism*) was calling attention to the tendency of science in certain departments to eliminate 'substance and cause' from its analysis of nature. He cited from Mach's *Popular Scientific Lectures* a definite avowal of this aim: 'I hope that the science of the future will discard the idea of cause and effect, as being formally obscure; and in my feeling that these ideas contain a strong tincture of fetishism I am certainly not alone.'

Ward described the elimination of Cause as being at that time 'at last complete' in the sphere of the higher mechanics which he was reviewing; but the movement has extended and developed far since he wrote. Sir Arthur Eddington, lecturing thirty years later on the same foundation as Ward, has recently explained to us that the science of our day is unable to distinguish between

---

[1] *Hibbert Journal*, July 1932.
[2] *An. Post.* 71 b 9.
[3] *Logic*, III. v. 2.
[4] Ibid.

cause and effect. For the one-way relation of *causation*, with its inevitable reference to what he calls 'Time's Arrow', it substitutes a symmetrical relation which he takes leave to name *causality*. This revised causal notion, however, is only fully operative in 'primary physics'. 'Secondary physics can distinguish cause and effect, but its foundation does not rest on a causal scheme and it is indifferent as to whether or not strict causality prevails.'[1] Again he says: 'Whether or not there is a causal scheme at the base of atomic phenomena, modern atomic theory is not now attempting to find it; and it is making rapid progress because it no longer sets this up as a practical aim.'[2] Here the retention of the causal notion in a modified form for primary physics and the suggestion that there may after all be a causal scheme at work in the atom are obvious signs of reluctance to break with the tradition altogether; but it will probably be agreed that the general argument of the lectures implies a more complete rejection of causation than these sentences alone suggest. Professor Eddington's metaphysical speculations contain much, of course, that other scientists would dispute, but in their distrust of causation they seem to represent a general tendency of the scientific thought of the day. A recent attempt to state the outlook of science for the general reader says quite generally that the 'elimination of the causal relation . . . is characteristic of all the more advanced sciences'.[3]

It is certainly much to be desired that some one possessing the necessary scientific competence should carefully investigate the developments of scientific thought to which I have referred. I am not myself competent for such a task. The defects of my scientific education debar me from anything more than an external and necessarily superficial view of what is happening. But the questions raised are of such general importance and affect so profoundly the total philosophical situation that the mere layman, like myself, finds it difficult to stand aside altogether, and

[1] *The Nature of the Physical World*, p. 296.   [2] Ibid., p. 299.
[3] N. Campbell, *What is Science?*, p. 55.

may perhaps comment without offence. For the purposes
of this paper I am adopting a very wide and general point
of view. I wish to estimate the tendencies of the present
in the light of the past. The causal notion has passed
through many changes in its long history, and it is possible
that we shall be better able to appreciate what is going on
under our eyes if we recall certain features of this history.
Let us begin, then, by going back to Plato and Aristotle,
the chief legislators of our philosophical terminology.

It seems that both Plato and Aristotle were disposed to
describe their special and distinctive contribution to the
thought of Greece as a reinterpretation of the notion of
cause. In the *Phaedo* Plato's Socrates represents himself
as starting from an attempt to understand things in terms
of their physical components and antecedents, and as ending in the view that the ground of the beautiful was to be
found in beauty itself and nowhere else, i.e. in the principle
of its own organization. In passing he discusses his own
decision to wait quietly in prison for the poison which is to
end his life instead of accepting the proffered means of
escape. Its cause, he says, is plainly a resolve of his, inspired by a certain conception of what is good, and the
contractions of muscles and other physical phenomena in
which many would find its explanation are secondary and
instrumental to this resolve. He represents himself as turning from physical analysis because he was blinded by excess
of light. But this is ironical: the evident aim is to reduce
the physical and material to proper subordination. The
same theme forms the thread on which Aristotle's review
of the past, contained in the first book of his *Metaphysics*,
is strung. Previous thinkers, apart from Plato and the
Pythagoreans, were practically confined to a material
conception of cause. The only way of accounting for the
behaviour of anything that they could think of was to find
out what it was made of. The historical development for
Aristotle was the progressive supplementation of this form
of causation by others; and with his own discrimination
of the four kinds of cause the development was complete.

Thus, building on Platonic foundations, Aristotle formulated the famous doctrine of the four causes, presenting it as the completion of a natural historical development. First of all, he said, men thought to find the clue to nature in that of which all things were made—'the first from which they come to be, the last into which they are resolved'.[1] They sought a common material substratum for all bodies. Then they came to see that such a substratum, if they found it, could not well be supposed to control its own modifications: they had to look, then, further for a cause of the movement which was set up in this material. But having advanced so far, 'truth itself', as Aristotle says,[2] forced them a step further. The things thus generated exhibited in their different degrees goodness and beauty. What of these values? They could not be credited either to the material substratum itself or to that which was supposed to have introduced movement into it. On the other hand, 'so great a matter' could hardly be attributed to mere chance. Thus thinkers were led, though clumsily and with no clear understanding of what they were doing, to introduce a principle directed to order and goodness. In this way the good or end was recognized as operative in nature; a necessary supplementation was demanded from the final cause. And in a similarly halting and indecisive fashion other thinkers, of whom Plato was the greatest, came upon the chief of all the four causes, the Form or Essence. When this cause is added to the other three; when the relation of the four causes to one another is clearly grasped and the primacy of the Form over the rest is established; then for the first time the path is opened to a satisfactory knowledge of nature and her works.

The early modern thinkers inherited not so much the Aristotelian doctrine as a terminology derived from it. In their impatience with a burdensome philosophical tradition, which they felt they had outgrown, they hardly troubled to go back to the fountain head, to see whether they could make more of the Greek than of the Latin in

---

[1] *Met.* 983 b 8 (tr. Ross).   [2] Ibid. 984 b 10.

which the Middle Ages had swathed it. 'But as the inventions of men are woven, so also are they ravelled out. . . . The Analysis or Resolution is by the same way; but beginneth with the knot that was last tyed.' So says Hobbes,[1] speaking of Pope and Bishops; but the saying applies equally to this story of the four causes. Indeed, in this very book, the *Leviathan*, Hobbes himself proclaims his eagerness to untie the first knot by declaiming against 'abstract essences and substantial forms'. These he dismisses as 'Jargon', typical of that study 'which is not properly philosophy . . . but Aristotelity'. Hobbes has his conclusion ready. 'The World', he says—and he explains that he means by the world, 'the Universe, that is, the whole masse of all things that are'—'is Corporeall, that is to say, Body . . . and . . . every part of the Universe is Body, and that which is not Body is no part of the Universe.'[2] So the first knot was untied. The next step was to reject the final cause; and this was done with energy and decision by Descartes and most of his contemporaries and successors. There remained only the material cause and that which Aristotle called the kinetic cause. But of these matter, in the sense in which Aristotle had used it, became almost meaningless by the suppression of its correlative, form. Thus the way was opened for the state of things in which we were all brought up, in which cause has special reference always to change and movement. The efficient cause might still be distinguished, in academic studies which deferred to the old tradition, from formal cause, material cause, and final cause; but in fact these other three applications were felt to be archaic and artificial. When cause was used without qualification in what was felt to be its proper and natural sense, it was used of an event which made possible or necessary a subsequent event.

II

In the development which I have briefly described above there is, of course, much more than a mere change of

---

[1] *Leviathan*, ch. 47.   [2] Ibid., ch. 46.

terminology: profound metaphysical issues are involved. In a sense it may seem that the modern world merely simplified the issue. Where Aristotle had prescribed a fourfold method of inquiry—for explanation on all four lines was for him essential—the moderns concentrated on one. By this, it might be urged, they avoided the confusion incidental to the fact, pointed out by Aristotle himself, that if cause is used in all four senses, one of a given pair of things may be both cause and effect of the other, e.g. we take exercise to improve our health. Exercise, then, is the efficient cause of health and health the final cause of exercise. Again, the notion of final cause, with its obvious roots in human purpose, may be suspected of irrelevance outside the sphere from which it was originally drawn: once more possible confusion is avoided if it is, at least initially, excluded. But such considerations are at home rather in science than in philosophy. Philosophy has no business with convenient simplifications and initial exclusions. Science does not deny that what is initially excluded may turn out in the end to be an essential element in the final statement of the truth; and philosophy is concerned with the final statement.

The fundamental opposition between the two points of view is in the attitude to time and change. For Aristotle in the end there were only two causes, form and matter; but form has, as it were, suffered diremption into three varieties of expression—a diremption due to that resistance of matter to which the phenomena of change and development are a continual witness.[1] For him there was a region, that of the heavenly bodies, in which matter made no resistance, where things therefore did not change; and there was also pure Being, that of God, from which matter and motion were altogether excluded. Thus no mark of Time's Arrow is to be found on Aristotle's ultimates. The last understanding of a thing is the knowledge of what it timelessly is; and events, so far as they are intelligible, are illuminated by a light reflected from this knowledge.

[1] This point is well made by Mure, *Aristotle*, p. 13.

For the moderns, on the other hand, time and change are
everything. Centres of opposition to such a view may be
found in religion, art, morality, and even from time to time
within science itself; but once the first step is taken the conclusion is inevitable. And the conclusion is what Hobbes
announced—'every part of the Universe is Body, and what
is not Body is no part of the Universe'. In order to understand a thing, what you need is to be able to tell the parts
of which it is made and how they came to fall into the
pattern in which they now are. The pattern itself is an
effect, not a cause, and knowledge is a knowledge of causes.

The scientific determinism of the nineteenth century
represents a climax in the triumphant progress of this
modern view of the world. This phase of its development
is to be found faithfully recorded in the writings of J. S.
Mill, particularly in the account of Causation in his *Logic*
and in his various discussions of the Freedom of the Will.
It is axiomatic, first, that the present determines the
future, and, second, that the parts determine the whole.
Cause has been narrowed to a single point. It is that in
any present state of things which explains a selected aspect
of its future. There is a nexus between successive states or
events, which is somewhat surreptitiously and apologetic-
ally characterized as unconditional or necessary. The
work of exploring nature in this sense is likened to the work
of unravelling the tangled fibres of a rope. In that simile
the many fibres stand each for a separately intelligible
causal sequence, and it is assumed that the aggregate of
the knowledge of each sequence will yield a knowledge of
the rope as a whole—this, of course, in virtue of the axiom
above referred to that the whole is determined by the
parts. Applied to the world as a whole, then, this conception of causal explanation involves an indefinite temporal
regress. Mill speaks, it is true, of primeval causes, of
primitive facts, and even of original causes: in these and
other phrases he seems to hint at some first term. But it
appears on analysis that by such phrases he only indicates
factors which in a general sense are supposedly present

throughout the whole stretch of time covered by our calculations or facts, which have to be accepted as data from which to start. Any starting-point is, in fact, arbitrary; and wherever you start you require to know two things— (1) the distribution of the natural agents at work, (2) their properties, i.e. 'the laws of succession existing between them and their effects'. Given this knowledge, the prediction of the whole subsequent history of the universe is theoretically possible. The only obstacle is the limitation of 'human powers of combination and calculation'.

This scheme presents us with an ideal of human knowledge, reducing it fundamentally to the composition of two factors, which may be called respectively physics and geography. Physics is required to give us an ordered list of the various elements at work in the world and of the laws of their combination. Geography is required to tell us of their actual distribution at a given time. But the geographer required by this theory is only a surveyor, recording particular facts. It is not his place to formulate any laws; and his services are required only once. But, you may say, what of man? what of the human mind, of will and purpose? These have to conform to the scheme. The mind is only a series of events; and the laws of their causal nexus have already been to a large extent formulated by the psychological school, developing from Hobbes, Locke, and Hume, through Hartley to James Mill's *Analysis of the Human Mind*. The relation of these laws to those of matter may be doubtful, but in their general type and character they conform to the scientific ideal. And, as to will, one has only to see that a motive is an event determining a subsequent event called an action, to convince oneself that the same principles apply here too. Nor does this involve any derogation from human freedom. For what is asked in the name of freedom is only assurance that the motive does really determine the act; and this is not denied. No doubt in this region reliable laws are not easily formulated; but this is only to be expected, since the more complex forms of being are built out of the simpler, and yield, therefore, in general later to scientific treatment than they. But Mill hoped, when he wrote his *Logic*, himself to lay the foundations of a science of character, both individual and collective (*ethology*, he proposed to call it), which should formulate the laws of motivation and form the basis of a scientific ethics and politics. Thus the last stronghold would be stormed; and the mind of man would itself at long last be brought within the sweep of scientific method.

The larger movements of scientific thought during the nineteenth century, so far as they affected the general outlook of the time, all served to reinforce and confirm the attitude to which Mill's writings give characteristic expression. It was precisely on this account that developments in the field of Geology, and somewhat later Darwin's *Origin of Species*, aroused such bitter and prolonged controversy. In the last edition of his *Logic* which he revised for the press (the eighth) Mill added some paragraphs commenting on the new generalization of the 'Conservation or Persistence of Force'—a 'great advance', he says, 'an imposing edifice of theory, the building and laying out of which has for some time been the principal occupation of the most systematic minds among physical inquirers'. In this generalization he is careful to distinguish the element of 'ascertained fact' from that of hypothesis, and he is disposed to make some reservations in respect of the hypothetical element. But in the main the doctrine was in such full accord with the presumptions of the attitude he has previously taken up that he could hardly fail to accept it gratefully as a confirmation of its correctness. The 'irrefragable fact', he says, contained in the new doctrine is the 'mutual interchangeability of the forces of nature according to fixed numerical equivalents'. Difficulties and obscurities no doubt remained—Mill was sceptical with others as to the propriety of the term 'potential energy'—but by this generalization the disparateness of the various forces of nature was broken down. 'Now that they are known to be convertible into one another without loss, they are spoken of as all of them the results of one and the same force, manifesting itself in different modes.' Thus, every event in nature, from the fall of a pebble to the composition of Browning's *Strafford* (which Sir Richard Owen calculated cost him fully *two ounces*),[1] could now be regarded as the transformation of some part of a single total quantum of energy from one to another of its innumerable disguises, according to laws derived from the nature of that energy itself. The philosopher-scientist of the nineteenth century had certainly no place for chance, and unlike Aristotle, he saw no difficulty in crediting any matter, however great, to his substratum.

III

Even within the camp of science itself this view of the world was never able to secure quite unanimous acceptance. Biologists were slow to fall into line; and when at last they gave in, they were not able to prevent the periodical recrudescence of various forms of vitalism, testimonies to a suspicion that the laws of physics and chemistry were not sufficient to account for life, without the assistance of some supplementary principle drawn from life itself. But the degree of unanimity was sufficient to give the philosopher pause, and to make it difficult for him to question the assumptions on which the whole construction rested. The result was that, in those philosophers of the nineteenth century who rejected a dogmatic materialism and were not satisfied with mere empiricism or scepticism, a tendency declared itself to surrender the sphere of nature altogether to the scientist and to erect over against it a spiritual or supernatural order which legislated for itself. This tendency had already appeared, perhaps for the first time, in certain parts of Kant's *Critique of Pure Reason*, and these elements in Kant's thought received one-sided emphasis and development in the idealism of Mill's younger contemporary, T. H. Green. Not that there were wanting in Mill's own lifetime determined efforts to grapple directly with the scientific point of view and

[1] *Fox Papers*, II, p. 22.

to show its inadequacy. In Germany philosophy always managed to hold its own; and though the scientist might feel that in Hegel and the Hegelians his case was evaded rather than met, he could hardly say that of Hermann Lotze, who began publishing his *Mikrokosmos* as early as 1856. But England could not produce a thinker with Lotze's combination of scientific knowledge and philosophical depth; and Lotze's own writing was not of the kind which forces itself very rapidly into notice. Probably for most Englishmen of the later nineteenth century the main alternatives to scientific materialism were these three —first: an agnosticism, which relied on an unknowable thing-in-itself to redress the defects of the phenomena as known; second: a dualism of the natural and the spiritual; third: the old-established alternative of a more or less Berkeleyan immaterialism, which denied the independent reality of nature altogether.

But in this twentieth century the scene has changed rapidly and almost completely. All these options, including scientific materialism itself, are dead or as good as dead. Lotze and others had sown seeds which, without any new impulse from the side of science, were quite capable by themselves of growing into new philosophies; but these lie somewhat away from our present path and may here be ignored. It was the French philosopher, Bergson, whose trenchant criticism, formulated with astonishing literary skill, delivered what proved to be the decisive blow. The blow was made the more effective by the credentials and antecedents of the man who dealt it. This was no misty German metaphysician, but a trained biologist whose philosophical affiliations were with the straitest sect of the empiricists; no defender of innate ideas and *a priori* certainties, deducing on such grounds the untenability of scientific presuppositions, but an experimentalist who claimed to show by observation and experiment that the principles in use could not but make insoluble the problems which they were devised to solve. The main emphasis of Bergson's attack was on his demand for a reconsideration of the notion of time; and in striking here he struck at the very centre of the whole construction. With dramatic propriety he accused those for whom time and change were everything of having reduced time and change to nothing. If the time-series is such that accurate knowledge of the present makes possible exact prediction of the sequel, then 'tout est donné' and the time-process is reduced to meaningless repetition. But when the nature of time, as revealed in experience, is frankly faced, it is at once evident that repetition is the one thing definitely excluded. This means that the ideal of prediction has to be surrendered. The future is unpredictable; for life is self-creative, and time is either invention or it is nothing. Thus evolution is made to confute determinism. The mechanistic philosophy of the nineteenth century had found no difficulty in accepting the theory of the origin of species presented by Darwin. His book had seemed merely to burst another barrier to scientific advance, making it possible for the first time to see how all the variety of animal life which inhabits the earth could have arisen incidentally to the continual passage of energy from one form to another. A purely mechanical Darwinism, though discouraged by Darwin himself, was in principle easy to formulate; and such a doctrine was, in fact, preached by many, if not most, of Darwin's professed followers. But the new conception of 'creative evolution' declared open war on any such interpretation of reality.

Since 1909, when the publication of Bergson's *Évolution Créatrice* made him the most popular philosopher in Europe, the break-up of the old order of ideas has proceeded with increasing momentum on a variety of lines. Already in 1896 James Ward was able to claim that the old mechanical view had been robbed of its foundations by developments within the field of theoretical physics itself. The 'extended, solid, indestructible atom' which had 'always been the stronghold of materialistic views of the universe' had proved unequal to the demands which increasing knowledge made upon it. What he said then is clearly much more true now; but to go into detail on this side of the

matter is beyond me. I will mention only one or two
general points. (1) The tendency to treat time as a fourth
dimension encourages, perhaps owing to a misapprehension, the view that to conceive the future as determining
the present is no more absurd than to conceive the past
as determining the present. (2) This view of time tells in a
sense opposed to that of Bergson's attack on the tradition.
It is a further step in the spatialization of time against
which he protested. It seems to make more difficult the
task of conceiving the time-process as creative. (3) The
quantum theory, as described by Eddington and others,
with its questionable relation to the 'classical laws', is
clearly a half-way house to something not yet fully disclosed, and it would be premature for laymen to base anything whatever upon it; but it shows an unmistakable
tendency to accept the exclusion of the possibility of exact
prediction: the scientist can at most expect to be able
to calculate the relative chances of this development or
that. (4) 'Much of the apparent uniformity of Nature', says
Eddington,[1] 'is a uniformity of averages', and he goes on
to explain that what reaches us through the senses is only
total resultant or average effect depending on a very large
number of minute activities, which as such are not perceived. 'Regularity of the average', he suggests, 'might
well be compatible with a great degree of lawlessness of
the individual.' Elsewhere he cites as an analogous case
the calculations as to the expectance of life at various ages
on which life-insurance policies are based. 'The eclipse in
1999 is as safe', he says, 'as the balance of a life-insurance
company; the next quantum jump of an atom is as uncertain as your life and mine. . . . Averages are predictable
because they are averages, irrespective of the type of
government of the phenomena underlying them.' The individual case, he insists, is really uncertain: it is not merely
that we cannot expect to obtain the full data on which to
calculate. 'The future', he says, 'is a combination of the
causal influences of the past together with unpredictable

[1] *The Nature of the Physical World*, p. 244.

elements—unpredictable not merely because it is impracticable to obtain the data of prediction, but because no data connected causally with our experience exist.' He further notes that so far as science adopts this position, it 'thereby withdraws its moral opposition to free-will'.

While revolutions on this scale are in progress in the world of physics, it is not surprising that in other departments of scientific and philosophical thought a wide freedom of speculation, and even a certain anarchy, should become apparent. Whitehead's various books constitute perhaps the most ambitious attempt to frame a metaphysic adequate to the present situation. We may note that the status of Time and its place in reality is the subject of vigorous controversy, stretching far beyond the ranks of the professed philosophers. Wyndham Lewis finds in the prevalent idolatry of time the chief cause of the malaise. with which this generation is afflicted:[1] and quite a considerable group of writers and critics range themselves more or less on his side, attacking the scientific point of view and attempting or demanding a more spiritualist philosophy. The theory of emergent evolution, sponsored by Professor Lloyd Morgan, is less radical in its reaction from the older scientific view; but if it does not question the dominance of time and the axiom that the present determines the future, it certainly questions another side of the tradition, viz. the principle that the parts determine the whole. A similar tendency is observable in Köhler's interesting 'Gestalt-Psychology'. Köhler is in conscious reaction against the atomizing of sensory and other vital processes which follows from the traditional assumptions. 'How empty and dead', he writes,[2] 'does the organism appear in this theory! Dynamically it has nothing to contribute to the monotonous elementary currents conducted compulsorily from a point of stimulation to a point of reaction. So it becomes an indifferent stage for actors indifferent to the stage as well as to each other.' He proposes to restore the 'functional whole'. This less radical type

---

[1] In *Time and Western Man*.   [2] *Gestalt Psychology*, p. 119.

of reaction is well represented philosophically by General Smuts's book, *Holism and Evolution*, which proposes to philosophers a return to the Aristotelian cosmology, modified by a recognition of the reality of time and process.

IV

I return now to the question from which I started. What is happening to the notion of cause? Is it any longer true that every event has a cause, and, if so, in what sense? If Professor Eddington is right, this proposition is no longer true of the world of physics. We have lost cause where we lost substance, in the atom. 'We have chased the solid substance from the continuous liquid to the atom, from the atom to the electron, and there we have lost it.' There too, apparently, we have lost cause: for cause implies law, and what we find, or conjecture, at the end of our chase is individuals with ways of their own. Lawlessness, it seems, is to be regarded as characteristic of individuality.

It is possible to regard this conclusion with satisfaction, as the recognition by reflective science of its own limitations, with perhaps the further implication that the scientific goal and method themselves need some redefinition. Such an attitude can claim support on both sides from Eddington himself. He is quite ready to ridicule the scientific atomism which pursues the infinitely small in deference to some *a priori* prejudice that the problems which baffle us on the larger scales will there find simple solution. In certain developments of modern physics ('entrophy' is the magic word here) he sees signs of a reverse movement. This means that the 'geography', of which we spoke earlier as the necessary complement of an ideally completed physics, is no longer to be the work of a mere surveyor who is needed only once. It becomes a science, and must indeed be prepared to break up into any number of sciences; for there is no *a priori* limit to the kinds or order and arrangement, to the variety of wholes into which the atom may enter. If once it is admitted that the parts do not determine the whole, the simplicity of the scheme is gone.

But in such developments there is no affront either to reason or to common sense. They may be held, indeed, to promise, if not actually as yet to present, a theory of nature more harmonious with human prejudice and with the actual organization of human knowledge than the materialistic monism which was formerly the orthodoxy of science. What is disquieting in the situation as disclosed by Eddington is that the emphasis of the argument is almost wholly on its negations. There are things, evidently, of which Eddington—not as a scientist but in other capacities—is strongly convinced. He loves beauty, he admires character, he feels the thrill of poetry and art, he believes in God. For all this the utmost that he can get out of science is a *nihil obstat*. Now it would not be in any way surprising or amazing to find that science cannot *completely* account for these things. Indeed, when the extreme of materialism is once surrendered, the necessity of some supplementation of the scientific point of view is at once evident. But if the sciences have any truth, and if the world has any unity, it should surely be possible to show that the fundamental, but possibly preliminary, truths of science provide some positive basis for these further beliefs. It is surely something of an affront to reason to be told that only at the margin, where science breaks down and reaches the end of its tether, these things have room to creep in. (I say this in no spirit of disrespect to Sir A. Eddington, from whose books in common with many thousands of others I have drawn great profit and pleasure; but if it is only through the crevices of his science that his philosophy creeps in, that philosophy cannot but lose some of the authority which his scientific eminence would otherwise earn for it, and the tendency of his philosophy is to discredit natural science as a body of truth.)

But, however that may be, the question which this paper is intended to raise is a quite general one concerning the notion of cause; and it is time that I attempted a final formulation of the issue. Looking back on the development of thought during the last few generations, we find it governed at the start, as I have already said, by a dual assumption—that the present determines the future and that the whole is determined by the parts. It may no doubt be questioned whether these two principles are logically inseparable. It may be argued that what holds them together is a questionable presupposition that the simple precedes the complex in time, or alternatively, perhaps, that science for some reason is compelled to work mainly by the method of analysis and can therefore only represent nature as the result of composition. But in any case the historical concomitance of the two principles seems not to be open to serious question. It appears that in recent times this dual assumption has been falling into increasing discredit as to one or both of its articles. The question is, what are we to make of this? It might mean, and some scientific writers suggest that it does mean, that the notion of cause is being superseded and suppressed; that a time is approaching when science will no longer seek to interpret nature in terms of causation at all. I cannot myself believe that this result is likely. I cannot guess how science proposes to make change intelligible without the notion of cause, nor can I find the germs of a notion to put in the place of cause. In this I may easily be wrong; but for convenience I assume that I am right, that cause in some form will remain. The question then arises as to possible revisions of the notion of causation. Such revision would be bound, I suggest, to have for its aim the formulation of a causal notion of universal application, such as the old notion claimed to be; for to say that events in Nature are in certain respects uncaused is equivalent to saying that in those respects they are inexplicable. Cause must cover the whole field or it must go.

Now the dual assumption to which I have referred has as its dialectical antithesis the twofold assertion that the present is determined by the future and the parts are determined by the whole. We are so embedded in the ways of thought in which we were brought up that these two principles seem to have little to recommend them. The first of them, indeed, which asserts the real dependence of the present on the future, would probably be dismissed by most men at sight as a mere paradox, not deserving a moment's serious consideration. It is only with an effort that we realize that these two propositions represent fairly accurately about half of what Aristotle was trying to say in his doctrine of the four causes. They represent the operation of his final and formal causes. The form or essence as determinant of all the varied aspects of a thing's being—this is the whole as cause of the part; and his final cause gives us the future as cause of the present, in the sense that every natural process is determined not merely by its point of departure but also by its goal. There was another half to the doctrine, of course: two more causes were required to complete the account; and it is evident that these two causes are represented to about the same degree of adequacy by the two principles which are the precise antithesis of the two last stated, and which we have taken as standing for the old orthodoxy of our modern science. Thus Aristotle held firmly to both sides of the antithesis we have constructed. Of the two, however, differing herein from us, he held more firmly to the second. The vital truth for him, on which knowledge chiefly depended, was the dependence of present on future, of part on whole (to us somewhat far-fetched and paradoxical), not the dependence, so self-evident to us, of present on past and whole on part.

Are we then to conceive as possible or probable a return on the part of science to a more complex conception of cause, some retying of the knots which the age of Hobbes and Descartes so roughly untied? I do not know enough of science to answer that question with any confidence, and quite possibly the answer might be different for different branches of science, e.g. according as their object is organic or inorganic, animate or inanimate. But my conjecture, for what it is worth, is that the scientist is finding himself increasingly driven towards a notion of cause resembling the Aristotelian form or essence, and consequently away from the one-sided dependence of the present on the past which has hitherto tended to colour his whole outlook on nature. With the wider implications of such a change of view the working scientist could hardly be expected to concern himself: to explore these is the task of the philosopher. It would, I suppose, involve the surrender of the view that Nature is a mere series of events and would call for a metaphysic in which the temporal factor is strictly subordinated. I think there would be a gain in such a development. For it would mean also, surely, an appreciable diminution of the existing gap between science and common sense. I know that science is often described as only an extension and systematization of the common sense point of view. So in certain respects it is. But there is, and has been for centuries, a yawning gulf between the picture of human life and action which science has felt obliged to frame for itself and the conception of his own activity by which each one of us lives. The words, already referred to, of Plato's Socrates in his Athenian prison, and the whole free will controversy of modern times, are sufficient evidence of this. Now, in the words of Professor Max Planck,[1] science has to surrender a fundamental assumption, viz. 'that the course of a process can be represented by means of an analysis of it into its spatial and temporal elements. . . . It is thus the concept of wholeness which must be introduced as well into the field of physics as into that of biology, in order to enable us to understand and formulate the laws of nature'. This pronouncement clearly points in the direction which I have indicated. It is for the scientists to determine the precise form which this concept shall take; but whatever form it takes, I cannot doubt that its establishment will have the effect of lightening for the philosopher the task of reconciling the findings of science with the data of moral experience. And in that case, with any luck, the Eddingtons of the future will not need to look only to the chinks and crevices of their science for evidence of the reasonableness of their faith.

[1] Cited by Woodger, *Proc. of the Arist. Soc., 1931-2*, p. 112.

VI. MATERIALISM IN POLITICS

I

Materialism

EUROPEAN thought is governed still to an unknown extent by the framework supplied by Aristotle, and it is doubtful whether the current uses of the word 'materialism' could be fully explained except by reference to his theory of causation. Materialism is sometimes defined, for example, as the doctrine that matter alone is real. But, if this is right, why should the principle of the economic interpretation of history, preached by Karl Marx, be regarded as a form of materialism? It is true that Marx did in fact lay stress on the importance of physical conditions, and especially of the tools of labour, as determining the direction of human effort and the forms of social organization, but on analysis these are seen to be significant only in relation to human needs and desires, so that if these needs and desires were removed from the world, the tools would not exist, and the forms of social organization would disappear.

In the context, of course, of a two-substance theory of nature, which views matter and mind as wholly disparate substances existing side by side and in no way dependent the one on the other, materialism as defined above acquires a definite meaning. It means the denial of the alleged spirit-substance, and the attempt to show that the various phenomena commonly classed as mental or spiritual, such as the life of plants and animals, the emotions, thoughts, and desires of men, can all be interpreted as fundamentally physical in their nature. And it is, I suppose, this two-substance theory, propagated by the powerful influence of Descartes in the seventeenth century, which determines the immediate significance of the term 'materialism' as we use it to-day. Not that Descartes' theory was ever even so generally accepted that it could truly be said to constitute the orthodoxy of any period. But it was no mere invention of Descartes. It had ancient roots, going back ultimately, like much in his thought, to St. Augustine and Plato. His theory was only a rather extreme and provocative version of a belief which derived powerful reinforcement from the religious dogmas of resurrection and immortality. But those who held to these dogmas did not necessarily accept Descartes' account of the matter. In the same century in which Descartes wrote, Hobbes and Gassendi both avowed themselves complete materialists. In his *Leviathan* Hobbes writes:[1]

'The World (I mean not the Earth only . . . but the Universe, i.e. the whole mass of all things that are) is Corporeal, that is to say Body, . . . also every part of Body is likewise Body, and consequently every part of the Universe is Body, and that which is not Body is no part of the Universe. . . . And because the Universe is all, that which is no part of it is nothing, and consequently nowhere.'

Hobbes might be suspected of being an unbeliever, but later in the century John Locke, whose devotion to Christianity was unquestioned, writing normally in terms of two parallel substances, was yet evidently uneasy as to their separation, as is seen from his willingness to entertain the hypothesis that matter might be conceived as capable of thought.

But even if the immediate form taken by the modern conception of materialism is determined by the opposition of material and spiritual substance, there are in it also, I suggest, traces of an older opposition, which was formulated by Aristotle and comes to the western world from him. I mean the opposition of Form and Matter. It is this opposition, not the foregoing, which governs my understanding of the word. All natural objects are complexes of varying degrees of complexity, and a human being, with its rich variety of physical and mental functions and attributes, is merely a particularly complex physical object. Materialism, if it is to be regarded as a general theory of

[1] Hobbes, *Leviathan*, c. 46, p. 497 (ed. Waller).

nature, must be expressed as a general theory concerning the genesis and organization of these complexes. Such a theory Aristotle himself possessed. He expounded it in his doctrine of the Four Causes, a doctrine which has perhaps exerted a more continuous influence on European thought than any philosophical doctrine which has ever been formulated. Every natural thing, in his view, from the rock beneath our feet to the stars above our heads, was a specimen of formed matter. In all cases certain pre-existing materials had been moulded into a certain shape. Aristotle's view was that in all cases the operative principle in this process was not the matter, the pre-existing materials themselves, but the form which these materials were destined to embody when the process was complete. There was a materialism current in his day to which he, following his master Plato, was opposed. It was the attitude which insisted on a reversal of this last statement, insisting that the operative principle, in all natural processes, resided in the pre-existing materials, that these created spontaneously their own form out of themselves. This seemed to him and to Plato incredible because in the case of man it deprived human thought and will of all independent significance, and in the case of the world generally because it represented growth and progress as no more than a lucky accident.

My own philosophical inquiries, pursued over a number of years in various fields, seem to me to converge more and more on the point that if a tenable theory of the natural world is to be framed, it must be on the basis of a recovery of a conception of cause closely resembling the Aristotelian form. I feel, consequently, that the modern tendency which requires most urgently to be corrected is the tendency to a materialism which denies the possibility of such causation. This tendency is very powerful in every field to-day. It derives great support from the natural sciences, because it is the special function of science with its analytic methods to explain things in terms of their components and previous history, i.e. to exploit the material cause.

II

The Materialist as Democrat

In the field of politics there are two influential sets of ideas in relation to which modern materialism shows itself powerful to distort and pervert judgement, with results which are of practical as well as of theoretical importance. These are, first, the ideas connected with the word democracy, in which most of us profess to believe; secondly, the ideas connected with Marx's Dialectical Materialism, crystallized politically into Communism, with which most of us profess to disagree. I believe myself to be justified in advocating democracy and in repudiating Communism, but I also feel that the claims of democracy, in the form in which they are often advanced, contain a fundamental error which is in principle identical with that of the Communist. What I want to show is that both doctrines— the one sometimes and by a kind of inadvertence, the other always and deliberately—involve materialism in the broad sense in which I have defined it—the denial of the formal cause, the assertion that the materials are competent to provide their own form—and that so far as they involve this both are rightly rejected because they do not make sense.

Take first Democracy. This is one of the ideas which came into general currency about the time of the French Revolution, and were notably helped to spread by it. Its early European prophet was Rousseau, whose writings dominated much Revolutionary thought, and still exert a powerful influence to-day. He starts his political theory in its maturest form (in the *Contrat social*) with the problem how the chains of government are to be justified. That is to say, he takes it for granted that government involves restraint upon the citizen, and asks what makes such restraint legitimate. His answer is that these chains are legitimated when they proceed from the collective decision of a community which is legislating for itself. The citizens of a free country, therefore, will not delegate the legislative power. If they did, they would barter away their freedom. They will keep this power in their own hands, and legislating for themselves they will continue to be free in spite of the restraints on personal initiative which may be involved. In all this the word democracy is not mentioned by Rousseau, but the general idea is that government is not opposed to freedom where you have self-government, which he explains as meaning that a plenary assembly of adult citizens legislates for itself.

Rousseau's interpretation of self-government may be disputed, but his refusal to use the name democracy did not and does not conceal the fact that in arguing for self-government as a precondition of freedom he was voicing the fundamental democratic demand. He only uses the word democracy when he comes to consider what *he* calls the problem of government, i.e. (as we might say) the question how to constitute the other parts of government which remain when the function of legislation has been taken away. And when he comes to this question, he decides very properly against democracy. It is, he sees, impossible that a people should actually administer its own laws, and exact from individuals the punishments which are inflicted for the breach of them. Democracy in this sense is a baseless figment of the imagination, or, as he also says, 'Were there a people of gods, their government would be democratic. So perfect a government is not for men.' On this account he was attacked as a traitor to democracy in a contemporary pamphlet bearing the title, *Jean-Jacques Rousseau Aristocrate*.

Rousseau, as has been said, rejected representation. He was consequently opposed to the idealization of English parliamentary government which Montesquieu had made fashionable in his day. He looked for the realization of his ideas by the formation of small States like the City-States of Ancient Greece, and he made the further suggestion that the obvious inconveniences of such a change could be obviated by some scheme of federation. But he did not work this out, and those who were inspired by his ideas were inevitably forced to come to terms with representative government. The line they took was (if I may use current terms) to interpret representation as delegation. In places like England where representation was an effective political factor, the representative had by this time won his freedom. Burke's famous speech to the Electors of Bristol is dated 1774. It shows that the relation was still a matter of controversy, but claims confidently for the Member of Parliament a freedom which in practice at that time he was always granted, and which since that time, in England at least, he has never been refused. But the followers of Rousseau in the French Conventions of the revolutionary years had not the evidence of this development before them, and probably would not have perceived its significance if they had had it. Holding fast to the idea of a people as self-governing, or at least as determining its own laws, they regarded it as obvious that freedom on the part of representatives meant unfreedom on the part of the represented. The people of England, Rousseau had said, are free only at the time of a general election, i.e. when the representative body does not exist. Therefore they welcomed any proposal tending to make the representative conceive himself as the mouthpiece of his constituents. The constituents should be able, they argued, at any time to cancel the representative's mandate, if he should be seen to vote contrary to their wishes. In the National Convention of 1793 Robespierre urged the necessary and *physical* responsibility of all public functionaries including the members of the legislative body.

'A people,' he said, 'whose representatives have not to account to any one for their conduct, has no constitution. A people whose officials are accountable only to inviolable representatives has no constitution, since it is in the power of the latter to betray it with impunity and to allow it to be betrayed by the former. If that is what representative government means, I confess that I accept all the anathemas which J. J. Rousseau pronounced against it.'[1]

---

[1] Esmein, *Traité de droit constitutionnel*, vol. i, p. 448.

It was these tendencies which led the Convention, when the followers of Rousseau had failed to secure their majority, to make the curious constitutional provision (since then incorporated with slight variations in many later constitutions) that the deputy was to regard himself not as the representative of a constituency, but of the whole nation.

In modern times the Rousseauistic strain still survives; it even seems indeed recently to have gained in strength. Its typical expression is to be found in a whole series of constitutional projects and provisions which have for their common object the prevention of divergence of opinion between the electorate and the elected body. The representative system has of course as one of its main features a device for securing this end. It provides in all cases that each member of the elected body shall only enjoy the right of participating in legislation and government for a limited period, at the end of which he has to seek fresh authority from the electors. The calculation evidently is that this situation will make him want to serve and please them, and thus tend to win for the word representation more than a mere legal significance. Legally no doubt he has power to consent to anything on their behalf, and they will be bound by the decision which results from the votes of him and his fellow representatives; but his dependence for continuance in office on the votes of his constituents will lead him to consider carefully their wishes and their interests, and to vote on lines which are likely to be generally agreeable to them.

But the followers of Rousseau think that this does not go far enough. They argue that he should have an explicit mandate from the electors for each vote, or for the more important of them; and since the growing complications of the work of Parliaments have made the imperative mandate an obvious absurdity, they seek to secure a substitute for this by increasing use of the device of the Referendum, by which a matter is taken out of the hands of Parliament altogether and referred for decision to the

votes of the electorate. By an extension of this device
they provide that legislative or constitutional changes can
actually be initiated outside the representative body on
terms which reduce that body to an almost equal degree
of passivity. A century ago, again, they were pressing for
the principle that the intervals between elections should
be made as short as possible. The Chartists asked for
annual Parliaments. This demand also the growing responsibilities of Parliaments have reduced to absurdity. So
now, by way of substitute, they fall back on constitutional
provisions by which exceptional dissolutions of Parliament, before the fixed term has expired, may be effected
by popular demand. You can all probably think of other
illustrations of this tendency to qualify and limit in
various ways the freedom of the representative and of the
representative body. There is no sign of its cessation. The
post-war constitutions are full of it. The recall has not,
so far as I know, had any trial on a national scale, but it
was embodied in the original Soviet constitution of the
Russian Federation, and it has had a considerable vogue
in the smaller units of government in U.S.A. The pene-
trating studies by Mr. and Mrs. Sidney Webb of trade
union history and organization show this conception or
misconception of democracy at work on almost every
page.

This is the most dangerous and the most persistent of
the fallacies of democracy. It may be called (after Shaw's
Apple Cart) the fallacy of the rubber stamp. It ignores
the fundamental fact that democracy is a form of *government*, converting it into a form of no-government or
anarchy. That is really what Rousseau meant when he
said that only a people of gods could be governed demo-
cratically. He was accepting the notion common to his
age that government was only occasioned by human weakness and wickedness, with its corollary that a community
of perfectly good men would not require to be governed
at all. It is thus that his two statements which I have
quoted about democracy are reconciled. He said first that

it was impossible, secondly that it was too good for men. If he had expressed himself fully, what he would have said was that where any form of government other than legislation is required, it must be provided on some principle other than the democratic principle, and that such forms of government will everywhere be required while men are men. And in all this he is assuming of course that the problem of legislation has already been solved on democratic lines, that the community in question has laid down for itself (possibly, as he rather inconsequently adds, with the assistance of a divinely inspired legislator) the principles of social organization, and further that (if only human frailty did not obstruct) these would be so graven on the heart of the citizen that no force or penalty would be needed to secure their observance.

Now it is certain that there can be government where there is nothing that we should call law. First comes government, then by slow degrees law, then the machinery of consent, growing by elaboration over centuries into the formidable representative apparatus with which we are familiar. The whole secular process has as its starting-point the fact of government, which remains its ultimate presupposition. Government is not necessarily by law, and to this day is in different countries in very different degrees bound by law. Law is not necessarily dependent for existence on the prior consent of the subjects, and even in the most democratic countries is never fully dependent on it. In all cases from the extreme of absolutism to the mildest of parliamentary régimes the fundamental fact is the relation between certain people who have authority vested in them and the mass of people over whom they have authority. Through the whole historical development this relation persists, but it suffers in its evolution two great and fundamental modifications, the first when it accepts the rule of law, the second as it provides increasingly for the consent of the governed. These two developments on the original stock of government both owe their origin and vitality to the idea of freedom. The very fact of government is a standing threat to the desire of subjects to be free to go their ways. The rule of law binding the governors gives the negative guarantee that (as Locke says) the governed will not be 'subject to the inconstant, uncertain, unknown, arbitrary will of another man'. The principle of consent, as it develops, establishes more and more firmly the guarantee of a more positive freedom, securing that they shall always have the opportunity of contributing to the substance of the rules to which governors and governed alike are pledged to submit.

The important point is that these two great modifications of the original idea of government are accretions upon it which only make clearer its real nature: they are in no contradiction with it. The primitive government which preceded the invention of written law was not the arbitrary rule against which Locke protests as no government, and against which law guarantees the subject: it was only a form of government which contained no explicit features precluding such perversion of the relation of ruler and subject. Similarly the lawful governments of predemocratic and undemocratic times and countries are not governments which do not rest upon consent at all: they are merely governments which make no explicit provision for securing the consent of the governed to law and policy. But enthusiasts for these relatively recent developments, law and democracy, often overstate their case. Thus there is a famous and oft-quoted statement of Aristotle's concerning Law.[1] 'He who bids the law rule may be deemed to bid God and reason alone rule, but he who bids man rule adds an element of the beast; for desire is a wild beast, and passion perverts the minds of rulers, even when they are the best of men.' But note the words 'may be deemed'. Aristotle knew quite well that this opposition was false. The question is not whether man or law shall rule, but whether man shall rule through and by law or not. Similarly enthusiasts for democracy found themselves in ancient Greece at odds with the principle

[1] *Pol.* iii. 16. 5.

of the rule of law, since the sanctity of law seemed inconsistent with their idea of freedom, and ultimately at odds with the fact of government itself, so that for Aristotle and Plato democracy in its extreme forms approximated to anarchy. But what they were fighting was not surely democracy but a misreading of it. If democracy is to be a principle of *government* it must be so construed as to preserve the rule of law and the fact of government.

Let me now try to translate some of the controversies which we have reviewed into the more philosophical terms from which we started. Where is the form and what is the matter of a Commonwealth? The matter evidently is the lives of its citizens, which are to be seen, so far as the political state is justified, as preserved, moulded, and enriched by the organized social context which the political authority exists to maintain and develop. The formative impulse has to come from the government, i.e. from certain persons told off to think for the community and to act in its name. A community will not and cannot organize itself. There is no possibility of a spontaneous generation by which matter provides its own form. But it can and will react, fruitfully or otherwise, to the formative activities of which it is the subject, and in so doing it will necessarily limit those activities and may profoundly modify them. The false dream which misleads the Rousseauistic democrat is the dream that this reaction may finally be converted into action, so that the formative activity may be dispensed with altogether. He sees this activity of government as something external, ignoring the fact that it falls within the community, and therefore sees it as a qualification on the self-determination of the corporate body. Thus in philosophical terms he is a materialist, denying the necessity of a formal cause. And in the end he, like his brother materialist in the field of natural science, is forced to leave growth and progress to chance. The atoms of the scientist had no thought of the world they were making: it represents only a pattern into which they happened to fall. Similarly in society the multitude of citizens can hardly be credited as individuals with thought and purpose in regard to the policy which their actions are generating. A mystical confidence in a super-individual General Will may conceal this weakness from those who accept Rousseau's position, but to those not so blinded it will surely be obvious.

III

The Materialist as Social Historian

Perhaps the best short statement of Marx's position is one which he wrote himself in the Preface to his *Critique of Political Economy*:

'My investigations led to the conclusion that legal relations as well as forms of State could not be understood from themselves, nor from the so-called general development of the human mind, but on the contrary are rooted in the material conditions of life, the aggregate of which Hegel, following the precedent of the English and French of the XVIIIth century, grouped under the name of "civil society"; but that the anatomy of civil society is to be found in political economy. The general conclusion I arrived at—and once reached, it served as the guiding thread in my studies—can be briefly formulated as follows:—In the social production of their means of existence men enter into definite, necessary relations which are independent of their will, productive relationships which correspond to a definite stage of development of their material productive forces. The aggregate of these productive relationships constitutes the economic structure of society, the real basis on which a juridical and political superstructure arises, and to which definite forms of social consciousness correspond. The mode of production of the material means of existence conditions the whole process of social, political and intellectual life. It is not the consciousness of men that determines their existence, but, on the contrary, it is their social existence that determines their consciousness.'[1]

There is, of course, much that is true and important for the student of politics in this statement. It is true that political and legal forms do not explain themselves, and

[1] *Handbook of Marxism* (ed. E. Burns), Gollancz, 1935, p. 371.

are not products of pure reason. It is true that their full explanation requires a careful study of the social and economic conditions in which they flourish. It is probably true, as a broad generalization, that of the external conditions of political processes economic processes are the most important. Marx's assertion of these truths further was salutary and timely; for though they are at least as old as Aristotle and had been reasserted with emphasis by Bentham, they were not truths which the mind of the time, nor even Bentham himself, had fully grasped. They are in fact truths which man is always apt to forget, and has therefore constantly to discover afresh. But none of these truths, nor all of them taken together, will suffice to constitute the doctrine of economic materialism with which Marx's name is inseparably connected. The second half of the statement formulates this principle with the aid of five terms: (1) material productive forces, (2) necessary productive relationships, independent of volition, between man and man, (3) economic structure of society, (4) juridical and political structure of society, (5) social consciousness. What is asserted is a necessity originating in material productive forces, determining irrevocably, through these three intermediate terms, man's social conscience and judgement of values. The correspondence asserted at each stage is clearly to be read as determination or necessitation by the preceding stage, so that the whole means that if the material productive forces were different, political and social ideas and practice would necessarily be different.

The intention is plainly to eliminate the human will as a true cause of the social and political order. This comes out at both ends of the statement—at the beginning when he says that the starting-point is in material conditions of production which necessitate certain relationships independently of volition—and again at the end when he says that these relationships form the real basis on which a legal and social system arises. It is true that judged by mere logic the last statement is harmless and could be accepted by those who refuse the offered principle of social analysis. Economic facts are certainly real, and equally certainly they are the basis on which legislators build. But the word real is clearly introduced to suggest the relative unreality, the epiphenomenalism, of the decisions taken by legislators and statesmen. The suggestion clearly is that while the accredited leaders seem to themselves to be deciding important questions, and controlling the development of society, the material productive forces are developing on their own account and by their development forcing a parallel development of law and policy. Thus legislators and statesmen are carried passively by a material evolution to which they contribute nothing. This is clearly the general intention, but neither from this passage, nor from other statements of the position made by Marx and Engels, is it clear how rigid this exclusion of the human will, as a real historical cause, is to be taken as being. Most of their statements seem to leave room for some small residual freedom, such as the earlier materialism of Epicurus provided for with his uncaused and unpredictable swerve of the atom. But at least the assertion is that the main movements of history can be accounted for without attributing any originative power to the human will. Generally (though not necessarily without minor qualifications), the material conditions of man's social existence determine his ideas and consequently his line of action.

The correctness of this interpretation is confined by the following concise statement of the position made by Engels in his Anti-Dühring:[1]

'The Materialist conception of history starts from the principle that production, and with production the exchange of its products, is the basis of every social order; that in every society which has appeared in history the distribution of the products, and with it the division of society into classes or estates, is determined by what is produced and how it is produced, and how the product is exchanged. According to this conception, the ultimate causes of all social changes and political revolutions

[1] *Handbook of Marxism*, p. 279.

are to be sought, not in the minds of men, in their increasing insight into eternal truth and justice, but in changes in the mode of production and exchange; they are to be sought not in the philosophy but in the economics of the epoch concerned. The growing realization that existing social institutions are irrational and unjust, that reason has become nonsense and good deeds a scourge, is only a sign that changes have been taking place quietly in the methods of production and forms of exchange with which the social order, adapted to previous economic conditions, is no longer in accord. This also involves that the means through which the abuses that have been revealed can be got rid of must likewise be present, in more or less developed form, in the altered conditions of production. These means are not to be *invented* by the mind, but *discovered* by means of the mind, in the existing material facts of production.'

Here, quite explicitly, the ultimate causes of social change are found in natural facts external to and independent of the minds and wills of men, to which these minds and wills are forced in the end to conform. It is further, however, recognized that the old ideas and habits may persist after the material conditions have made them obsolete, and from the tension thus set up in the body of society arise the revolutions that figure so prominently in history. In each of them new economic relations break violently the bonds of an obsolete legal and social order, and in each the new economic forces produce, after longer or shorter delay, new legal and social forms appropriate to themselves. It is to be noted that here human social ideals are credited with a certain power, but only with the negative power of delay and obstruction, due to the fact that they are apt to be rooted in the past rather than the present. They have no positive contribution to make, and therefore are not reckoned among the causes of social development.

It will be remembered that in Aristotle's theory of causation, matter, though reckoned a cause, is not an active agent. The only active agent is Form, of the realization of which matter, in virtue of its receptivity, is a *conditio sine qua non* (οὗ οὐκ ἄνευ). The only independent contribution matter can make to the result shows itself as defect and failure, and is due to matter's capricious resistance to the activity of form. For Marx and Engels conversely the material conditions are the real causes, receptivity is the best that can be said of mind, which also has the power of resisting and delaying the forces of material evolution. Thus Marx turns Aristotle, as well as Hegel, upside down.

This interpretation of social development, which denies all positive contribution to the political factor and ulti- mately to the human will, is recommended by its advo- cates as a *scientific* conception of history. In Russia to-day it is passionately advocated in this sense, as an interpreta- tion which is in line with the work of Charles Darwin and the other great triumphs of nineteenth- and twentieth- century science. And though many of the greatest scien- tists, including Charles Darwin himself, might have strongly resisted this assessment of their work, it cannot be denied that there is much truth in it. The scientist generally works by a method of analysis which always in the result, so far as it is successful, exhibits large-scale visible pro- cesses as the necessary resultant of small-scale processes which are not revealed to the eye at all or revealed only through the microscope. This means that the active forces at work in any process are not the substances familiar in common speech and natural history, but always certain other substances which belong to a lower structural and evolutionary level. For the change of scale does not bring into play other substances of the same kind, but substances of a more primitive character, which are the vehicle not merely of this large-scale process but also of innumerable others as well. Ultimately the scientist takes us back to atom and electron which are to be conceived as the uni- versal basis of all physical processes whatever. It is surely quite clear that the retreat of the economic materialist to the material productive forces for a ground of explanation of social changes is of precisely the same order as the retreat of the scientist to the atom. In these he hopes to

find the common ground of all social changes and con-
formations whatever, and so to be able to get rid of principles of explanation, like national character, racial type,
dominant ideas, outstanding personalities, which have a
more restricted range or have their application only within
the selected field. To get this common ground he, like the
scientist, has to fall back from the higher to the lower
structural level. Material productive forces, in which he
finds the real basis and true cause, are avowedly below the
level of life; and when mind enters into his account of the
matter, it enters primarily in respect of those primitive
needs and impulses, such as those connected with food and
sex, which are most universal among men and provide the
preconditions of man's higher life. That higher life is
regarded as merely the resultant echo of these more primitive processes, which are themselves creatures of the
material conditions of life. If we give the terms higher and
lower a strictly evolutionary significance, so that the lower
is what is necessary for the existence of the higher and the
higher is what is built upon the lower as its precondition,
we can say that the principle is the explanation of the
higher without remainder in terms of the lower. Or, to put
it otherwise, no principle derived from a given level of
being is to be accepted if a principle derived from a lower
level of being will fit the facts.

From this we see, to put the matter in a few words,
that the economic interpretation of history is an attempt
to introduce the materialism which is characteristic of
natural science into the fields of history. An attitude or
rule of method which has for centuries been traditional
and normal among scientists is introduced into company
in which it appears as a paradox or even as an outrage.
For the historian sets out to tell the story of man and his
doings, and his natural basis is the assumption that men
are of some importance, at least to men, and that their
actions have, for men at least, some creative power. If
this doctrine is true, the historian is now found to have
been wasting his time under the spell of ancient romantic

delusions. He has only to borrow the scientist's microscope to find all that he has laboriously deciphered from stone and parchment, from letters and documents, all the narrative that he has constructed with more than detective ingenuity from these and other sources, rendered unnecessary and inaccurate by the simpler and grander story of the material productive forces and their development. But the historian knows in his heart that if he accepts this, he commits suicide: for this story, when it is written, will not be history at all: it will be a chapter in the book of science. By its original commission history must tell the story of man, and if man is the mere creature of his environment, man has no history.

Thus materialism applied to history destroys history, as in our previous example materialism applied to democracy annihilated government.

IV

Conclusion

I believe it can be shown that materialism in all its various forms is false, in that it offers a theory of the world which does not make sense of it. The material factor is not, as the theory would have it, the real agent in physical and social change. There is always a formative factor of a higher order at work on which growth and development wholly depend. But I am not concerned in this lecture to develop an alternative general theory of the causal process. I wish to confine my view, as far as possible, to the two examples of materialism which I have brought forward and to the social field to which they belong. In these concluding remarks, which must be brief, I want to call attention to the practical harm which these false ideas have power to do, and to the practical gains which would accrue if they could be disposed of.

The two doctrines have the common characteristic that so far as they are believed man's sense of responsibility is seriously weakened. A statesman who accepts Rousseau's conception of democracy no longer has any important questions to decide for himself: his business with them is merely to see that they are decided for him. A voter inspired by the same doctrine will make no painful personal sacrifice for a principle when he finds the majority against him: he will see at once—so Rousseau actually argued— that he has made a mistake of fact: that he was in error when he gave his vote. In voting he was seeking to formulate the general will, and this now turns out to have been the reverse of what he thought it was. The responsibility is corporate: the individual, whether voter or statesman, escapes it, and it is impossible, as Burke observes, to indict a whole nation.

From the doctrine of economic materialism, similar consequences even more evidently follow. How can a statesman who believes that it is not he that thinks and wills but material forces that pursue their inevitable course through him attach independent value to his fears and scruples? How can he measure his work otherwise than by its actual efficacy? He can have no independent standard or ideal by which to judge the facts, only those prejudices which birth and upbringing have ingrained in him; and a conflict between these and immediate urgencies can be no more than the vain struggle of the past against the present. Hegel's[1] dark saying now gets its full value— *die Weltgeschichte ist das Weltgericht*; or, as we might put it more bluntly, from fact there is no appeal.

There thus arises a mood of fatalism, which is one of the most prevalent and disabling weaknesses of the modern world. We look at the disquieting phenomena of our day objectively and scientifically: we study with care and exactness their genesis and their dimensions. We follow them to their roots in human folly and weakness, and in the faulty conditions of life of which these are bred. We see them as the incidental outcome of a secular process which in its continuation in the course of centuries may incidentally extrude them. Where our fathers would have

[1] Schiller's.

said: 'Here is a wrong to be righted: let us see what can be done about it', we in our greater wisdom say: 'Yes, the case is bad, but it has a long history, and no one is really to blame: it will get worse for certain before it gets better', and satisfied with having diagnosed the disease and prophesied the disaster, we leave the cure to nature.

It is often said in these days that the weakening of principle, which is so plain a feature of this post-war world, is a consequence of the diminished hold which religion has on men's minds. How far this may be so I do not know, but it seems to me that what the modern world wants to arrest its rake's progress is two things, which are really one, a belief in the efficacy of ideas and a belief in the freedom of the human will. This is the faith that under the spell of scientific materialism we are in danger of losing, and I doubt if any revival of religion could be guaranteed to win it back for us. The trust in reason which is the first article of this faith is inseparably bound up with the consciousness of freedom which is the second. For if thought is not free, if it is only a mirror held up to nature, then will is not free either. And the will which is not controlled by reason must be totally immoral and irresponsible. It is true that man is in large measure the creature of circumstance. Reason itself helps to bind him more tightly to circumstance, since it is essentially a consciousness of fact, and a reasonable creature can be seen to differ from one that is unreasonable precisely in the range and rapidity of its adjustment to fact. But it is also of the essence of reason that the consciousness of fact is always at the same time a valuation of it, and therefore the adjustment to environment includes always the effort to transform it. Here is the salt that gives the savour, the yeast that leavens the lump. This is the creative form, of which materialism is the denial.

H

VII. ON THE NEED FOR A SOCIAL PHILOSOPHY[1]

I

IN Boswell's *Life of Johnson* the following entry may be found under the year 1755: 'In July this year he had formed some scheme of mental improvement, the particular purpose of which does not appear. But we find in his "Prayers and Meditations", p. 25, a prayer entitled "On the Study of Philosophy, as an instrument of living", and after it follows a note, "This study was not pursued."' Johnson at the time was forty-six years old. What crisis evoked this pathetic and abortive appeal to philosophy for guidance, Boswell clearly did not know. He makes no comment on the final note in which the hope of assistance from this source is finally dismissed. It is as though the Master had proved his strength once more by overcoming yet another temptation. I sometimes wonder whether this entry in Boswell is not typical of a very general attitude to philosophy, characteristic of most men at most times, and of nearly all societies. For the most part, it is something with which they need not concern themselves and can safely leave alone, which raises unnecessary questions, interesting, perhaps, to intellectual busy-bodies, but better ignored by practical men, questions probably not capable of final solution and in any case of little moment for the guidance of life. At times, however, things go wrong, and a suspicion stirs them that in these remote unsolved problems the secret of their perplexities and the solution of them may perhaps be found. Then they may for a time take up 'the study of philosophy, as an instrument of living'. But for most of these, after a longer or shorter time, a new equilibrium is reached, and the study of philosophy is 'not pursued'.

If this is at all true of the single individual, it is natural that it should be more true of man in the mass and of the

[1] *Proceedings of the Aristotelium Society*, N.S., vol. xxxvi.

societies which men form. One would expect to find that periods of great stability and security would be periods in which the public interest in philosophical speculation was at its minimum; that some deep and far-reaching disturbance of the social equilibrium on one of its many sides would be necessary before the philosopher could claim general attention for his doctrine or find ready assent to his own estimate of the importance of the questions with which he deals. I think there is pretty good historical evidence that this is in fact the case. The chief period in which the English people was deeply interested in political speculation was the period of the Civil Wars and the Commonwealth, when English political institutions were in the melting-pot, and the astonishing outburst of ethical speculation which characterized the first half of the eighteenth century in this country was preceded by a powerful movement of religious scepticism which loosened the hold of religious sanctions on the educated mind of the time. The ferment which accompanied the events of the French Revolution at the end of the eighteenth century in nearly every country in Europe is another example, but in its later stages that disturbance cut too deep, and philosophy itself was thought to have been discredited by its excesses. Hazlitt, who had himself, as he put it, seen the sun of liberty turn in France to blood, described the Revolution as 'the only match that ever took place between philosophy and experience'; and Macaulay wrote of the reaction that followed: 'Freedom was regarded as a great delusion. Men were willing to submit to the government of hereditary princes, of fortunate soldiers, of nobles, of priests: to any government but that of philosophers and philanthropists.' But there is no need to multiply instances. The point is simple and probably obvious; some profound disturbance of the social and intellectual climate is required to bring philosophy into general attention; at other times it remains in the background, respected perhaps, but ignored by those who manage the affairs of men.

These trite reflections have a certain actuality. For we

are at the moment living through a period of profound disorder and disturbance; and if there is any truth in what has been said, these disturbances should have produced or be producing an increased demand for the services of the philosopher in the regions affected by the disturbance, if not an unusual outburst of philosophical speculation in matters relevant to it.

It is, in fact, difficult to point to any considerable portion of the field of thought and conduct which is wholly untouched by the radical scepticism and instability characteristic of the time through which we are passing. Everywhere is fluidity, insecurity, lack of final authority and of untroubled certainty. Perhaps one is inclined in retrospect to exaggerate the complacency and stability of the late nineteenth century. But though there were problems then, and though pessimistic observers of politics, like Leonard Hobhouse, saw the presage of disaster to democracy in the hectic imperialism of the Boer War, and acute interpreters of scientific thought, like James Ward, saw signs of growing weakness in the imposing façade of scientific orthodoxy, yet they were far from carrying every one with them; and even they must have been surprised before they died at the scope of the revolutions which they saw in progress round them. In the nineteenth century natural science made spectacular advances in every part of its field. Problem after problem was successfully formulated and solved. Methods were devised and perfected by which, as it seemed, this process could be continued indefinitely. The whole field was divided up; for each part of it appropriate methods and principles were found. All that was needed further was a sufficient number of industrious and intelligent workers, who, working each in his own little plot, in co-operation would gradually uncover the last mysteries of nature. Whether there were, as philosophers said, or were not, as many scientists were inclined to think, further important questions about the world, which such methods as these were impotent to answer, did not really matter. In either case, the scientist could go on with his work safely, without troubling his head with them. Metaphysics could be left to metaphysicians.

There can be no doubt that during this present century the confidence of the scientists in their ability to exclude ultimate metaphysical questions and solve the problem of nature by the cumulative effect of piecemeal advances has seriously weakened. They have found themselves forced more and more to question their fundamental assumptions, and thus to enter ground which had been previously reckoned metaphysical. Not unnaturally, the philosopher has been tempted to intervene in these discussions, and sometimes, advancing with more zeal than discretion, he has run the risk of appearing to claim the position of legislator for the sciences. There has in fact developed a kind of No Man's Land where scientific philosophers and philosophic scientists engage in controversy as to the propriety of which neither science nor philosophy is assured. The signal example of this tendency is, of course, mathematical physics; but it is not the sole example. There is also the field of biology, in which the old mechanism is questioned by working scientists as well as by philosophers.

More relevant to my present subject is the field of conduct, and here the situation is essentially the same. Our time is plainly characterized by widespread doubt concerning the principles of action, to which the late nineteenth century offers no parallel. In those days the philosopher felt in a sense no great responsibility in this field. His task was merely that of providing a theoretical basis for practical principles securely established and generally recognized. These formed the secure starting-point and the pre-determined goal of his speculations; his differences with his brother philosophers were differences of interpretation. He might accept the Utilitarianism of the Benthamite or the Law of Duty as preached by the followers of Kant, and feel that practically the choice was of little moment. Thus, here, as in science, the philosophical question was isolated and fenced off, after a fashion made possible by the existence in the field of a massive series of immediate certainties, which rightly or wrongly were taken as beyond question. To-day, these immediate practical certainties seem no longer to exist; the principles of action are themselves questioned and found to need proof. The philosopher therefore does not know where to begin. He is asked to face the novel task of creating his own point of departure. This means that mere interpretation is no longer sufficient; he is called to perform a work of construction. It means, to put it otherwise, that while formerly his work had merely theoretical significance, it now has, or is expected to have, practical importance. He is asked not merely to speculate, but also to preach and edify. Thus once more, as in ancient Greece, the question 'what must I do to be saved?' is addressed to the philosopher; he is expected to commend to his followers a way of life. The task which the advent of the Christian religion seemed to have relieved him of for ever comes back upon his hands.

Equally in politics and in sociology generally, not excluding economics, the foundations are shaken and the old certainties have become matters of dispute. There is little trace to-day of any parallel to the splendid confidence with which, before the first Reform Bill, James Mill constructed a deductive science of politics from a few propositions of psychology. All theoretical deductions are paralysed by a general doubt which reaches to their fundamental principles. In politics, the geometrical method (to give it John Mill's description) was surrendered long ago; but it was reserved for our own time to disqualify the theoretical economist as well. He is now shown to have been making sociological assumptions to which he had no right, and to have lost his limited application in a changing world. And this general distrust of deduction is not balanced by any compensating confidence in the promise or performance of the inductive method. Plans for positive sciences of politics and society were frequent enough in the nineteenth century; but to-day little is heard of them. No such sciences exist or seem likely to come into existence. The secure basis for political action, which so many seek, seems very unlikely to be found by any extension of the methods of the natural sciences. Meanwhile, the world clamours for guidance in its pressing perplexities. Never has the theorist been so much in demand, and never has he been so uncertain of his own inspiration.

To a great extent, of course, the social and political confusion is simply the same phenomenon, written in larger letters, as the ethical confusion previously described. Weakness or lack of principle creates a general fluidity favourable to novel and even repulsive experiments. All sorts of things traditionally censured as morally, socially, or economically improper and pernicious are shamelessly done. There is simultaneously a tremendous outburst of wild and often stupid theory, seeking to justify novelties already adopted or to recommend innovations even more daring. In no part of the field is there an orthodoxy, a body of principle, strong enough to stand up against this restless questioning and undisciplined speculation, able to distinguish authoritatively true from false, right from wrong. The German version of Fascism, with its explicit advocacy of the Follow my Leader principle, betrays more obviously than the Italian form that it is only a violent cutting of the knot. The mood is that of Wordsworth's lines—'Me this unchartered freedom tires, I feel the weight of chance desires: I long for a repose that ever is the same.' Duty and obedience, blind obedience to the Leader, is the alternative offered and widely approved. Fascism, of course, in Germany claims to have a *Weltanschauung* which will fill the void to which it owed its opportunity, and demands that every German shall be educated in it, but the content of this creed is very slight, and Italian Fascism admits that it is purely opportunist. I cannot see that this violent cutting of the knot can do anything in the long run but aggravate the disease from which it offered release. If the disease was a generally disabling doubt, hysterical assertion without conviction will not cure it. The machinery of representative government which the Fascists have scrapped made evident the fact that no one knew what to do. There was so little clearness as to end and means that none of the committees on which such government rests could evolve any settled policy. In such a situation a committee is an almost insuperable obstacle to action. Fascism pushes these obstacles aside and so formally restores the power of action. But the problem is only transferred to the one who leads, and where shall the leader find his inspiration? He can give the people parade and spectacles and a great show of business, but it soon becomes apparent that after all he knows no better than any one else what to do. In Germany, as in Italy, we are faced by the ultimate prospect of a people (in the pathetic refrain of a song current in 1914) 'all dressed up and no place to go'. The other popular solution of the day, dogmatic Marxism, is also, as it seems to me, a violent cutting of the knot; but it is also certainly much more of a solution, because it is capable of answering every question and it has a constructive long-range scheme of reorganization on which men's hopes may well continue for generations to be fixed. It is, therefore, capable of lasting as Fascism is not. But apart from the details of the dogma offered, Marxism as we know it is irredeemably dogmatic, and dogma as such is repulsive to any speculative mind. Must we choose, then, we ask with Kant, between scepticism and dogmatism, or is there a third and better way?

II

The only answer to this question, it might seem, which is open to the President of a philosophic society, is an endorsement of the famous thesis which is the centre of Plato's *Republic*. 'Until philosophers are kings, or the kings and princes of this world have the spirit and power of philosophy, and political greatness and wisdom meet in one, and those commoner natures who pursue either to the exclusion of the other are compelled to stand aside, cities will never have rest from their evils—no, nor the human race, as I believe—and then only will this our State have a possibility of life and behold the light of day.' But this is an Aristotelian, not a Platonic Society; and Aristotle showed reason for thinking that in this as in other respects Plato seriously over-estimated the power of philosophy. I am disposed to agree with Aristotle's criticism; but in any case before we can profitably consider the possible contribution of philosophy to the reconstruction of belief, it is necessary to give some attention to the more general question, what the power and function of philosophy is.

In a well-known aphorism, F. H. Bradley has said that 'metaphysics is the finding of bad reasons for what we believe upon instinct'. Bertrand Russell once declared that 'philosophy should show us the hierarchy of our instinctive beliefs. . . . It should take care to show that, in the form in which they are finally set forth, our instinctive beliefs do not clash, but form a harmonious system. There can never be any reason for rejecting one instinctive belief except that it clashes with others; thus, if they are found to harmonize, the whole system becomes worthy of acceptance.'[1] There is no need to examine closely the word instinct which figures in both statements. I quote these two very diverse authorities only because they seem to agree on a point which if true is vital to our present discussion. Philosophy, they both imply, has its task set to it from without, by activities quite independent of itself; these activities are represented as spontaneously generating a set of beliefs or principles, of which the practitioner need not apparently even be conscious, which, in any case he is unable to question, and the principles thus generated are represented as constituting the philosophic problem. Now if this, or something like it, is true, it follows that a period of uncertainty and disorganization in the primary activities must necessarily be an unproductive period in the secondary activity of philosophy. The looms will stand idle for lack of raw material, or work

[1] *Problems of Philosophy*, p. 39.

to little effect because of its inferior quality. But we have already noticed that at such times of disorganization in the primary activities the demand for philosophy is exceptionally great. So we get a practical paradox of a familiar type. The demand for philosophy is at a maximum when its possibilities are at a minimum, and vice versa. Just as, on the Stock Exchange, shares are always offered at bargain prices when we have no money to buy them, and when we have the money they are apt to be so dear as to be hardly worth buying.

Let us take once more a fleeting glance at the frontiers of philosophy and natural science. If at any point the inquiries in which the life of science consists break down and come to a stand, I cannot see that the philosopher by means of his philosophy can make any direct contribution to their revival and re-establishment. If it were the case that the sciences rested, even in part, on fundamental premises supplied by philosophy, the situation would be different; but does any one now believe that this is so? Recent philosophical discussions of physics give no support to any such view. On the contrary, they show the philosopher in this region always as in principle receptive, waiting upon the physicist. It is for the physicist to decide; philosophy can at most criticize. The reason why philosophers intervened was, first, as has already been suggested, because the physicists appeared to be engaged in disavowing what had previously been taken to be their 'instinctive beliefs'—a manœuvre as suspect to a philosopher as a manipulation of the raw cotton market is to a cotton-spinner; secondly, because physicists in questioning and modifying these fundamentals of theirs were inclined to suggest certain generalizations of the new principle which took them admittedly outside the sphere of physics altogether and were in fact metaphysical theorems. With regard to these excursions into metaphysics, the physicist, of course, was the trespasser, and it was for philosophy to decide, but the decision of the other question rests entirely with the physicist; it is for him to say what principles he needs for the solution of his own problems. The philosopher can only await judgement, and though he may be said to criticize the result, he has no right to impugn the validity of the principles in their own sphere. It should be noted that the restriction of philosophic competence above asserted does not depend upon the acceptance of a Kantian conception of metaphysics. Even if metaphysics in the pre-Kantian sense is possible, it still does not follow that metaphysics can legislate for science. Conceivably the human mind may be able one day to determine what being in general must be; but it is by no means certain that on that basis it would be able to determine what the several spheres of being must be. Aristotle maintained that being was not in that sense a genus, and if that is so, the sciences still retain their autonomy. Anyhow, in practice the fact is evident that the scientific world is self-governing and will not submit to the dictation of philosophy.

The point I wish to make is merely that a similar restriction of competence debars the philosopher from constructive action in the practical field. The most obvious difference here is that while some philosophers are physicists, all philosophers are to some extent practical men, and, as practical men, actually take part in establishing and maintaining the standards and principles which as philosophers it is their duty to investigate; but this only makes the confusion of the two sets of questions more likely to occur and more difficult to avoid. And, further, since action is inarticulate, and since the practitioner in any region is only too apt, when he does give an account of his own procedure, to misrepresent himself, there is a kind of gap between conduct and philosophical reflection upon it, which has no parallel in the case of science. There is room here for a variety of descriptive work, recording how the men of a given time and society actually live and act, how their societies are organized, how their political institutions are ordered and administered, and so on. There is room also for all the many kinds of hortatory literature, sermons, tracts, projects of reform, &c., recommending reorganization and revaluation. Both kinds of literature, both the descriptive and the hortatory, are commonly produced by persons who make no claim to be philosophers, and contain in fact a minimum of philosophical reflection. But the philosopher, when his subject is conduct, is seldom careful to remain on his own side of the gap. For one reason or another he commonly prefers to fill it himself. It is even perhaps exceptional to find a work on Ethics or (still more) Politics by a professional philosopher which is to any great extent philosophical in character. Much the greater part of Aristotle's Ethics, for instance, is descriptive or analytical of the ethical valuations of contemporary society; a good deal of it is hortatory. Hardly any of it is philosophical. But this is perhaps not a fair instance, since Aristotle did not believe that ethics was a part of philosophy.

My object in the foregoing remarks is not at all to criticize philosophers for their treatment of the problem of conduct; I am charitable enough to suppose that they have good reason for what they do. I only want to show how I understand their performances in this region and to explain something which must, I think, have struck every student of philosophy, viz. the relative impurity of works of practical philosophy. (It is, of course, precisely this impurity which makes ethics and politics the best gate of entry for the non-philosophical student into the philosophical field.) The point is highly relevant to the present discussion. For by reason of this impurity the moral philosopher does in fact assert ethical values, recommend lines of action, advocate reform of existing institutions— all things which as a practical man he has a perfect right to do, but none of them in themselves activities pertaining to a philosopher. The philosopher, I should say, in virtue of his philosophy cannot prove anything to be good or bad. If men really think that vice is better than virtue, that justice is a dream or a triviality, that all significant relations between states can be expressed in power equations, philosophy can only register these facts and explore their implications. By cross-examination of those who say these things the philosopher may in fact be able to show that they do not really mean what they say. That will no doubt be a useful service, but it is not itself philosophy. It is a preliminary rectification of something offered as a starting-point for philosophical reflection. The refutations of such moral nihilism to be found in philosophical works, as in the *Republic* of Plato, for instance, are largely exercises of this order, i.e. demonstrations that the thesis in question is meaningless. So far as they are not that and really claim to prove, for instance, that virtue is better than vice, they are either question-begging, in the sense that they are substantially only the assertion of a divergent valuation, or what they prove is not what they pretend to prove.

I see no reason at this stage to consider politics separately. I assume that what is said above applies equally in both fields. And I proceed to register the immediate conclusion that if there is scepticism and disorder in the practical field the philosopher is totally unable to remedy it and reconstruct the shattered fabric of belief. If the world asks this of him, it asks something which he cannot give. The very nature of the philosophic task precludes him from any such service. The certainties on which he builds are certainties developed and tested by practical men in the conduct of life. If these are lacking, it is not in his power to create them.

III

But, as the title of this paper implies, I cannot rest in this negation. I began by pointing to a need and a demand; I went on to explain that in my view the demand is not one that philosophy can meet; what I want to do in conclusion is to show that the philosopher is, nevertheless, in a position to give some real assistance in the practical field, and to urge therefore on my colleagues the advisability of giving fuller and wider attention to that side of their responsibilities.

In the economy of human thought it seems that philosophy and science (i.e. the complex of the natural sciences) are the natural complements of one another. Being mutually complementary they advance normally, as would be expected, hand in hand. The philosophic synthesis and the scientific analysis are interdependent and inseparable. The sciences make progress by minute subdivision of a field which the philosopher has always to consider as a whole. But this subdivision presupposes a plan of the whole, which the sciences may be said collectively to affirm. Yet this plan, on which they work and which they are said to believe in, is something which they have never had before them at all; it is revealed for the first time by the subsequent efforts of philosophic reflection. It is hardly more than a pattern into which the scientists fall as they go about their business of exploring nature. It comes from no supreme directing brain and is administered by no general staff. It is a pure product of empirical opportunism, and any necessity it may claim is a necessity of fact. Now, this pattern or plan is, in fact, constantly being disturbed and developed, but mostly in its minor features only, which represent its adjustment to the more superficial features of nature. The general plan remains over long periods the same, and these minor adjustments leave it unaffected, a reliable foundation for the co-operative labours of the scientific hive. More far-reaching adjustments are at times necessary, and these must of course dislocate research on a more extensive scale, by enforcing revision of its assumptions, and thus endanger to some extent the whole co-operative enterprise. It is at such times that the frontiers between philosophy and science become doubtful, and the philosopher finds himself exceptionally in a position to do some small service to the scientist. Of such crises we may perhaps say that they represent a phase in which, to a greater or lesser extent, a new synthesis has to be made before the work of analysis can profitably continue.

On the practical side, I would suggest, the special

responsibilities and opportunities of philosophy depend similarly on the generally recognized fact that social organization means division of labour. Plato, who was one of the first to point this out, immediately demanded and sought to give a rational justification for such division, and his scheme for a rational division of labour became a scheme for a complete social revolution. But neither philosophy nor science is in a position to say authoritatively how social functions ought to be allotted, though each may offer facts and theories which are easily turned into criticism of the actual allotment. Here, too, we have, in fact, co-operative work on a large scale based on a plan for which no one is responsible—a pattern into which human life has somehow fallen. And it sometimes seems that society can only keep running smoothly and happily so long as every one takes the plan so much for granted that no one even asks what it is. As soon as attention is directed to it, a justification is of course demanded, and little discussion is needed before every citizen and every group of citizens is profoundly convinced that the plan gives him (or it) a position in society wholly incommensurate with his (or their) deserts. Yet more and more in the modern world social self-consciousness increases ; more and more eagerly men search for some principle on which social functions shall be justly distributed, some principle of higher authority than economic necessity or historical accident. In our own day, the consciously planned society is often said to exist or to be coming into existence. But it is probable that no individual and no society can plan more than a very small fraction of its life, however important that small fraction may be.

From the social point of view, each one of us is a highly specialized worker, tied to his own little niche in the general scheme. In that respect we are products of an analysis for which as individuals we are not responsible and over which we have no control. But decisions have to be taken for society as a whole, with due regard to all the varied interests which it comprises, and this synthetic activity is of course the subject-matter of politics. In the name of the democratic principle an attempt is made to induce every adult citizen to take a part in this work of synthesis, and so far as this is successful he gets some understanding of the whole and of his place in it. This is clearly a valuable corrective of the inevitable specialization of function, and that is one good argument for democratic institutions. But there is another reason for aiming at a democracy which perhaps goes deeper. Democracy may be regarded as essentially the product of political and social empiricism. If it were the case that the human mind could formulate completely and indisputably all the principles and possibilities of human nature, the argument would be impossible to resist that one wise man, or a group of such, ought to be put in charge of each society; but this is not so, and the imposture of collective wisdom, of which anti-democrats talk, is less of a swindle than the imposture of individual inspiration, which is their alternative, when it is not anarchy. The empiricist is modest in his claims for reason, and it is not collective wisdom that he means to assert when he supports democracy. He is looking for an arrangement by which the natural growth of a society will be as little obstructed as possible, by which at the same time all constructive ideas can find easy expression, considering that the human intellect at its highest is mainly exercised in guiding and correcting movements which it did not originate.

These remarks lead me a little aside from my main point, but they are not irrelevant, since they should explain briefly how I understand the work of political synthesis on which the health of societies so largely and increasingly depends. The work itself must be left mainly, even in a democratic State, to professional politicians. The question is whether in this extremely difficult and critical work they might not be given more effective help than they now receive, and whether in particular the philosopher might not help them.

It is not a question of expert advice. The politician is

himself an expert in the political machine and its possibilities, and experts in any desired field are easily found
or made. These and the specialist social sciences, like
economics, belong to the analytic distribution of social
effort and represent material which politics exists to
synthesize. It is a question of assistance in the work of
synthesis itself. The question is, where is this to be found?
It seems to me that there are only two established disci-
plines from which the required assistance could possibly
be expected. These are history and philosophy; and of
the two philosophy appears to have much the greater
possibilities. Both have it in their power to restore to due
proportion a perspective distorted, as that of the practical
man must always tend to be, by the pressure of present
emergency. Both can contribute effectively to the achievement of that distance and detachment which is so necessary a condition of genuine statesmanship. Some men, no
doubt, of high ability, have a constitutional aversion to
philosophy, and for them history will be the only resource.
But where this aversion does not exist, and both roads lie
open, the superiority lies surely with philosophy. For the
benefits derived from history are mostly indirect; its only
essential service is in the close neighbourhood of the problems at issue, and generally in bringing home that continuity of present, past, and future which makes Society,
in Burke's words, a partnership 'between those who are
living, those who are dead, and those who are to be born'.
Otherwise the reader has to make his connexions mostly
for himself, and in so doing he is apt to fall into questionable and even dangerous analogies. But in a philosophical
analysis of society the subject-matter is the more permanent aspects of those very problems which the politician
is himself employed in handling, and the mode of argumentation used is largely of the same order as that which
he himself in facing these problems is forced to use. Philosophy, I mean, by its refusal to abstract and its insistence
on taking everything into account, is forced to put aside all
idea of exact calculation and mathematical demonstration

I

in respect of its central assertions, and the practical man or statesman, however much he may employ these in the preliminaries, has in the end to do the same.

If I am right in the view of philosophy which I have outlined above, if its primary task is to exhibit the constitutive principles of theoretical and other human activities, which came into existence without its help and are in no sense subject to its rulings, it follows no doubt that these activities will continue to go their own way, and there can be no guarantee that their progress will always be perfectly orderly and consistent, or wholly satisfactory to the philosophic critic. But it does not follow that philosophic criticism is of no assistance to their progress: on the contrary it may still be at times almost indispensable. For philosophy on this showing has the task of expounding to them on the evidence of their activities what their fundamental beliefs are, and that task, which may seem almost otiose when all is going well, becomes important as soon as things begin to go badly. When the foundations are shaking, it is as well to know what they are. These considerations apply in my view over the whole field of philosophy, but they apply, for reasons already given, with especial force on the practical side. If philosophers were to cease, *per impossibile*, to take any interest in the progress of the natural sciences, no very serious harm would result. The scientific world would respond by evolving, as to a large extent it already does, its own critical apparatus. But in the practical field proverbially the sign of strength is silence, and a call to reflective criticism is resented as an interference with the practical programme and a solvent of effort. The man of action has little leisure or inclination to discuss the principles on which he acts. Therefore his critical thinking has to be done largely for him. And my case is that a social philosophy is needed for this purpose—a philosophical synthesis specializing in the social field as philosophers also specialize in science or the field of art. This post-war generation is, I think, in urgent need of such a synthesis. Our young men and women are attracted in large and probably increasing numbers to the Marxist creed, not so much because it is adequate and theoretically unanswerable, as because it is the only coherent body of doctrine that they can find. Many, probably most of them, are not philosophers, and possibly they are rather repelled than attracted by the philosophic side of the creed. But that side of it is very important and its adequate discussion is a real need. What is wanted is a philosophic discipline, encouraging and promoting the careful exposition and discussion of the presuppositions of social organization on every side. No such discipline exists in this country at present. If it existed it might of course tend to the endorsement of the Marxist case; but if so it would be a more intelligent Marxism than we commonly meet to-day. But those who believe, as I do, that the Marxist position contains fundamental falsehood, will be confident that it would be able to show those who are drawn towards it a better way—not by preaching an alternative ideal, or by inventing a rival Utopia, but by showing them on the evidence of the actual achievements of humanity what man's fundamental beliefs really are, and by showing further how little of all this is honoured in the Marxist solution, and how much is excluded. I take Marxism only as a highly topical example. My point is that our generation is not being given in these matters the tools necessary for coming to a sound critical judgement, and that philosophy alone has the power to give them these tools. When men do not know the faith by which they live, they will be apt inadvertently to betray it.

VIII. CAN PHILOSOPHY DETERMINE WHAT IS ETHICALLY OR SOCIALLY VALUABLE?[1]

THE problem raised by this question is to my mind fundamentally the problem how far and in what sense the philosopher is in a position to give assistance to the practical man in his action; in particular, whether he is rightly expected to prescribe the end or goal or principle of action for men as moral individuals, or for societies as responsible for organizing and directing the lives of their members. I answer the question with a qualified negative, i.e. I think that the philosopher can be of assistance to the practical man, but not in the way suggested. Perhaps a further personal explanation may be in order, since it will show how the question in fact arose and why I am asked to open the discussion though my answer is to this extent negative.

At the beginning of this session I wrote a paper for the Aristotelian Society under the title 'The Need for a Social Philosophy', concerned largely with this very point. In the course of that paper I called attention to the fact that large portions of the books written by philosophers on ethics and politics are not strictly philosophical in character: to a large extent they are descriptive, occupied in recording relevant experiences, and in much of the rest they are apt to be hortatory, occupied in recommending this or that reform or line of action. From a strictly philosophical point of view there is a high degree of impurity in such works, which may be generally desirable and justifiable and certainly makes them more attractive to the non-philosophic reader, but is apt to cause confusion in the reader's mind as to the task of philosophy and the contribution to be expected from it. I went on as follows:

'by reason of this impurity the moral philosopher does in fact assert ethical values, recommend lines of action, advocate reforms of existing institutions—all things which as a practical

[1] *Aristotelian Society*, Supp., vol. xv.

man he has a perfect right to do, but none of them in themselves activities pertaining to a philosopher. The philosopher, I should say, in virtue of his philosophy cannot prove anything to be good or bad. If men really think that vice is better than virtue, that justice is a dream or a triviality, that all significant relations between states can be expressed in power equations, philosophy can only register these facts and explore their implications. By cross-examination of those who say these things the philosopher may in fact be able to show that they do not mean what they say. That will no doubt be a useful service, but it is not itself philosophy. It is a preliminary rectification of something offered as a starting-point for philosophical reflection. The refutations of such moral nihilism to be found in philosophical works, as in the *Republic* of Plato, for instance, are largely exercises of this order, i.e. demonstrations that the thesis in question is meaningless. So far as they are not that and really claim to prove, for instance, that virtue is better than vice, they are either question-begging, in the sense that they are substantially only the assertion of a divergent valuation, or what they prove is not what they pretend to prove.'[1]

My task in opening this discussion is to re-state and explain these contentions, and explanation is clearly desirable on two main points—(1) as to the conception of philosophy presupposed, (2) as to the relation of philosophical reflection to the grounds of practical judgement and decision.

I

Philosophy and its Task

I agree substantially with the conception of the philosopher's task which Bertrand Russell adopted some twenty-five years ago when he wrote his *Problems of Philosophy*.

'Philosophy', he said, 'should show us the hierarchy of our instinctive beliefs. . . . It should take care to show that, in the form in which they are finally set forth, our instinctive beliefs do not clash, but form a harmonious system. There can never be any reason for rejecting one instinctive belief except that it

[1] See *supra*, pp. 108–9.

clashes with others; thus, if they are found to harmonize, the whole system becomes worthy of acceptance.'

Russell had in mind chiefly, when he wrote those words, fundamental common-sense assumptions, such as that material bodies exist. Whether he would have attached any special value to the word 'instinctive', which I do not much like, I do not know; nor do I know what else, if anything, he would have asked the philosopher to do besides exploring and exhibiting the system of these beliefs. When he says that no such belief can legitimately be rejected except on the ground of its inconsistency with others, he seems to imply that the philosopher's constructive task is exhausted in this. However that may be, I see no reason why the conception should not be generalized so as to include not merely the practical presuppositions of common sense, to which the word 'instinct' is not inappropriate, but also, e.g., the principles of induction, which he goes on later in the same book to investigate, and the complex assumptions which underlie the scientific interpretation of nature, in regard to which the word 'instinct' seems to be rather out of place. And with that extension, if it is an extension, and with a request for a better word than 'instinctive', I am prepared to accept the description as fitting the philosophic task.

Philosophy, as I understand it, is essentially a reflective activity of thought, in contact with reality, so far as reality is other than mind, not directly but through primary and pre-existing mental reactions to it. These primary activities are of various kinds, but all alike come into existence without the philosopher's assistance and go their way independently of him. He has no power or title to regulate or control them. Each of them has its own actuating principles and its own fundamental constitutive beliefs. These last are not a set of clearly formulated principles, which can be set out once for all, like the axioms of Euclid, before the activity begins, but rather principles and beliefs developed experimentally as the activity develops, and justified for the experimenter by the success of the experiments in which they are operative. The task of the philosopher is (1) to determine the precise character of the principles, (2) to pursue their implications, (3) to consider all questions arising from the interrelation of the pre-suppositions of human thought, theoretical and practical, in its different fields of exercise. The first of these three tasks calls for special familiarity with a particular field, and thus accounts for a certain degree of specialization on the part of philosophers. The specialization may be lasting or it may be, so to speak, periodical. One philosopher is specially at home in the field of science (or the philosopher at one period devotes himself to this side of thought); another philosopher (or the philosopher at another time) concentrates on art or religion or history or on the problems of the practical life in ethics and politics; and in this way are produced philosophical treatments of these depart-ments. But, if the treatment is to be philosophical, the specialization cannot be absolute. In executing the first of his three tasks the philosopher must have in mind the second and the third; for it is his business, as a philosopher, not merely to understand the procedure of the artist or the scientist, but to procure an insight into the nature of reality in its universality. This differentiates his work from that of the specialist proper. An artist will sometimes discuss the principles of his art, an experienced politician will attempt to expound the lessons of his experience and the principles which have guided him in his work: either of them may in fact have something of the philosopher in his composition, and if so that will complicate the formula; but primarily, and so far as they are true to their own specialities, each will have in mind his own successes and what made them possible: each will be making a contribu-tion to his own speciality with a view to improving its practice. The philosopher is facing in the opposite direc-tion. What interests him is not the consequences of these principles in operation, but their presuppositions: his question is, What must the world be to make this possible? To say this is, of course, only to generalize the theorem concerning the opposite movements of philosophic and scientific thought which Plato formulated in his *Republic*. In terms of the triple task formulated above it means that while both the specialist proper in his reflective moments and the philosopher will appear to face the second of the questions enumerated, viz. that of the implications of the principles, they will be concerned, so far as each is true to his nature, with a different set of implications. The considerations which specially concern the philosopher may be called the metaphysical implications, and these do not concern the practitioner as such.

I would only add, with no emphasis, because it is not very relevant here, that it seems to me to be clear that the main philosophical controversies are incidental to the third of the tasks set out above. The successes of science, for example, are represented as requiring or implying a materialistic interpretation of nature; action, on the other hand, and the principles of moral judgement upon it, are represented as demanding a conception of the material as malleable by a will which is not material. Thus there is a conflict, real or apparent, between the implications of two different kinds of human experience, out of which prolonged disputes connected with terms like materialism, the freedom of the will, &c., are born. To accept such a conflict as inevitable and irreconcilable would be to surrender the faith on which knowledge depends, and therefore in attempting to reinterpret the rival theses so as to remove their apparent conflict the philosopher is undertaking a necessary task, which has to be performed if the several activities which are in apparent conflict are not to be paralysed by fundamental doubts.

II

The Practical Field

If the foregoing definition of the philosophic task is correct, it follows at once that the first duty of the philosopher in any field which he may enter, and therefore specifically in the practical field which is here in question, is to determine a question of fact. If a normative science is one that sets out to formulate ideals which are in no determinable relation to current practice, his is not a normative science. With ideals and principles of action he is certainly concerned, and equally certainly these ideals and principles of action are not always and everywhere effective in action, but if they are nowhere effective it is difficult to see what right they have to their name. His first task is to determine by the appropriate evidence what the operative principles of conduct actually are and what are the limits of their operation. It is his business to find out what is thought obligatory, not what ought to be thought obligatory; what is considered good, not what it is good to consider good. It is no more his business to put himself in the place of the agent or politician, and think out his problem for him afresh, than it is his place to go into the scientific laboratory and attempt a new solution of the scientist's problem. He is concerned only with the reflective interpretation of a given activity, and such interpretation must start, like any interpretation, from determination of fact. It merely happens that in this case the relevant facts are essentially valuations; and this creates a confusion in some people's minds, who cannot conceive a valuation as a fact requiring accurate definition and analysis.

Another source of confusion here arises from a tendency, which seems to be natural to the unsophisticated human mind, to a utilitarian interpretation of conduct. If all differences of practical valuation are reducible in the last resort to differences in acceptability between the probable results of action, then the obvious conception of ethical and political theory is the conception of it as directed to determining the general considerations on which such acceptability depends or should depend. Men will thus go to ethics and politics (to borrow Aristotle's metaphor) like archers in search of a mark. Nearer objectives they have no doubt in plenty, based on blind instinct, example, tribal custom, and other questionable foundations; but to bring order into their lives and achieve the full freedom of a planned life they want an ultimate objective in reference to which these others may be systematized and regulated. On this view the philosophical theorist is conceived as thinking on precisely the same lines as the man of action, but as carrying the thought further and deeper than the man of action is willing or able to carry it. He will be telling the practical man, who has no leisure to complete the answer to his own perpetual question, what in the long run is really worth having. But even if the utilitarian view is correct, this conception of ethics and politics does not necessarily follow. It may still be the case that the philosopher has no authority from his philosophy for pronouncing that this is better than that, and that when he propounds a definition of the human good, the evidence for the truth and adequacy of this conception is to be found in the more limited judgements of the man of action, of which it is the continuation and justification. In this case the philosopher will after all be occupied in substance in deciding a question of fact: he will be telling the practical man what he really is aiming at all the time. Aristotle's own final conclusion was really that this is what the ethical and political philosopher actually does.

But, it will be said, even if the first step is the determination of fact, which may well be true, the philosopher cannot surely stop at that. Surely it is his obvious duty to criticize these judgements of value, to correct errors and misapprehensions, to recommend the right principles of action, and so contribute to the making of a better and happier world.

This is the type of objection which in one form or another is always brought against any one who puts forward such a conception of practical philosophy as I am now advancing. I have come to the conclusion that its real root is the failure to realize what a difficult task in the practical field this initial task (as I have called it) of determining the facts is, and how little therefore relatively remains to be done when it is satisfactorily accomplished. The idea that the commands and principles of morality are as plain as a pikestaff may be a convenience to rulers and teachers and other lovers of docility, but it is a long way from the truth and a serious obstacle to any one who wishes to establish a sound practical philosophy. The material which must form the empirical basis of any theory is rich and various. It consists of acts and judgements—acts of our own and of other persons, judgements upon acts and projects of action of our own and of other persons. Each of these acts and judgements is essentially atomic and isolated, as the judgements of aesthetic appreciation are also atomic and isolated. Each has reference to a particular performance and situation, and no other. Consequently there may be any degree of inconsequence and inconsistency between them. How many people judge themselves and other persons by the same measures, or hold consistently to one standard of judgement over a period? Further, the specifically moral factor in action and in judgement is so inextricably mixed up with other factors that its separate operation is not in fact conceivable and its theoretical isolation is a matter of extreme difficulty. The moral diagnosis of any act involves necessarily the ascription of motives to the agent, and how can we, who find by experience that we cannot pronounce confidently as to our own motives, identify with any confidence the motives of some one else? There is obviously an enormous gap between this chaotic material and the tidy ethical systems which philosophers offer us as the result of their reflection upon it. The philosopher does not trouble much to show the steps by which from that starting-point he arrived at this result. It often seems as though he had been content to generalize from his own limited practical experience, assuming that it was typical or authoritative. But whether the field from which the material is drawn is wide or narrow, it seems clear that the determination of the facts, which is the first step, is no simple straightforward matter, but a difficult and complicated undertaking.

My first answer, then, is that the question of fact, the question what are the ideals and principles actually operative in the field of practice, is by itself a question of sufficient magnitude to occupy justifiably the main part of an investigator's attention. My second answer is that such correction and criticism of current practice and belief as is logically justifiable will be given implicitly in the attempt at a systematic exposition of the facts. Everything turns here on the question how the valuations on which the decisions of the agent or statesman depend are established or confirmed. If they are capable of systematic *a priori* exposition and proof, then I suppose the philosopher might undertake this and so formulate a body of doctrine, like Locke's Law of Nature, which would be 'an eternal rule to all men, legislators as well as others'. By it as standard he could judge the actual practice of legislators and others, and show wherein it fell short. But I see no reason to suppose that any such body of *a priori* law is attainable. A more laborious empirical method has therefore to be devised. This means that the would-be theorist of conduct has to face the mass of material above described and attempt to reduce it to some degree of order. He has to show that this multiplicity is at bottom a unity, that this unorganized sequence of decisions and judgements has none the less its own inner organization and can be plausibly regarded as the expression of a single principle or of a few fundamental ideas which are in intelligible relation to one another. Now the fundamental principle of any empirical method, as John Stuart Mill rightly pointed out, is this: 'we have no ulterior test to which we subject experience in general; but we make experience its own test'. Mill was thinking of the scientific exploration of nature. The principle is no doubt sound there, but it is far more directly and obviously applicable when the object to be tested or judged is an expression of human effort and reason. Every such manifestation of mind must necessarily be an attempt to achieve something which is not in fact fully achieved. To state its aim and motive is to state a fact: this is what the agent, the painter, the poet, was actually aiming at. To describe the achievement is also to state a fact: this is what he actually achieved. The perceived interval between the first and second of these two facts is a main ground of favourable and unfavourable judgement upon actions and upon the products of art.

The only way we have of *persuading* other people (as distinct from inducing them by threats, bribery, bullying, &c.) to desist from some course of action is to show them that its continuation will obstruct certain things which they also desire, or that it implies the acceptance of principles and beliefs irreconcilable with those implied by other actions to which they are also committed. The practical man generally, and the politician in particular, is very sensitive to charges of inconsistency, and will resort to the most transparent devices to prove the straightness of a most obviously tortuous course of action. If it were not for this 'instinctive belief' in practical consistency, if practical decisions were really as independent of one another as they often seem to be, the reflective analysis of the philosopher, however interesting and necessary as theory, would be of no importance for practice. But given this demand and belief, his possible influence is very great, and arises directly from the exposition of fact in the sense already explained. Let me illustrate this by an example from political theory. Locke in his *Civil Government* says that 'the great and chief end of men uniting into commonwealths' is the preservation of their property, i.e. 'life, liberty, and estate'. With this principle in his hand he proceeds to condemn this constitutional or other provision and approve that. He thinks that his starting-point is in human reason, i.e. in that which is evident *a priori*, and would probably demur to the suggestion that it is taken from the facts themselves. Yet surely in truth what he did was to reflect on the principles and practice of government in England—and no doubt in other countries—as known to him, and in the course of that reflection convinced himself that the more permanent and constructive features of that government implied fundamentally the observance of some such principle, while disorder, disaster, and weakness entered in so often as public action was taken which implied its suspension or rejection. And having thus obtained his principle from the facts he uses it to judge the facts. What is accepted is accepted as necessary and helpful, what is rejected is rejected as harmful and obstructive to this 'great and chief end'. For a long time after it was written, Locke's work was very influential in the political field. The extent of Locke's influence was due, not to theoretical conceptions, already half obsolete, like the law of nature and the social contract, but to the superb judgement with which he discerned and expounded for his contemporaries the central currents in the turbulent stream of events through which he lived. It was this that gave him his hold on future practice, and enabled his teaching to work for its strengthening and purification.

III

Conclusion

The practical values, in my view, are created, sustained, and developed by practitioners who are in direct contact with the external world at the requisite point. Theirs is the only authoritative and responsible judgement as to what is valuable, and all generalization upon the nature of value and the valuable has to recognize its dependence upon them. New and unforeseen developments at these points of direct contact are always possible, and in such cases it will always be difficult to tell wilful caprice from fruitful innovation. Rules of a kind may be formulated to govern practice, but they have no theoretical foundation: they are essentially generalizations from practice, without power to bind future practice, and without value except for beginners. Reflective analysis by the practitioner of his own practice is no doubt in some degree a persistent element in the practice and contributes to its efficiency, especially by increasing its coherence and consistency. More elaborate attempts at such analysis are undertaken occasionally by the practitioners themselves and persistently by philosophers in treatises devoted to the subject. In their nature these efforts are identical with those of the self-conscious practitioner, and their possible service to practice is of the same order as that of his reflections. But when they are philosophical they have a further aim. They are not directed essentially to the improvement of practice, but to the definition of the principles of practice with a view to clearing up the nature of the world and man's place in it. In any case these reflective efforts are not directly creative: they do not open up new spheres of value: that function is reserved for the practitioner. They are not legislative, producing principles binding on the practitioner: the practice is autonomous. The only sense in which philosophy can be said to determine what is ethically or politically valuable is this, that in its critical examination of the practice and in its exposition of its principles it is attempting to make explicit and evident assumptions as to the nature of good which are for the practitioner largely concealed within the concrete detail of his judgements and decisions. It is only so far as the man of action is reflective that the philosophical analysis links up directly with his thought: towards the answer to his primary question, What shall I do?, philosophy contributes directly nothing.

IX. THE PHILOSOPHY OF DEMOCRACY[1]

I TRY in this paper to give a philosophical account of democracy, which is a thing rarely attempted. That is to say, I begin by stating a general theorem, which originates in other fields and applies to many other things besides politics, and I go on to show how it applies to politics and how in the light of it the principle of democracy may be satisfactorily stated and defended.

(1) In early modern philosophy there was a prolonged dispute concerning the part played by sense and thought respectively in the genesis of knowledge. Some were inclined to give the primacy to the senses, and these were called empiricists, because they stressed experience, actual contact with things. Others rejected the senses as untrustworthy and argued that the most important ideas, e.g. that of God and the fundamental conceptions of mathematics, could not be traced to the senses, and therefore required another pedigree. Therefore they were disposed to assert the independence of the human reason, its ability to evoke knowledge from its own being and resources. The clearest and most certain truths at least were of this order, and the thought directly connected with the use of the senses they tended to regard as an inferior activity: sensation for them tended to be equivalent to confused thinking. This tendency is called rationalism. In the eighteenth century Kant attempted a solution of this age-old conflict by means of the ancient opposition of Form and Matter. He propounded the view that these two cognitive functions are complementary; that there is accordingly no cognition in the full sense which does not owe something to both, sense contributing always certain material which submits to organization, and thought contributing always the organizing form and principle. Thus every genuine judgement in Kant's view has two parents and presupposes a mind which

[1] *Hibbert Journal*, July 1936.

is at once passive and active. As passive it is sensitive to its environment and receives the necessary material, as active it gives the material shape and form. 'Thoughts without content are empty: perceptions without conceptions are blind.' By this formula he seeks to reconcile the two opposed tendencies, recognizing that each party was engaged in over-emphasizing one side of a complex truth. The one side, empiricist or sensationalist, had seen the passivity only and exaggerated accordingly the role of sense; the other had seen the activity only, exaggerating in consequence the role of thought. By his formula he is able to do justice to both factors.

(2) There is a similar antithesis in regard to human equipment on the practical side between desire (appetite, instinct) and will. A desire stands for a tendency to action of a certain type, which is at least in its more primitive and inescapable forms—hunger, thirst, &c.—for a reasonable being a mere datum, a fact which requires to be recognized and taken into account, a limit on his rationality. Here again, there are two one-sided solutions of the resulting problem—on the one hand, a rationalism which violently asserts man's freedom against the appetites which limit it and seeks to prove that freedom by systematically denying them all. That is the erroneous extreme of asceticism. On the other hand, a naturalism which deifies the instincts, spurning this independent reason as a morbid perversion of human nature, and proclaims that intelligence is only healthy when it is their faithful servant. 'Reason', wrote Hume, 'is and ought only to be the slave of the passions.' Here again the antithesis of form and matter may be invoked to effect a compromise and a reconciliation of the two opposed tendencies—a mean position from which justice may be done to the half truth involved in each. For instinct and desire are evidently in their pure form blind, devoid of plan and forethought, sure to lead those who trust them to frustration and disaster. What they offer to a reasonable being is the shapeless material out of which a course of constructive and consecutive action may be

K

made. As thought is both the master of sense and its servant, so will is both the master and the servant of desire. As thought which is not fructified by sense is empty, and sense which is not organized by thought is blind, so the life which denies desire is empty of substance and delight, while the life that concedes everything to it and denies the sovereignty of reason, blunders blindly in the dark. The moral life depends, as Aristotle argued against contemporary exaggerations of asceticism, on the proper discipline and organization of the natural appetites.

(3) My argument in this paper depends on my being allowed to apply the simple considerations concerning individual thought and action which I have just advanced to the case of a community of men organized under government. I ask the reader to let me make that application, without asking too closely for the moment what he is allowing me to do. To make the application I shall have to speak of such a community as though it were a unity possessing these attributes of thought and action. The question how far this assumption is correct is a legitimate one and any results which the argument may reach must subsequently be qualified and corrected in the light of the answer to it. But there is no harm, as far as I can see, in reserving the question for the present. The only use I want to make of this point now is to observe that from the point of view of extreme individualism (or pure social nominalism) no fundamental defence of democracy is possible.

(4) If a whole community, as organized under a single government, can be said to have a will at all, its government must surely be that will; and by the term government we must understand the whole complex of sovereign authorities which have the right to make the laws of the land, to decide points of law, to execute and administer the laws, or to take any other action in the name of the community. These various forms of government activity will in fact be in complicated relations of interdependence, of control and subordination, with one another, as the law and practice of the constitution may determine; but these com-

plications can safely be ignored. For our purpose it will be sufficient to regard the whole complex as what it is always trying to be, a unity, a single will, declaring in its various concurrent expressions a single purpose and policy; adding perhaps that in modern times it is usually taken for granted that in the formation of policy the legislative body plays in some sense the preponderant part. This government, then, dominated by a representative legislature, may be taken to embody in its decisions the reasonable will of the community so far as such a will exists.

My further suggestion, on this basis, is that if the community is united and healthy, and if the principle of representation is working satisfactorily, the corporate decision embodied in government action will be the resultant of the fruitful interaction of two factors, viz. *first*, incipient tendencies to corporate action arising in the general body of citizens; *second*, proposals for corporate action on the part of the central authority, formed largely in the hope that they will meet and satisfy these tendencies. These tendencies are of course demands and desires of various grades of definition and urgency. My suggestion is that the fruitfulness of the interaction of these two forces—on the one hand a representative government anxious for a mandate, on the other hand a mass of people ready to give one— depends on this, that the interaction is a process in which matter receives form, in which the spontaneous and unorganized movements of desire and impulse in the body of the people are ordered and articulated till by a continuous process they issue in a conscious corporate decision which is a law or an executive act.

(5) Democracy, reduced to its simplest terms, is the principle that every one shall have a say in matters of common concern. Under a representative system this principle encourages every citizen to play a part in the selection of the representatives who have power to decide such matters. The election of representatives is conceived as the first stage in the continuous process by which out of the unco-ordinated and inconsistent impulses of the

citizens is produced a definite national policy and line of action. Consequently the decision of the representative body and of any smaller body, such as a cabinet, on whom they confer or with whom they share power, is not a wholly free decision. They do what they think best in the circumstances, the chief circumstance being these popular impulses above mentioned, or, as they more commonly say, the state of public opinion. That is to say, their range of decision is severely limited (as the choice of form must always be) by the material available.

These considerations give us the first and fundamental justification of the democratic principle. Its invitation to every citizen to take a part in the selection of representatives is justified because by this invitation it provides an opportunity for the citizens singly and in groups to make known to those who will be their representatives what is stirring among them by way of protest or demand. Legally the citizen may (as by the laws of England) have no other opportunity of making his wishes felt beyond this opportunity which comes at each election time. But the formal opportunity provided by the occasional election is expected to create both in electors and in elected a state of mind favourable to the informal application of such pressure in the intervening periods. So that by this simple piece of machinery a situation is created in which we have a people continuously interested in the larger matters of common concern and continuously expressing its desires in regard to them, and a government continuously sensitive to such expression and continuously active in transforming the material thus provided into corporate action by which the community stands committed.

If the general body of citizens were provided with no such formal right of interference, if, that is, no element of democracy entered into the constitution, the informal give and take between ruler and subject might still subsist. The citizen body might nevertheless attend to what was being done in its name, and the rulers might pay considerable regard to their wishes. To some extent they certainly would, because laws which no one wants are apt to be ineffective. But *first*, the chances of these conditions being realized would obviously be much diminished, and *secondly*, almost inevitably the rulers would tend unconsciously to be unduly dominated by the opinions of the circles with which they were in daily contact, those of their friends and of their neighbourhood. If England lacked the democratic machinery, the opinion of London, for example, would be far more influential on policy in comparison with that of the rest of England than it now is. The democratic machinery corrects this tendency to some extent. It ensures further, generally, that the representatives shall feel these popular impulses, each so to speak directly and in his own person, and it makes the political life of each of them depend on his responsiveness to them. (But in very small bodies, like social clubs, literary and dramatic societies, effective democracy is compatible with the complete absence of any such machinery for the simple reason that the officers are in continuous contact with the members.)

(6) The interpretation of democratic government outlined above can be shown to resemble the Kantian formula from which I started in this, that it effects a reconciliation and combination of two sharply opposed extreme views of the political problem, to which men are at all times prone, and does fair justice to the half truth contained in each. Let us have a look at these two extremes. The first one exaggerates the necessary receptivity of the central authority until it makes government merely the faithful register of a popular activity; the other exaggerates the formlessness and incoherence of popular movements until they cease to have any positive significance, so that the government becomes sole creator and sustainer of national unity and only begetter of law and national policy.

This exaggeration of the central function, of the activity of the government, is analogous to rationalism, and if will is rationalistically interpreted—i.e. understood as action infused by knowledge, as it was by the Greeks—the doctrine becomes simply a form of rationalism. Accordingly we find that it is an attitude to which rationalistic philosophers are prone. Plato's plea for the philosopher king in the Republic is paradoxical not because it suggests that philosophy is the best education for a statesman—Berkeley said almost as much as that[1]—but because it argues that the ruler should be guided rather by the pattern in heaven than by the facts on earth, because it maintains further by implication that in an ideal state ideally well governed the body of the people would have no positive contribution whatever to make to the conduct of state affairs. On the first of these two points—the pattern in heaven—the theory which I am expounding has no great quarrel with Plato: its difference is mainly one of emphasis. Plato seems to take delight in emphasizing the philosopher's detachment from the world, and his disdain for earthly affairs and ignorance of them. This may be regarded only as a kind of superficial perversity, but I think it goes deeper. My account on the other hand emphasizes the necessity in the ruler of extreme sensitiveness to earthly affairs. As to the pattern in heaven itself it is difficult to believe nowadays in absolute political forms, and metaphysical issues also come in to complicate the issue: thus the detail may be questionable; but on my account also the ruler has to supply the Form, and therefore requires in some measure the detachment and independence which Plato claims for his philosopher king. The other point of difference is much more serious. To deny that the body of the citizens have a positive contribution to make is to reduce them to the level of mere brute matter, like the marble or bronze of the sculptor, which imposes on his work only fixed and distant limits capable of being discounted once for all before he begins to operate on it. But animal and still more human material is far from being so simply malleable as that. The general point has already been made and the argument

---

[1] 'Whatever the world thinks, he who hath not much meditated upon God, the human mind, and the *summum bonum*, may possibly make a thriving earthworm, but will most indubitably make a sorry patriot and a sorry statesman' (*Siris*).

need not be repeated. I would only add here that this fundamental error and misapprehension—as I regard it—is made worse in Plato's case by the fact that it is incidental to the definition of a perfect polity. If he had merely argued that ordinary human nature, as he knew it, was incapable of making the positive contribution to policy that democracy requires, and that attempts to encourage such contribution in the name of democracy were therefore futile or disastrous, there would have been much to be said in favour of his view. Even to-day there is something to be said for such a view. The point anyhow could have been challenged and investigated on the plane of fact. But to elevate such incapacity into an ideal principle is to accept as desirable the sharp division of the community into rulers and subjects, an active minority and a passive majority, and thus to destroy once for all its unity and its power of corporate action. This result becomes even clearer, when the rationalist interpretation of will is withdrawn, so that idealism gives place to materialism and the political formula in consequence is merely authoritative force as the sole condition of social unity and effective corporate action. Such is the view of Hobbes and of his modern imitators in Italy and Germany. What the ruler's source of inspiration may be is now no longer apparent. It is hardly a pattern laid up in heaven. But from their subjects they ask only obedience, and it would seem that for them, as for Hobbes—'the Common People's minds, unless they be tainted with dependance on the potent or scribbled over with the opinions of their Doctors, are like clean paper, fit to receive whatsoever by Public Authority shall be imprinted on them'. They have shown that the 'potent' and the 'Doctors' can be broken or silenced, and that obedience can be obtained on these lines, but at what cost and for how long the world does not yet know. The simplest name for this extreme is Despotism.

(7) The other extreme view consists in the exaggeration of the peripheral activity, of the positive contribution from the side of the citizen body. When Aristotle gave his

account of the virtues he showed each as a mean state standing between two opposed extremes which were both vices. Thus the virtue of courage was in opposition on the one hand to the vice of foolhardiness and on the other hand to the vice of cowardice. He commonly noted that one of these extremes was a good deal nearer to the mean than the other, so that it was in practice often confused with it. Thus foolhardiness is quite easily mistaken for courage, but cowardice not so easily. These two extremes with which I am dealing behave in this same way. The one I now come to, which exaggerates the periphery, is the one nearer to democracy and is often confused with it— so often indeed and so persistently that the theorist is often tempted to give up the struggle and choose another name for the principle in which he believes. But he can't do that in fact because the struggle for the name is really of far-reaching practical importance, and also because it is necessary to show that this pseudo-democracy, which represents itself as merely democracy made completely logical and consistent, is actually no alternative principle of government at all, but something which simply is not and cannot be actualized in practice. To revert to my parallel with courage—*if* courage means only absence of fear where most men are afraid, foolhardiness is extreme courage, something like total absence of fear, and must accordingly be a better not a worse state than courage. Similarly *if* democracy means simply a belief in the popular contribution to policy, it provides no ground for accusing any one of exaggerating the extent of that contribution. Those who believe in it more are simply more democratic. They may be wrong, but to prove them wrong some other principle independent of democracy and forcing limits on it must be introduced. If we accept these two definitions, of courage and of democracy, we must also accept these absurd or unpleasant conclusions, but we have the alternative of amending the definitions, and this is the sensible thing to do. To that point I will return later; first, let us look this whole-hearted democrat, as he styles himself, in the face.

This view is the exact antithesis of the last. For that the government was active and the people passive; for this the people are active and the government passive. On the one view the government asks of the citizen only that he shall obey: on the other the citizens ask of the government only that it shall obey. The conception is frankly ideal: it does not pretend to be a picture of fact; but ideally democracy is taken to mean that a people governs itself, instead of appointing or accepting persons who shall govern it. Its officials are thus reduced to relative insignificance; their personal responsibility for what is done reaches vanishing point, except in matters of administrative detail. This is the goal to which the true democrat looks forward, the standard to which, if progress continues, democratic practice will increasingly approximate. Some such view of democracy as this is inevitably suggested by the hackneyed concluding phrase of Lincoln's fine Gettysburg speech— 'government of the people by the people for the people'. Its currency in modern times owes much to Rousseau's *Social Contract* and to the French Revolutionary leaders who were inspired by Rousseau's ideas. Many of the more unproductive features of modern democratic institutions are due to its continued influence, and much of the unsatisfactory working of such institutions is attributable to the false demands and expectations of those who work them connected with this set of ideas. Their examination and correction is therefore a matter of some practical importance, especially at a time when we are asked to observe a general break-down of democracy. For what has broken down may well turn out to be, in part at least, not democracy, but something else.

In terms of the account which I have given, the fundamental inadequacy of this extreme is at once obvious. The one extreme asserts Form without Matter or requires Form to supply its own Matter: this extreme asserts Matter without Form, or requires Matter to supply its own Form, which is equally absurd. As the one extreme is analogous to a rationalist theory of knowledge, so this extreme has its analogue in the sensationalist theory of knowledge, which gives the senses the monopoly of truth.

(8) This theory of democracy seems to rest theoretically on the ascription of magical and as I think highly improbable properties to what it calls the General Will, and it culminates logically—though it is not often pressed so far—in what William Godwin looked forward to, the euthanasia of government. With regard to the term General Will, it is worth while pointing out that a will is to be found only where there is an act: consequently if General Will is rightly asserted there must also be General Action. Further will is pre-conditioned, according to the classical analysis which has never been superseded, by desire and deliberation; and deliberation is the typical act of practical thinking, in which means and end are seen in causal relation. Consequently, there must also be General Desire and General Thought. If, I insist, we are to take seriously the proposition that a people does or can govern itself, we must be satisfied that all these things are or may be true; and it is not easy to see how we can receive this satisfaction. Rousseau, it is true, was cautious enough to introduce a number of qualifications which go far to neutralize his hypothesis and deprive it of applicability to the states with which we are familiar. A General Will, he argued, was only realizable (though he did not stick to this) when all the adult male citizens are collected together in a single assembly: he therefore asked that states should be made very small, consisting if possible of a single town and the country round it. He refused to require, further, that there should be unanimity, that desire, thought, and will should be identical in each voter; he required only that each should ask the same question— what is the common interest?—and try in good faith to answer it. In the assembly he supposed by some mysterious mechanical or chemical process the different answers would be fused into a single majestic unity of result. He saw again the absurdity of supposing that the general body of citizens, assembled or otherwise, could take

responsibility for the execution and administration of its own laws: he therefore confined the General Will to the act of legislation and provided for the appointment of what he called an aristocratic executive. In these and other ways Rousseau made so many concessions to common sense that he may even be said to concede implicitly that government of the people by the people is a wholly unrealizable idea for a nation state. But Rousseau's followers forget or ignore his qualifications. Arrangements are made all over a country on a given day that every citizen, male and female, shall have the opportunity of voting: it may be in a general election, it may be in a referendum or initiative, it may be in a presidential election. Each goes into his little secret box and marks his cross. Busy clerks total the result. For these democrats forthwith the will of the people is manifest, and all the magical properties of the General Will are immediately credited to it. The decisive step has been taken: the rest is mere routine. Further, any general activity of the citizen body is saluted impartially as an expression of the General Will, and that country is regarded as the most democratic which gives its citizens the most frequent opportunities of putting a cross on a ballot paper.

(9) The only answer to rash and reckless theory is the twofold one, a closer study of the facts and the formulation of an alternative theory more adequate to their complexity. My own view as to the inadequacy of this theory and as to the correction which it requires has already been indicated in general. It is a fundamental error to suppose that will can emerge spontaneously from the citizen body, for will is form imposed upon desire and impulse, and desire and impulse are powerless to generate of themselves the form which will order them. But this general answer requires now some restatement and also on one particular point some supplementation.

In my account of democratic government I started by saying that the will of a community, if it exists, will reside in the government of the community, and by the government of the community I explained that I meant primarily the representative legislative body. Rousseau would, in fact, probably accept this statement as true in a sense. He would be ready to admit that what will there is in such a community is embodied in its government. He would merely add that in his view the will of a community has no effective existence where legislation is delegated to representatives. This objection will be met if it can be shown first, that a central authority must be created before anything of the nature of a corporate decision can come into being; secondly, that in the ideal case (i.e. where circumstances are favourable and everything works smoothly) the decision of such a central authority can reasonably be regarded as a national decision. The view on the second point implied in my earlier statement was that in a favourable case such an interpretation is seen to be reasonable when it is remembered that parliament's decision is not fully free, but is preconditioned by an elaborate process of give and take between the representatives and the electors, in which process the germs of will present in the citizen body may be regarded as gradually passing by a continuous process into definite considered action. I am far from saying that this is always so; I am only saying that it is what we as democrats are aiming at, and what we already to some extent achieve. This statement contains also by implication my answer on the first point. It is this process of give and take between the responsible politician and the relatively irresponsible citizen which is in my view the essence of democracy, because if anything of the nature of a general will is to come into being it must by this process be *created*. The idea that a general will exists, and that the political problem is to find a means of expressing it, is mere mythology. It has to be made before it can be expressed, and the political problem is to find a way of making it. The failure to see this point is the essential flaw in the Rousseauistic misinterpretation of democracy, on which blind faith in the referendum, the recall, proportional representation, and a dozen other things depends.

Once it is seen they fall into their place, as relatively un-important devices which may in certain conditions assist, but are more likely under present circumstances to hinder the democratic aim.

(10) At this point I must introduce, by way of supple-ment to my original statement, the necessary qualification to which I referred before. In that statement I over-simplified the case by representing the impulses in the body of the people to which a democratic government gives form as so to speak ready-made facts, pre-existent, which the government recognizes and incorporates into its deci-sion. But though no doubt there is always a certain priority on the side of the matter, as sense has always priority in relation to thought and desire in relation to will, this priority is not like that of, say, infancy to childhood, childhood to manhood, &c., where the earlier term ceases to apply precisely in proportion as the later begins to apply; it is the priority rather of the necessary condition in relation to that which may find in it occasion for actualization. This may seem technical and obscure; but it is really quite simple. Desire is, let us say, a necessary condition of will. Every desire might pass by a continuous process into will, but not all do. Desire is only an oppor-tunity for willing which is not always taken. But granting that many or most desires are abortive, i.e. do not issue in action—a fact which is generally recognized, but ex-plained differently by different theories—it may still be maintained plausibly that will is the child of desire. The statement is plausible, and is indeed true, if it is recognized that will, like the human child, both needs and has a second parent. The active formative principle which trans-forms desire into action begins its work from the moment when the blind impulse first raises its shapeless head. The abortive desire is not an impulse on which this principle has never worked, but one on which at a certain point it ceased to work, so that the impulse never came to maturity as will. Another and blunter reply to the view that will is the child of desire would be to point out that it is at least

as plausible to say that desire is the child of will. This reply comes in the end to the same thing: for what it asserts essentially is that in a somewhat different sense of priority action (or will) is prior to desire.

The application of these considerations to politics is, I hope, fairly obvious. The practical point, which acquires special importance from the prevalence of the misinterpretation of democracy now under discussion, is this: that a democratic government is not required by its principles to be at any stage of its dealings with the public purely passive and receptive. On the contrary theory shows— and practice amply confirms the lesson—that the part it has to play is essentially active and formative from beginning to end. The demands which it registers and meets with seeming docility are demands which it has itself evoked from the citizen body—not perhaps what it wished to evoke, but then no man's children are quite what he dreamed they would be. If the government sinks into inactivity and seeks to play a merely passive part in relation to public opinion, the popular movements at once begin to lose unity, relevance, and coherence; they become feeble and spasmodic; finally perhaps increasing bitterness and frustration leads them to seek elsewhere the lead which government refuses to give, until by violent revolution the government itself is swept away and a new political situation is created.

All this is merely the formulation in terms of politics of the famous principle laid down by Kant that 'thoughts without content are empty: perceptions without conceptions are blind'.

(11) I do not claim for the theory which I have been expounding that it opens up any startling new truth, or suggests the need for any drastic alterations in the practice of parliamentary government: on the contrary I claim that in the main it only confirms principles which the wiser of our democratic leaders have for generations consistently put into practice. The substantiation of that claim would surely constitute the best possible recommendation of the

theory: but I will not attempt it now. I would only, in conclusion, call attention to two general advantages which the theory seems to me to possess, the first of a more practical, the second of a more theoretical, order. On the practical side it has the merit that it gives the democrat an answer on both fronts. It gives him a case which he can state without asserting the imposture of collective wisdom, which excites the ridicule of one set of opponents, or the still more flagrant imposture of the inspired superman, which infuriates the other. Democracy seen as the fruitful interaction between rulers and ruled gains in definition and ceases to be one of those slippery principles, so common in politics, in the application of which the politician can always be outbidden by a rival who takes a more extreme or leftward position. But practice after all must look after itself and will not pay much attention to the theorist. It is the theoretical implications which interest me especially, and in particular this. If the account above given of democracy is correct, there is a close natural connexion between the prevalence of democratic ideals in politics and the practice of methodical empiricism in science and other fields of thought. This empiricism, which is eminently characteristic of the modern era, had to fight its first battle with a rationalism which would lay down the law *a priori* for nature; and always it has had to resist a tendency encouraged by misinterpretation of its own successes to distort this empiricism into the absurdity of sensationalism. How similar is the history of the democratic idea, which during this same period has made steady and uninterrupted progress towards general recognition in Europe. Further, it is striking to observe that those countries in which the empirical tendency in thought has been most persistent are also those countries in which democracy has struck deepest root. It is surely no accident that among the Great Powers of Europe, France and England are at once the most democratic and the most empirical in their outlook on the world, while Germany, which is the least democratic, is the most friendly to ambitious metaphysical systems. This can hardly be mere coincidence, and it seems to me to provide a further confirmation of the substantial truth of the theory which I have been stating.

If then I am asked, finally, what is the philosophy of democracy, I would answer, taking the question now in a rather different sense from what my title intended, with the one word—empiricism. The natural temper of a democratic government is empirical, or, as we commonly say in practical matters, opportunist. It will with difficulty look very far ahead, or undertake very drastic and ambitious schemes of reconstruction. Its greatest achievements will tend to be anonymous in the sense that all alike will depend on the disciplined co-operation of immense multitudes of men, so that even the leader at the decisive point will see afterwards that he built better than he knew.

X. THE PRINCIPLES AND LIMITATIONS OF STATE ACTION[1]

PHILOSOPHY cannot define with any sharpness a question of the kind suggested by the title of this article. At times philosophers starting from certain premises have tried to lay down hard and fast rules as to what the State may do, what it should do itself, and what it should leave to individuals, but it is now generally agreed that those attempts were failures and that they carry no clear lesson for the present day. There are a variety of reasons for that; perhaps the main one is that philosophy is really interpretative, occupied in trying to understand what exists, and if you try to twist it into something creative, into an attempt to determine the lines on which things ought to develop, you turn it from its true purpose and introduce at once a sophistry into the argument. Another reason is that the State is not constant or absolute. The State, whether that term is confined to the central government or includes Municipalities and Local Authorities generally, is constantly changing, and the most rapid rate of change is that which it has gone through during the last hundred odd years since the French Revolution, and which it is still going through with probably increased acceleration at the present day. During that period the State has gradually, and it is probably true to say reluctantly, come to accept a wider and wider view of its responsibilities and of its possibilities; it has come to extend its functions in all sorts of directions. Protests in the name of *laisser-faire* have been pushed on one side by the logic of facts. The political authorities have found things that urgently needed doing and have done them, whatever academic authority might say. Simultaneously with this widening of the function of the State these hundred years have witnessed a progressive development in the direction of political demo-

[1] *Social Service Review*, June 1931.

cracy. I say in the direction of democracy, because I consider democracy to be an ideal which we have not reached, which it may be that man will never reach. What we can say is that we have made enormous strides with astonishing rapidity in the direction of democracy. These two parallel developments are connected. The progress towards democracy makes more possible and less dangerous the extension of State activity which conversely tends to make democracy more solid and more practicable. A hundred and twenty years ago Government was a force foreign to the citizen and something of which by ancient tradition he was suspicious, if not afraid. I do not think people sufficiently realize the enormous change which has come about. In these days the ordinary man in the street tends to think of the Government as his Government, and of whatever it does for him and his fellows as done in general with their consent and authorization.

It is as well perhaps to begin by thinking of one or two things which the State must do if they are to be done at all, or which it is clearly desirable that the State should do. There are some things which individuals, as individuals or by voluntary association among themselves, cannot do. These are things which require a certain universalization as a condition of their being effectively done. For instance, individuals alone or in combination cannot satisfactorily under modern conditions provide themselves with fresh drinking water. Obviously, they cannot provide themselves with sanitary and satisfactory drainage. These are things which require to be universalized; their provision requires an element of compulsion; and unless they are done everywhere, especially in the case of drainage, they are hardly done at all. No one would question the propriety of the public authorities taking over duties on behalf of the citizens in such matters as that. These are the clearest kind of cases, and where the element provided is capable of sale you get the element of monopoly coming in, which has always been regarded as a fair ground for State action. We may pass to a class of enterprise in regard to which the

propriety of State action is more questionable. There are
things which individuals alone or in association can provide
for themselves, but which it is thought they cannot provide
for themselves as well as the State can provide it for them.
If they provided it for themselves, either they provided it
badly or perhaps they got it on very expensive terms.

Take the provision of public education. Compulsory
public education was objected to in principle by quite
serious thinkers, though many advocates of *laisser-faire*
made an exception in this case. It was objected to on the
ground (among others) that it was interference with freedom. If you take freedom in the more positive sense you
may claim for the parents the right to choose between
different types of education, to suit their children with an
education adapted to their requirements, and so on. By
providing a single public pattern, so to speak, and making
it compulsory, you are limiting this reasonable freedom
of choice. Of course the unanswerable argument in that
case, at the particular moment when the controversy arose,
was provided by detailed investigation of facts. It was
bodies like the Manchester Statistical Society who went
out into the towns of Lancashire and found out exactly
how many children were being educated and where, and
reported conditions, who provided the best arguments for
the new departure. The thing was not being done sufficiently either in quality or in quantity.

Private enterprise had broken down just as it has broken
down in our own time in housing. We have been compelled
to build houses simply because the houses were not being
built. Houses had to be produced and private enterprise
was not doing it. Another case one might take here perhaps
is the case of transport. A lively controversy arose at a
rather later date over the tendency which declared itself
towards the end of the nineteenth century for Municipalities to take charge of the transport of the town by running
municipal trams and buses. There you had, of course,
something which was more or less being done and which
plainly could be done by private enterprise; but clearly, if

a town is to plan itself, if it is to settle where houses are to be placed and therefore indirectly where its citizens are in large numbers to live, it is very important that it should have the opportunity of arranging transport so as to make living in those places possible for persons of certain means. As soon as the general question of town planning arose the necessity of the control of transport by the municipality became obvious.

I might mention a great many more examples, but keeping these few in mind, let us now consider whether there are any principles that we can lay down to govern State action. John Stuart Mill, when he recovered from the fanatical Benthamism of his youth and from his violent reaction against it, came in effect to put another goal of State action in place of the maxim, 'The greatest happiness of the greatest number'. He said that in his considered opinion the source of all progress, the source of all advance and improvement in human life was individual energy and initiative; and therefore he took as the criterion of social welfare and as the test and goal of government the abundance in a society of what he called 'individual vigour and manifold diversity'. Perhaps he laid too great stress on mere difference or peculiarity; he certainly suggests at times that merely to be different from your fellows is to be a benefactor to the community. But the important point is this. We are a community, focused in this general human organization which we call the State, and the force at the disposal of that organization is simply the force of individuals. The individual is no doubt modified by contact with other individuals, new energies are no doubt evoked by the associations which the State creates and facilitates; but the vigour of individuals is the only force at the disposal of the community through the State. Hence the aim of all State action should be to encourage independent development; its task is that of guiding the energies and activities of the individual members of the community; whenever it checks or retards these it is definitely inflicting a loss on the common life. It has to stimulate and canalize these energies, it has to guide and direct them into fruitful channels, with the minimum of coercion or restraint. Keeping this in mind, it seems that one may offer a better test of State action than the greatest happiness for the greatest number. What is wanted is a test of the value rather than of the legitimacy of State action. Following Mill's hint, one may think of State action as justified to the extent to which it evokes and makes possible the energy, the activity of the members of the community affected by it. These energies and activities are the real wealth of the community. The money wealth is only a surface phenomenon, and the economic problem has behind it the much deeper problem of getting the energies and capacities of the people on to fruitful lines.

One is tempted to think that any action of the State which is not so justified is a loss and a damage to the community. Of course some forms of labour and effort are in a real sense worth while and others are not, though it is hard to say which are which. If a person is hard at work preparing for an examination or getting up a lecture he may be sure at the time that the labour is not worth while; and yet afterwards he may very well change his mind. There may be work not worth doing of which the State may properly simply relieve the citizen. But it is quite possible for the State to act in ways which definitely call out the energy of individuals, and these are the things that we wish specially to look for. Here may be mentioned the question of the 'dole'. This is really the same question, at least in part, that was the subject of such very acute controversy in the first Reform Parliament of 1832, when the Benthamites set themselves to a policy of abolishing outdoor relief for the able-bodied. In the course of about sixty years they very nearly succeeded in doing it by the Poor Law Act of 1834 and its sequel. With regard to that question it is quite plain that the worst possible form of State action, as it is plainly the most unjustifiable according to the principle already laid down, is the form of State action which simply distributes money to the citizens. It

has no justification in itself; it calls forth the minimum of
activity from those who receive it; it gives the minimum
of encouragement to future activity. (Incidentally, much
private charity is open to the same objection.) The objection to this form of State action is in principle absolutely
justified. If you make any community into a benefit society
which distributes largess to its members you are simply
corrupting the members. If and so far as there is any
element of contribution on the side of the recipient, the
danger is at once diminished and very soon totally disappears. As soon as the recipient can feel (even if the feeling is to some extent not justified) that what he receives is
due to his own effort, the matter assumes a totally different
complexion. Then the prospect of getting the reward becomes a positive encouragement to effort and activity on
the part of the member and he has a proper feeling of pride
in receiving the reward when it comes. It therefore seems
unquestionable that the proper basis of all these money
payments is what may be called in a wide sense of the
word a contributory basis.

The business of any community, therefore, is to stimulate and evoke the energies of its members and to guide
them on to fruitful lines. One ought to judge any project
of Government action by that principle before any other.
Further, the agents of voluntary associations, in the work
they do for those who happen to be less fortunate than
themselves and whom they are called upon to help in
various ways, ought to adopt this as a guiding principle in
all their actions. They ought always to try so to act as to
call out the maximum of activity from those with whom
they come into contact. During the last couple of years
there has been an attempt in Manchester to organize a
Community Association on a new housing estate. As a
result of a great deal of effort and about two years' work,
last October the Association succeeded in erecting on a
piece of ground placed at its disposal at a rent by the
Manchester Corporation a small hall sufficient to hold
about 120 people; this hall is now quite inadequate for

current requirements. There was an alternative possibility. The City Council, instead of renting the piece of land and saying that the Association might do what it could with it, might have said, 'We will give you the land and we will put a hall on it'. Now, if it had done that, there would have been no guarantee that any one on the estate would have had the slightest interest in it, and probably the building, even if no bigger than the present one, would have been too large. The value of what has been done is largely in the work that has been undertaken to do it. The action of the public body should be so calculated as to evoke the responsive activity of the citizen; for this activity is the thing of supreme value to which all public policy should be directed.

Some of those who have experience of social work may bring up against this argument the misery of the slums, and may claim that it cannot be dealt with on these terms. In part this may be admitted, just as it may be said that the 'dole', though an evil, is in our present position a necessary evil. Of course one has to recognize that our great towns are diseased and deformed, and constitute in a large measure pathological cases which require surgical treatment and other drastic action. But surely we should not think of this diseased and disordered condition as a permanent situation or as a general situation anywhere; and, above all, as determining the general lines and character of State activity. It is, on the whole, the soundest as well as the politest assumption that human nature is much the same everywhere, that the way to treat other people is the way in which one would wish to be treated oneself. Those who have the misfortune to live in slums are also capable of being roused to fruitful activity, as those who have seen some of them rehoused well know.

XI. LEISURE[1]

I

Aristotle's View

'IT is commonly believed,' says Aristotle in his *Ethics*, 'that happiness consists in leisure: we forgo leisure that we may have leisure, just as we go to war in order that we may live in peace.'[2] This statement has a paradoxical air. War is a disturbance of social life, an abnormality, a more frequent and familiar intruder no doubt to a Greek of the fourth century B.C. than to a modern European, but yet an unwelcome intruder, which no decent person can value for itself but only, if at all, for something of quite opposite nature to it, which, in given circumstances, it may help us to get. Are we to accept this analogy? Are we to believe similarly that leisure is the normal, natural, and wholly desirable state or situation, and that work and whatever else is its opposite is an unwelcome disturbance of life, frequent perhaps but still essentially inferior and second-rate, of value only for what it contributes to activities in which it has no part whatever?

The instructed reader will already be on his guard. He knows what a tricky business it is to transfer a thought to another language, century, and society, and that sufficient ingenuity in the choice of what are at best only approximate equivalents will sometimes turn a commonplace conventionality into a striking paradox. Such tricks can no doubt be played, but I am not playing one of them here. The explanations which I am about to give will show, I think, that when all deductions have been made, there still remains in the sentence above quoted a sharp challenge to much modern thought and practice. Aristotle had, of course, a developed theory of life, what it was and what it ought to be, and his theory was in positive relation with

[1] *Hibbert Journal*, July 1935.   [2] *Nic. Eth.* 1177^{b}4.

the actual practice and the half-conscious ideals of his contemporaries. Few modern thinkers have so complete a scheme, and the practice of our contemporaries is—or at least seems to us—particularly incoherent. We are inclined in despair to give up all attempts to determine the purpose of life, or, making a virtue of necessity, to adopt a theoretical irrationalism which enjoins blind confidence in the thrust of the will and the urgency of natural instinct. For such a view there is no challenge in Aristotle's statement, except in the blasphemous underlying assumption—common to his and most philosophies—that there is something to be hoped from intellectual analysis; but for those who still wish to understand even if they almost despair of doing so, a valuation of life which seems to run counter to their own is a challenge that has to be met, and they will be prepared to meet argument by argument.

Aristotle's leisure is not opposed to activity. This follows from his first statement that it is commonly identified with happiness, for Aristotle himself defines happiness as a form of activity. Thus, in so far as this common belief is justified, leisure is also a form of activity. Further, he distinguishes leisure from two things which are also excluded from its opposite, unleisure or business, viz. play (amusement) and recreation. This implies that by leisure he means the actual use of time in certain ways. The playing of games is not one of the uses consistent with the conception of leisure, nor is recreation, by which he means, as he explains, things done to remedy the overstrain of strenuous effort. Games may no doubt be played as recreation in this sense, or they may be played for their own sake; but in either case they are neither business (unleisure) nor leisure. Play and recreation thus constitute a third division of life, necessary and legitimate within its limits, since man is so made that he is not capable of continuous effort, but subordinate to the plan of the whole which is set by the claims of leisure.

What, then, are these claims of leisure? To put it briefly, they are the claims arising from man's power of self-determination in thought and action. Aristotle calls this man's rationality, regarding it as that which distinguishes man from the lower animals: hence the famous definition 'man is a rational animal'. But man is not always and purely self-determining. His peculiar gift of reason has two sides, original and derivative. As original, it enables him to think things out for himself and plan his own life. As derivative, it enables him to accept ideas and orders from others, to co-operate as a subordinate in a plan not of his own devising; for this also is something that none of the lower animals can do. This distinction within reason corresponds to the distinction between business and leisure. Leisure comprises those activities in which man is truly creative and self-determining, which have their excellence in themselves, not in something else which it is hoped to get out of them.

These are, of course, conceived by Aristotle as the highest activities of man, and since natural growth is always an ascent from the lower to the higher, they are not immediately accessible to the young and immature. Hence the vital importance of education and the inevitable responsibility of governments in regard to it. These highest powers, of which the young are not yet conscious, have to be safeguarded for them; and the necessary development of the lower powers has to be so regulated that it shall not hinder but actually promote this final freedom. This is where states in fact, in Aristotle's view, tend to go wrong. Under force of external circumstance, in surrender to pressure of public opinion or to what they see as urgent needs of the state, they substitute a nearer end. They fall back ignobly on what promises immediate utility and pecuniary profit. Like Sparta they make everything contribute to victory in war, forgetting that war is at best a means to something not itself, and that the activities of war are typical examples of unleisure. But facts as well as arguments prove, says Aristotle, that the statesman should direct all his military and other measures towards leisure and peace; that the business of the state is to develop in the citizen the capacity for leisure. Since, however, man is physical as well as spiritual, and irrational as well as rational, and the former in each case before he is the latter, education should begin with the body and mould the non-rational powers of mind before it attempts the fortress of reason itself. Business is justified ultimately by leisure, but in the order of growth business is the foundation of leisure. The freedom, which is leisure, has to be won from life's necessities by the discipline which they enforce, and that discipline is the basis of this freedom. The moral demands of war are great, but those of peace are greater.

When Aristotle makes war the symbol of unleisure, he has in mind, no doubt, the limitation of choice, the narrowing of the field of action, which a state of war brings about both for the statesman and for the ordinary citizen. War is a situation in which life itself is endangered. The very foundations are threatened, and this being so the main concern is naturally food and the other elementary conditions of mere existence. The higher concerns, which in normal circumstances occupy our minds, resting upon these as their unseen substructure, are for the time being forced into strict subordination—rightly and inevitably so; for though without these life would not be worth living, clearly there must first be a life to be lived. Thus in war we are driven back to our physical beginnings and the rational afterbirth is suspended or undone. All this is, I think, unexceptionable. War is an occasional intruder on life and when it comes it affects every citizen in his degree. But there is also the question of the peace footing, the permanent organization of society, with its demand for different services from different classes of person; and here we reach more disputable ground. Aristotle argues that there are certain forms of occupation and employment which put leisure definitely out of a man's reach, and it turns out on further inquiry that in these are included nearly all the occupations to which the bulk of a modern society is irrevocably tied.

Probably we should not object to his statement that

there is no leisure for slaves. He does not mean, of course, that a slave leads a specially energetic and active life; only that his life is, as it were, incorporated into the life of another: he is the 'living tool' of another will. The slave has no life of his own: slavery, in short, by definition excludes freedom. But he carries this principle of exclusion much farther. To the lower-grade artisan he attributes a specialized and limited slavery. I suppose he has in mind here such a case as that of a leather worker who mends shoes or saddles to order, opposing his case to that of the sculptor, for instance, whose craft gives greater scope for free invention. Such work is regarded as slave-like, because, though the craftsman does not give his whole life to any one man, yet throughout the greater part of his life each single piece of work is a submission to external commands and subserves the purposes of another life. His activity gets a general passive colouring from its strict dependence on external demand. Now, clearly this mark of passivity is found in a greater or less degree in all employees and wage earners. We have only to add to this the principle that a citizen is required to contribute positively to the life of the city to get the result, which Aristotle expressly formulates, that artisans, shop-workers, and farm-labourers should be excluded from full citizenship. For a positive contribution to social life can only come by independent activity and initiative, and these classes live in a fashion which precludes these things. In short, they have no leisure, and leisure is the condition of fruitful political action. The passivity which marks their lives should mark also their participation in politics.

Aristotle is quite aware of the economic implications of this line of thought. It is sufficiently obvious that if you have no property of your own you must work for some one else, and if working for others excludes leisure, leisure therefore presupposes what we call private means. Aristotle's social thought, of course, always presumes slavery in some form, and for the rest he does actually urge the desirability in any city of the widest possible distribution

of property. These are the two main external conditions
on which he relies to make leisure possible for the citizen
body. But, of course, they only make it possible: they
cannot create it. Riches are plainly no guarantee of the
initiative which Aristotle requires of his citizen: the richest
man may live in slavish subservience to the whims of
others and the dictates of circumstance. We may also
doubt, on the other hand, whether the habitual acceptance
of orders from others, either in the military sense or in
the form of business commissions, is rightly construed as
definitely exclusive of the necessary independence. If it
were, how could a subaltern officer ever develop into a
general? There is only one condition, it may be suggested,
arguing from his analogy of war, which, on Aristotle's
showing, finally removes all possibility of leisure, and that
is extreme poverty. For to be very poor is to be in danger
of life: it is to be perpetually preoccupied with the necessities which are the basis of life. While the struggle to live
holds the field, the higher concerns, which are in the end
what makes life worth living, are forcibly subordinated to
the elementary conditions which make life possible. In
such a position what room is there for arts or letters or
philosophy, or for any positive achievement which may
enrich social life? Riches do not create leisure, but the
struggle with poverty definitely excludes it.

II

The Ethical Problem

In the doctrine which I have been reporting there are
two strands which, though closely connected, are yet
separable. On the one hand, there is asserted an ethical
ideal, a conception of life as culminating, at least for a
select few, in spiritual freedom; on the other hand, certain
principles of social structure are laid down and the political
organization which follows from them. There is some
evidence which makes it probable at least that Aristotle
modified these political ideas in his later life, while he seems

to have retained the ethical ideal to the end. But with that side of the matter, interesting as it is, I cannot here deal. I will discuss the doctrine as it stands, separating these two sides of it, and dealing with the ethical problem first. In both cases, the extreme opposition of business and leisure seems to me to be the fundamental flaw, and I shall be chiefly occupied in suggesting ways in which this opposition may be and is in some degree overcome.

The special characteristic of animal life in the world of nature is for Aristotle the ability of the animal to move itself. All lower beings, even plants, stay where they are till they are moved: with the animal begins local freedom. Within the animal world the gradations asserted when we call this animal higher and that lower may be regarded as variations in the scope of this freedom if we include in it those powers of adjustment—sense, appetite, reason—which are bound up with it or built upon it. The structure of nature thus points in a sense to freedom as the goal or end, and the conception of leisure as the goal of human effort is simply the application of this conception to human life. The humblest of mankind is endowed by nature with capacities for thought and action which give him a freedom such as no other animal possesses. But the law of development applies also within the individual life; and the higher the level of life the more it applies, in the sense that the more complex the organism, the greater the interval between maximum and minimum achievement. Thus the freedom man enjoys by right of birth is nothing to the freedom he may win by suitably directed effort.

The elementary condition of this development is a moral discipline as to the general nature of which the common sense of mankind has long ago come to general agreement. The instincts and emotions, which circumstance operating through the senses continually stimulates, have to be organized and controlled so that deliberate action may be possible and the firmness of character that belongs to it may be established. The popularly accepted virtues, courage, temperance, &c., are the different facets of this

discipline; and seven out of the ten books of Aristotle's
ethical treatise are devoted to its (and their) discussion.
So far the development is conceived as progressive mastery
of the self on its emotional side, and through that of bodily
movement, and so of the external environment which is
the field of action. But at the end of the treatise, by a
transition which is never fully discussed, we are asked to
regard all this practical virtue as merely instrumental to
a higher activity which has no intrinsic relation to it. The
higher activity is one which demands of the environment
only that it shall not be interfered with and is in that
respect independent of circumstance. It consists in contemplation of eternal perfection, and thus excludes all
passage and mutation, and with it presumably all human
life, from view. It is in fact an approximation on the part
of man to the life of God, who is conceived by Aristotle
not as an ordering providence but as a culminating self-
complete perfection engaged in the contemplation of itself.

This final abrupt transition on Aristotle's part from the
practical to the contemplative life has its roots of course in
the religious mysticism of his time and is only fully intelligible in its historical context. Its value and its relevance
for our present discussion lies in this, that it formulates
with particular sharpness a conviction of the insufficiency
of the purely practical point of view, which is never far
from the surface in any discussion of the ethical problem.
As agents we immerse ourselves in the flow of events, contributing this and that by way of insignificant supplement
and modification to a process vast beyond comprehension
and without conceivable end or beginning. If the value of
an individual life or of a social organization consists only
in its contribution to this process, then strictly no accurate
assessment of it can be made and in any case its value lies
beyond itself, in something else which it helps to make
possible. What is wanted then is, as the old Orphic pro-
phets put it, some delivery from the 'wheel of birth', and
in this ethical context that delivery depends on the discovery of some intrinsic value, of a good which is not

instrumental merely but self-justifying and which is in some sense independent of the flow of events, so that it does not pass and perish with them. It is this need which creates and maintains the close connexion of ethics with religion—so close that some think that if religion were to vanish all effective standards of conduct would vanish with it.

The attempt, however, to appreciate Aristotle's problem on such lines as these only makes us the more conscious of the inadequacy of his solution. The reader of his Ethics is struck by the contrast between the precise, rigorous, realistic analysis of character in the first seven books, based obviously on a wide experience of human nature in all its strength and weakness, and the brief vague generalities by means of which the ideal of contemplation is presented. The fact that Aristotle here makes one of his rare attempts at fine writing only makes the contrast more marked. It looks as if he were himself aware of the weakness of his case and tried in this way to conceal it from the reader. The inadequacy lies, of course, not merely in the contrast between the robust solidity of the virtues of practice and the nebulous mysticism of the higher activities in which they are to issue, but much more in the lack of positive relation between means and end. These are related in a fashion of which the relation of war and peace, offered as an illustration, gives only too exact a picture. So far as war comes in, peace goes out, and peace has no real need of war; if it had, perpetual peace would not even be conceivable. The interests of peace require that war shall be abolished, or if circumstances make that impossible, at least that it shall be kept at the lowest attainable minimum. Practice and contemplation similarly are in irreconcilable opposition. The more there is of the one, the less there is of the other; and the one can only enter when the other goes out. The only important difference between the two relations arises from the provision of human nature by which the gifts realized in contemplation develop late in life, so that no man can in fact reach leisure except through business. The relation then is that of war and peace, where the peace can only be reached in the first instance through war.

Where the relation between so-called means and end is as negative as this, the end cannot be truly said to perform the function which Aristotle's teleology requires of it, that of giving value and significance to the means. It would be stupid to say that our love of peace gives war a positive value, since it is quite obvious that war owes its negative value to that very love. Nor will this alleged end serve as director of action and determinant of the choice of means as an end should. In time of war a love of peace is not much of an asset: if it makes for war being better waged, that is only in the sense that it makes men wage it so that it shall end sooner and end in a better peace; and even that is not altogether beyond dispute, for here also more haste may mean less speed, and the dislike of war involved in the love of peace is apt to make a man a poor judge of the measures appropriate to a state of war. All this can be transposed easily and with effect into the terms of the other opposition, that of business and leisure; and such transposition reveals a similar absurdity. To put it briefly, it is not possible to find the meaning of business in leisure if these two are irreconcilable opposites. Business may need supplementation in some sense from without in order to acquire the positive significance which by itself it lacks, but such supplementation to be effective must invade the area of business or grow directly out of its activities. We should at least be able to say that business is done the better, not the worse, because of it.

Let us now review briefly the various marks by which Aristotle characterizes his leisure activities, with this point in mind, and see how far we are bound to accept or reject them as marks of such a supplementary principle.

First, it must invite to active effort, not passive enjoyment or mere relaxation. Work is not transfigured and redeemed, though it may be made more endurable, by the opportunities for amusement which it incidentally

M

provides. It is something, but by no means everything, that the wage one earns should leave a sufficient margin for the pictures, the football match, and other amusements. But by active effort is meant here the full use of all one's faculties, which in such situations is not in question.

Secondly, in this effort, the man must be no creature of another's will, but his own master. This is more difficult because no man is absolutely his own master. All co-operation involves some degree of subservience to the wills of others and all work done under direction allows of some degree of personal independence. If this requirement is pressed, therefore, it means the total surrender of the practical field, where these restrictions always operate, for some field of artistic creation or free speculation, where apparently at least they cease to operate. In the field of practice it can only take the form that the greater the scope left for personal decision and initiative, the greater the possibility of really good work.

Thirdly, unleisure for Aristotle involves continual dependence on circumstance, with consequent insecurity and unrest. The resulting requirement, like the last, forces in the end the desertion of the field of action altogether. The same reply must be made here as there, viz. that this insecurity cannot be eliminated but can be diminished. Aristotle has himself observed how the development of skill by intelligent practice effects the reduction of this insecurity, expressing itself in an opportunism which is yet internally coherent and consistent. Practical virtue itself is for him such an opportunism, and thus represents an ideal of mastery of circumstance opposed to his other ideal of escape from circumstance. We must keep the first of these ideals and let the second go.

Fourthly, this effort must be spent on something not merely productive of good but good in itself. Aristotle is helped to his result by taking this demand to mean that the mental activity must be directed upon something that is perfectly good, and since there is no perfection for him beneath the moon, the field of action is once more finally excluded. But the world of experience shows plenty of examples of things reckoned good in themselves, and since we refuse to leave that world we must look among them. Pleasures and amusements are valued for themselves, even if they are also valued for what may come out of them, and in this way they differ to common-sense humanity from work. Further, any thing or person to which a man is tied by affection acquires at once a value independent of its serviceableness or market price. The former class of goods is perhaps too unsubstantial, too transient, and too external to work, to confer a new meaning on it; but the latter class, those of affection, have surely some such power. We have to think not only of ties of affection formed in his work, such as pride in the firm and friendship with fellow workers, but also of the family life he is enabled to build up and the place in the wider community which he is enabled to establish on the basis of his work. For the employer perhaps these things are of value because they make a better workman, but for the workman it is these things that have value in themselves and his work is only their indispensable foundation. It is in virtue of all this that he is able to feel that he has a life of his own and is no mere cog in a machine.

A review, then, of the principles involved in Aristotle's conception of leisure tends to this tentative conclusion, that they can be and are satisfied to some extent (though never fully) within the practical field so far as a man succeeds in incorporating his work into a private life which is felt to have an independent value and significance. It is his own life, and in it he is active, not passive: it is not independent of circumstance but it represents a mastery over circumstance and a relative though not an absolute security against the buffets of fate. How far his private life is integrated with the work which makes it possible will depend on the nature and conditions of the work and all sorts of other factors; but so far as the integration takes place the work loses the taint of slavery which still clings to the notion of work, and becomes free service.

Thus the ideal seems to be a complete integration which is rarely achieved. Its full achievement would mean that the distinction between work and leisure had become quite external and unimportant.

III

The Political Problem

This side of the problem may appropriately be introduced by a familiar passage from *Ecclesiasticus*:[1]

'The wisdom of the scribe cometh by opportunity of *leisure*; and he that hath little *business* shall become wise. How shall he become wise that holdeth the plough, that glorieth in the shaft of the goad, that driveth oxen and is occupied in their labours, and whose discourse is of the stock of bulls? He will set his heart upon turning his furrows; and his wakefulness is to give his heifers their fodder.

'So is every artificer and workmaster, that passeth his time by night as by day: they that cut gravings of signets, and his diligence is to make great variety: he will set his heart to preserve likeness in his portraiture, and will be wakeful to finish his work.

'So is the smith sitting by the anvil and considering the unwrought iron: the vapour of the fire will waste his flesh; and in the heat of the furnace will he wrestle with his work: the noise of the hammer will be ever in his ear, and his eyes are upon the pattern of the vessel: he will set his heart upon perfecting his works, and he will be wakeful to adorn them perfectly.

'So is the potter sitting at his work, and turning the wheel about with his feet, who is always anxiously set at his work, and all his handiwork is by number: he will fashion the clay with his arm, and will bend its strength in front of his feet; he will apply his heart to finish the glazing; and he will be wakeful to make clean the furnace.

'All these put their trust in their hands; and each becometh wise in his own work. Without these shall not a city be inhabited, and men shall not sojourn nor walk up and down therein. They shall not be sought for in the council of the

[1] Ch. 38, 24 ff.

people, and in the assembly they shall not mount on high: they shall not sit on the seat of the judge, and they shall not understand the covenant of judgement: neither shall they declare instruction and judgement; and where the parables are they shall not be found. But they will maintain the fabric of the world, and in the handiwork of their craft is their prayer.'

On the political side, Aristotle offers us a society in which a certain number of superior people are relieved from the more elementary economic cares by a larger number of inferior people who work under their direction. The superiority is of course conceived not as a mere economic fact but as dependent on the possession of higher moral and intellectual capacities; and the leisure enjoyed by the superior is supposed to be justified by the work of direction which they undertake and is thought of as taking positive shape from the lofty capacities to which it gives opportunity of exercise. The superiors are the active citizens who enjoy positive freedom. In absolute opposition to them are the slaves who have no freedom at all. Between the two come wage earners who can only enjoy a negative freedom because the conditions of their life prevent the development of those higher gifts which make anything else justifiable. It is socially desirable in Aristotle's view that this last class should be as small as possible and the class of superiors as large as possible; but the artisan work has to be done, and if it is not done by free men it will be done by slaves, so that, other things being equal, this will mean an increase in the number of slaves, who commonly constituted at least half the population of a prosperous Greek city.

The civilization of Western Europe has never rested on slavery, like Greek civilization, and in recent times it has thrown off even the out-growths of colonial slavery which had attached themselves to it, so that we cannot procure leisure for our citizens in this way. Further, we have stretched the conception of the active citizen to its limits, demanding, formally at least, active participation in the work of government from every grown man and woman

permanently resident in the country. It seems clear that
the vast majority of these citizens must be employed in
ways even more open to Aristotle's objection, as precluding real freedom and initiative, than the small number
of free men in a Greek city who did work more usually
allotted to slaves. This being so, the Aristotelian theorem
forces on us the question, how do we justify our conception
of citizenship, or, in other words, what is the theoretical
basis of our belief in democracy? This question is not only
very important but also very actual. For there is in fact
a growing disbelief in democracy, an increasing reversion
to the belief that passive citizenship is the normal and
natural state of man in society, and those who oppose this
tendency are somewhat half-hearted in their defence of
democracy. They defend it not so much for what it was
and is, as for what it may one day be, and for that Utopian
future they rely on such external devices as that of reducing the hours of work so that every man shall have ample
leisure. But such leisure may be only a negation, a mere
freedom from work. Can we trust to chance that these
free hours will be fruitfully occupied? Can we afford to
ignore Aristotle's point that work is the preparation for
leisure? If this is true, the use made of leisure time will
largely depend on the nature of the work to which it succeeds. Such reflections lead in the direction of socialism,
on the one side, and scepticism, on the other,—and perhaps
they are none the worse for that—but at least they show
that democracy requires other defences. It will not be
saved by any change within reach, but depends now as
always on the reasoned faith of its defenders.

If the discussion is kept on the ideal plane which the
early Aristotle at least prefers, his case is hard to meet.
The world-wide vision, the sense of trusteeship for humanity,
which true statesmanship involves, can hardly be expected
of the humble craftsman, kept by the claims of trade and
family to a close routine in the few streets round his home.
And though such an attitude cannot be reckoned on with
certainty anywhere, it will at least have a better chance of

establishing itself where the economic basis is secure and unquestioned, so that there is liberty to travel and reflect and easy access to the accumulated records of human wisdom and experience. But when these things are translated into the hard cash of political practice, they take on a very different appearance. They tend in fact to come to little more than a distribution of political power which enables those who have private economic resources to determine, so far as law and government determine, the lives of those who have not. Any such arrangement is at once seen to be open to unanswerable objection in the light of Bentham's principle that in the long run no body of men can be trusted to look after the interests of another body of men. This cynical truth alone will not give us the democracy we want, but it gives us the starting-point. In the distrust of rulers is the beginning of democracy.

The man in the street, then, has to be given a part in politics, because if he has no part his interests will not receive attention from those who have. And it is evident, further, that lack of private resources makes a man more dependent on the public law and administration, so that the poor man has always in a sense more at stake in these public decisions than the rich. But when the political door is thus opened, the man in the street is not invited to come in and say what his interests are; he is asked to think in terms of social progress, national emergency, and generally of a common good in which he can have but a small share. In every question that comes up he sees once more the impossibility of dissociating his affairs and interests from those of others; and if he does not give up the questions altogether as too complicated for him, his thoughts are forced on to a plane of national or even world policy and interest. It seems almost old-fashioned now to stress this point, but surely one of the solidest grounds for recommending the widest possible participation of citizens in political decisions is the educational stimulus which even the most distant responsibility for such decisions provides. In the middle of last century this was popular ground, and subsequent experience has only verified its soundness. The last few generations have seen a rapid and progressive widening of the horizon for all classes, and in this development Parliament and the extension of the franchise have played a leading part. If leisure stands for the transcendence of the limitations—fundamentally physical—which position and occupation impose on each one of us, then representative government can claim to have made a real contribution to it.

We argue then on well-worn lines, first, that popular participation in government is required in the interests of justice; secondly, that such participation is beneficial in its indirect effects on the participants quite apart from its direct effects on policy. We must add, thirdly, the important consideration that a prime necessity of government is that it shall obtain widespread popular approval of its acts and decisions. The device of a popularly elected parliament, on which responsibility is concentrated, is the easiest, simplest, and least troublesome method of making such approval readily obtainable. The intensive propaganda of Fascists and Marxists, by wireless and posters, rhetorical exhortation and revivalist preaching, backed by the missionary efforts of armed and disciplined volunteers, exemplifies a different method of achieving this end; and for the time being at least they may appear to secure it more fully than we do. But with what effort and friction! Are they not in danger, to borrow a phrase which Burke applied to the French Revolution, of making the 'medicine of the constitution' its 'daily bread'? One may well doubt whether such efforts can be long sustained beyond the emergencies in which they arose, and feel sceptical as to their promise of providing a model for the government of a settled and prosperous community. Their fever heat must surely pass away, with the pathological conditions to which it belongs.

On these and similar grounds the expediency and even to some extent the positive value of popular institutions may be shown with some success; but Aristotle's main point still requires to be met. He implies that the State exists essentially for the safeguarding of certain higher interests and activities which he designates comprehensively by the term 'leisure'; that the greater part of humanity necessarily has no part or lot in these; and therefore that a State which entrusts its policy to a popular vote is false to its sacred trust, accepting the decision of the blind and ignorant where some degree at least of sight and knowledge is available. The Liberal of the last century would have had a short answer to this. He would have admitted that it was impossible to guarantee that a popular decision would be wise or fully instructed: it might be stupid and ignorant. He would have admitted that a popular government might be a bad government. But he would have maintained that self-government is itself a good, and indeed so great a good, that, when once a certain stage of development has been reached, no other political good counts in the scale against it. This answer is not now popular, even among those who still call themselves Liberals: its unpopularity is part of the recent decline of faith in freedom. But in any case, whatever truth it may contain, it needs careful examination before it can be accepted; and the examination must take us back to ethical ground. Aristotle's 'leisure' is also a conception of freedom, and in its name he condemns self-government. Plainly it is necessary to consider what these higher interests and activities are, on which the meaning of life in his view ultimately depends, and what responsibility falls on governments with regard to them.

  The best opening to an answer is perhaps to ask another question. Is it a tolerable and can it be a durable state of things in which the higher interests are so monopolized by the few that their value is not even accepted by the many? Granted that there is and should be differentiation, and that this differentiation will always involve to some extent distinctions of status, superior and inferior, the differentiations are normally made durable and intelligible by their correspondence with a need or interest which is generally or widely felt. For one man who makes shoes there are thousands who need them, and similarly for one man who is a professional scientist there are thousands who are interested in science. The security of the expert is in the multitude of laymen, and the greater their number the higher the degree of his security. In a society in which art is not generally appreciated the artist leads necessarily a somewhat precarious existence.

It is a commonplace of history that a slave economy is a precarious and unstable thing. The considerations which have just been advanced show some of the ethical and psychological grounds of this instability: the slaves are occupied in supporting an order from which they are excluded and of which they have no understanding. If they were given political power, the conditions of their life being otherwise unchanged, the social order would undoubtedly be in great danger. A similar instability must mark in some degree any social order in which large sections of the population are excluded from any interest which is of vital importance to it. The establishment of a political democracy in such a state of things does not create the instability, though it may perhaps bring actual disturbance nearer. But it has, or should have, another effect. It should have the effect of making the interests endangered by the indifference of those who previously had no share in them bestir themselves to widen their appeal and secure their future by winning the sympathy of the holders of power. Thus popular institutions tend indirectly to the raising of the general level of life and to an increasing equality, not by depression of the higher levels, but by enrichment of the lower. In modern Europe this process of the gradual enrichment of life at its lower levels has been going on steadily, as any honest man can see, for a long time, concurrently with the extension of political power; and it seems probable on the historical evidence that the extension of the franchise has been the leader and not the follower in the development, i.e. the gift of the franchise has been always less the recognition of a spiritual development already achieved than the immediate stimulus to such an advance. However unsatisfactory in many of its manifestations modern life may be, there is in this solid ground for pride and satisfaction.

This extension of political power is of the first importance in connexion with the ethical problem which we discussed previously. It opens to the ordinary man and woman a sphere of free activity, free not only in the sense that it is fully and indisputably voluntary, but also in the sense that it takes them for the time out of the narrow circles of purely personal cares into which the pressure of circumstance tends always to drive them back. It gives to that private life which they build up round their work a more than merely personal value and significance. The fact that they have this power tends indirectly, as we have seen, to open to them forms of leisure which would be otherwise closed to them; directly, so far as they use this power, its exercise is itself a leisure activity of the highest value. Thus there are important elements of intrinsic value in a democratic political organization, and the old liberal catchword that self-government is better than good government is so far justified. Of any other non-democratic form of government one can only judge by the fruits it produces, by the actual wisdom or unwisdom of its decisions; with reference to a democracy, if my analysis is right, this question becomes secondary: its mere continued operation is of value, and its natural momentum is towards a fairer and juster social order. Its principle might be characterized in three words as that of 'leisure for all'.

XII. LOCKE'S CONTRIBUTION TO POLITICAL THEORY[1]

I THINK you will all agree with me that the right way to form a judgement about a man is to adopt as one's standpoint the principles by which he claims to be judged. In attempting therefore this evening to form a judgement of the contribution made by Locke to political theory I propose to begin by quoting from his work one or two sentences which I believe show how the man himself wished to be judged.

First of all, you will remember that at the beginning of his *Essay* he described himself as content with the status of an 'under-labourer', occupied in 'clearing the ground a little and removing some of the rubbish that lies in the way to knowledge'. I think one may say that a profound and genuine modesty characterizes all his work, in the political field as well as in other fields. He said of himself: 'I flatter myself that I am so sincere a lover of truth that it is very indifferent to me, so I am possessed of it, whether it be my own or any other's discovery.'[2] I take it then that he would not want us to pay much attention to the question how far he could claim originality for his political doctrine; and that question I do not in fact propose at all to discuss. In another passage he says, 'I think everyone, according to what way providence has placed him in, is bound to labour for the public good, as far as he is able, or else he has no right to eat.'[3] He would wish us then, I think, in estimating the value of his political thought, to pay some attention to its actual contribution to human good.

Finally, and most significantly, he said, writing to

[1] Tercentenary Address, delivered at Christ Church, Oxford, in October 1932.

[2] To Molyneux, asking for his help in revising the *Essay* for a second edition, Sept. 20, 1692.

[3] To Molyneux, Jan. 19, 1693–4. In this letter Locke disclaims any love of writing for its own sake.

Molyneux, of a contemporary author: 'he is one of those sort of writers that I always fancy should be most esteemed and encouraged. I am always for the builders, who bring some addition to our knowledge, or at least some new thing to our thoughts. The finders of faults, the confuters and pullers down, do not only erect a barren and useless triumph upon human ignorance, but advance us nothing in the acquisition of truth. Of all the mottoes I ever met with, this writ over a waterwork at Cleve best pleased me —*Natura omnes fecit iudices, paucos artifices*'.[1] From this I think we may take it that he would wish to be judged above all else as a builder, in the full sense of the word, an '*artifex*'. His modesty would have made him hesitate to claim so high a status for himself, but he would be well content if we found ourselves able to claim it for him.

Taking these remarks of his own as a guide, what I want to do to-night is to re-state what I think (it is of course a matter of interpretation, on which different views are possible) are the main principles of his political creed, and in doing that to consider how they have fared in the two and a half centuries which have elapsed since he wrote. I want also to ask how they stand to-day, whether to-day he can still be reckoned with the builders.

Locke's political creed seems to centre from beginning to end in his conception of freedom. Again and again he returns to this conception, and his view of it is quite definite and precise. Freedom is not the possession of every human being, because it depends on what Locke calls reason, that is, on the power of independent judgement. 'We are born free as we are born rational; not that we have actually the exercise of either: age that brings the one brings the other too.'[2] Freedom, then, is something to which a man may make claim in virtue of his independence of judgement; it accrues to the child, for example, in proportion as the child acquires the power to act and think for itself. What this freedom brings is not merely freedom from something

[1] To Molyneux, February 22, 1696–7.
[2] *Civil Government*, ii. 61.

—as, in the case of a child, from parental control—but a freedom of something, of a realm which thought opens to one. This realm has its own organizing principles, which are the law of reason or nature. The child as it develops the power of reason takes upon itself a principle or group of principles which replaces the principles externally imposed in parental control. In obtaining freedom one is obtaining the opportunity of exercising one's power of judgement according to the law of nature, and of guiding one's life by this law.

If all men were true to their ideals in practical and social matters, there would, according to Locke, be no need for government: this law of nature or reason would of itself suffice. Government is needed only because men are unequal to their own ideals; it has its root in human frailty. But human imperfection is a fact: therefore government is a necessity. What shall it be? It cannot be the mere return of man to tutelage. It cannot be, as Hobbes would have it, the absolute surrender of the right of private judgement in matters of common concern. Government on such terms is not worthy of the name of government. It is dangerous, since the governed have no protection against their rulers; it is insecure, because it is imposed and maintained by force; and it is corrupting, because it undermines the independent judgement of the governed. Locke's view is that a government which deserves the name must be *based on* freedom and reason, based, that is to say, on the exercise of independent judgement by the governed, and must have the effect of strengthening that power in the governed.

Government of this kind, based on reason and having the effect of strengthening the power of reason, is possible under certain conditions, of which the chief are these. First, all political authority must be recognized as having its source in the governed, and therefore as capable in the last resort of being revoked and reallotted at the good pleasure of the governed. Secondly, the holders of authority must always recognize a higher standard than the law of the land; they must frame their policy according to the

obligations of the law of reason or nature, and accept appeal
to this law from any of their actions. Again, provision
must be made for continuously subjecting the exercise of
authority to public criticism, so that the principles upon
which it is exercised, especially those public principles
called laws, may receive the general endorsement of the
citizens. Further, all governmental authority must be
absolutely and unreservedly subject to law, and, lastly,
every act in which it finds expression must be directed to
the single end of maintaining the citizen in his independence, or, as Locke says, of the maintenance of 'property',
by which he means, as he tells us, the life, liberty, and
estate of the citizens. Under such conditions, government
may be fitly regarded as a guarantee of freedom. The civil
laws are no longer chains by which the citizen is bound
any more than principles of reason and conscience are. On
the contrary, Locke says that, under government, 'where
there is no law there is no freedom';[1] and again that 'the
freedom of men under government *is to have* a standing
rule to live by, common to every one of that society and
made by the legislative power erected in it'.[2]

I may fitly conclude this summary of Locke's principles
with two quotations. The first is from the first *Letter on
Toleration*:[3] 'Some enter into company', he writes, 'for
trade and profit; others for want of business have their
clubs for claret. Neighbourhood joins some, and religion
others. But there is one thing only which gathers people
into seditious commotions, and that is oppression.' The
second is from the preface to the same *Letter*. The words
may not be his: they may be the words of his excellent
translator, the Quaker, William Popple; but their spirit
is anyhow certainly his. 'Absolute liberty, just and true
liberty, equal and impartial liberty, is the thing that we
stand in need of.' Locke sought above all a form of government that would remove the fear of oppression and increase
the enjoyment of liberty.

There is one point in what I have said which needs further

---

[1] *Civil Government*, ii. 57.   [2] Ibid. ii. 22.   [3] i. 50.

explanation. That is Locke's use of the term 'property' in defining the general aim of government. In politics men are led by the nose by a word as surely as a donkey is said to be by a carrot; and this word property has at times played havoc with Locke's reputation. The word requires analysis, and Locke's own analysis is before us to prevent misunderstanding. The meaning he gave to it was, as I have already said, the life, liberty, and estate of the citizens. It was not property in the common narrower sense of the word, but all this, that was, in Locke's view, before all to be preserved by government. As far as I can see, the fundamental implications of this assertion are merely these. First, the supreme consideration for any government is, or should be, the life of the individual citizens, not some supposed mystical good of State or country independent of the life of the citizens. Secondly, all State actions should be aimed at securing the independence of the citizens; not at managing their lives for them, but at providing firm ground from which they can safely and providently plan their own lives. Thirdly, the most necessary of the conditions which government must ensure to make such independence possible is the certainty that every man will receive a due reward for his labour.

In the early part of the nineteenth century the doctrines of Locke's famous chapter on property received one-sided emphasis in two opposite directions from two opposed schools of thought. First, from the economic school of *laisser-faire*, which advocated the abdication of the State in the economic sphere and demanded a free field for private invention and initiative. Secondly, the early Socialists based themselves equally on Locke when they urged the right of the worker to the whole produce of labour. Locke's doctrine supports neither; both are one-sided developments of a part of his conception. Locke is content to define the end and aim. He leaves quite open the question how much or how little, in the attempt to secure this end, a State should itself undertake; how much it should leave uncontrolled and unregulated. His point, once more, is that the developing and strengthening of the independent life of the individual citizen should be the main principle of all State action.

I have stated what seem to me to be the main principles and the basis of government as conceived by Locke. What kind of State, then, we may ask, does Locke give us? He gives us a Liberal, or, if you prefer, a democratic State. But Liberal is the better word and has some sanction from continental usage in this meaning. Probably it is historically correct to describe Locke's *Civil Government* as the first adequate formulation of the principles of the Liberal State. It is a State which operates within limits. It is limited, first, in its actions both internal and external, by its submission to the law of nature. Externally, because by this law all men are united in one great and natural community, all alike bound by this law. The communities into which human frailty has forced them to form themselves have no absolute or final sanction, but only a relative justification from their convenience for the organization of human life. Internally, because every action of such a State must always be open to criticism in the light of this law, i.e. in respect of its justice. It is a State which is limited further and more drastically on the internal side by the requirement of consent. Consent is a vague term, to which theoretical precision can hardly be given, but it can have in practice a surprisingly sharp cutting-edge. Like the term freedom, it applies over a scale in which maximum and minimum are very far apart. Its exact measure for a given time and people can only be determined in use. Under a given constitution it will mean much or little according as the governed demand much or little in its name. But always it is a strong and drastic restraint on the actions of the State.

Historically the tendency has been towards increased pressure on government under this head. The demand has come to be one for the continuous and explicit endorsement of the general lines of government action (particularly of its legislative action) by the people through

N

some form of democratic machinery. A Liberal State cannot resist this demand. It is necessarily hospitable to parliamentary forms, though possibly, of course, other democratic forms may one day be invented which will take the place of parliaments. It follows immediately from this that our Liberal State is one that is tolerant and respectful of difference. It will be prepared to run very great dangers before it attempts to tamper with the freedom of opinion or generally with the independence of the citizen.

In these two and a half centuries since Locke wrote, the principles which he formulated have been continuously active in politics, never wholly dominant, sometimes more and sometimes less influential. They have had at all times to face bitter opposition from all sorts of sources—from the self-interest and self-seeking of nations, of classes and sections within the nation, of private citizens and public officials. They have had to reckon with the impatience of the reformer, intent on doing his people a great good, and reluctant to wait till the slow processes of persuasion have done their work. They have been in perpetual danger from the pressure of circumstances. The outbreak of a war causes them to be put aside till peace is restored. In any great emergency their application will be limited, and often legitimately limited, since rigid adherence to the principle of popular consent may well result in intolerable delay in action. But through all vicissitudes and in spite of objections well and ill founded, these principles have served the world well. They have helped to maintain peace between nations. They have increasingly dominated government on the internal side, and on that side, where they have prevailed, they have almost completely tamed or domesticated government. Government was no longer a fierce and predatory power which the citizen feared and hoped so far as possible to avoid; it had become a friendly and serviceable thing, more or less at his disposal, on which he relied. Governments in the past have been like wild beasts; out of the wild beast, by the power of Liberalism, has been made a beast of burden. That is, I submit, a considerable work, even though some of the constructive efforts in the public service have been badly bungled. Through two centuries and more this work proceeded, as Liberalism established itself ever more strongly and widely. That progress went on, although latterly with some signs of weakening, right up to the War of 1914. When our leaders said in that war that we were fighting 'to make the world safe for democracy', we thought, every one thought, that we were fighting for some such principles as these. We understood, as we were meant to understand, that those who opposed us held some other principles antagonistic to ours. What these principles exactly were we might not know, but we supposed that they were principles not really endorsed by the people of Germany and other enemy countries, so that defeat for them might be not without perceptible gain. Thus for more than two hundred years from its publication the principles of Locke's book stood always for the line of political advance. They were never replaced. They were never completely dominant; but they stood everywhere for the better mind.

Since the War there has been a change. On the one hand, the events which followed the end of the War seemed, on the face of it, to register the final triumph of these principles. Millions of people gained parliamentary government, in form at least and so far as constitutions are to be trusted, who previously had not. The principle of government by consent has now been at least formally adopted in every civilized country. That on the one hand. On the other hand, there is something like a general collapse in the faith by which such government is sustained. At this moment the forward movement in nearly every European country is one which spurns Liberalism altogether. It is composed of men who parade their belief that the days of Liberalism are ended and that something of a quite opposite tendency is required. In short, we are faced with the rejection of Liberalism and of the doctrines of Locke as the embodiment of the Liberal idea.

Now, as I have already said, up to the European War of 1914, the Liberal ideas for which Locke stood were operating over a great part of the earth, somewhat spasmodically and intermittently, no doubt, but yet substantially and effectively operating: and they were operating on the whole to the increase of human comfort and well-being. One might be satisfied to claim so much; to ask for due recognition of the good work done by Locke's principles in the past, accompanied by some appropriate expression of regret that man in his march had now left them behind and their day was over. Personally I am not satisfied with that conclusion. I am thus led to my last question, whether Locke's principles are still practicable and useful. These new political movements which are springing up in almost every corner of the world are all revolutionary, i.e. they all demand a going back on or cutting loose from the recent past. You will probably have noticed that every one of these modern, up-to-date movements, which have, or are seeking, power in Europe, however unlike they may be in other respects, are all united in bitter and complete repudiation of Liberalism. Bolshevism in Russia, Fascism in Italy, Hitlerism in Germany, all furiously and ostentatiously proclaim that they will have nothing whatever to do with any part of this whole set of ideas. It is contrary to their conception of government that its action should be hampered by the acceptance of any absolute principles of government whatever, except the principle, if principle it may be called, of the maintenance of the authority of government for the glory of the nation. (Some qualifications are here necessary for Russia; for Bolshevism is not nationalist. The leaders of Russia are true to the internationalism of their creed; but they are internationalist, of course, only on their own terms.) Therefore they allow the existence of no independent ground from which the actions of government may be criticized; there is no question of tolerating the expression of opinions hostile to its principles or to its practice.

Further, they advocate and practise a ruthless pursuit

of public expediency, unfettered by any moral limits or restraints. Humanity is a term of abuse in their speeches and writings, and the whole apparatus of the rights of man has been discarded and disowned. Everything must give way to the sovereign interests of the nation. There are no internal limits of State action. There is no need of consent. The function of the mass is indeed to help the work of the government, but only in an executive capacity; it is allowed no part in shaping the policy which it helps to execute. The State is organized on the military plan, by which authority passes from above downward, and there is no provision for a reverse movement. The opinions of the citizens have no prescriptive right to respect. A man's opinions, they believe, are simply the reflex of his environment. If they run counter to those on which the government is based, they are a legitimate ground for punishment. The environment is to be changed so that such opinions shall not flourish. The principle of the equality of all citizens before the law is frankly disavowed: there is no simple justice. Justice depends on one's origin, record, opinions, on all sorts of considerations independent of the matter which brings one into court. There is no hope of an impartial judge, since it is considered to be positively dangerous to separate the judicial from the executive and legislative functions of government. There is no equality of citizenship, but different grades of privilege. One of the first articles of Hitler's creed in Germany is that those who are not of pure German blood—particularly, of course, the Jews—shall not be admitted to citizenship. Thus, one after another, the principles which we were once taught to venerate are repudiated and cast aside as meaningless or pernicious restraints, obstacles to effective State action.[1]

[1] Lord Acton, in his striking, but over-rhetorical, youthful essay of 1862 on 'Nationality' (*History of Freedom and other Essays*, 1909), distinguishes three successive phases of the revolution begun in 1789, the democratic, the socialist, the nationalist phase. To him, rather surprisingly, with the very liberal nationalism of Mazzini before him, nationality was the most dangerous and destructive of the three prin-

What is the result of all this, and what is one to hope from it? It seems to me that the most obvious result will be the reversal of the process by which the government, to the extent to which it has been actuated by Liberal principles, has become a friendly thing, tame and domesticated; no longer an object of fear to subjects. We have become so accustomed by this time to the domestication of government that we have lost the fear of oppression. The very word has an archaic ring. But now, in all these countries, the fear of oppression is reviving, and it is reviving under modern governments armed with all the increased opportunities for spreading terror and pain which improved communications and the vast increase of mechanical resources put at their disposal. Thus we have now growing and spreading in Europe once more the fear of oppression. We have, actual in some countries and potential in almost all, a political system in which freedom cannot be taken for granted as a normal condition of life. If the process continues, perhaps the time will come when men will again turn to England, as they did in the eighteenth century, as the only country where freedom exists.

We may now return to Locke, and put our question once more. Is it true that his ideas have performed their full service and that we can now afford to dispense with them?

ciples. 'The theory of nationality is a retrograde step in history. It is the most advanced form of the revolution, and must retain its power to the end of the revolutionary period, of which it announces the approach. . . . There is no principle of change, no phase of political speculation conceivable, more comprehensive, more subversive, or more arbitrary than this. . . . After surrendering the individual to the collective will, the revolutionary principle makes the collective will subject to conditions which are independent of it, and rejects all law, only to be controlled by an accident. . . . Although, therefore, the theory of nationality is more absurd and more criminal than the theory of socialism, it has an important mission in the world, and marks the final conflict, and therefore the end, of two forces which are the worst enemies of civil freedom—the absolute monarchy and the revolution.' Acton's analysis of the revolutionary tendencies of his time is worth recalling in view of the bitter struggle between nationalism and socialism which is now in progress over a great part of Europe, scarcely masked in Germany by Hitler's attempt to combine both in the 'National-Socialist' movement.

I am willing to grant all sorts of weaknesses in his Liberalism, and still more in the actual government of those
European States which during the last century or so have
made some attempt to model themselves upon it. I admit
that at the present day a country, such as ours, which has
kept and still keeps close to the spirit of Locke's political
testament, is not saved by that alone; our free institutions
are at least in danger of showing themselves unequal to the
solution of vital problems which press on us. I readily
concede that Locke's principles need considerable supplementation in all sorts of directions. Out of such concessions, with sufficient disregard of changed circumstances
and historical development, a strong case against Locke's
political creed could be made out. But when all that has
been said, I still feel that we have in Locke the root of the
matter; that any political system which is to be healthy
and durable must incorporate almost without remainder
the principles he laid down.

When Locke wrote his book he wrote, as he frankly said,
with an immediate aim, that of helping to establish the
throne of King William, 'our great restorer'. He wanted
to assist a reform in the methods of government which he
believed to be of immense promise for the England of his
time. He was simple enough to think that the best way of
doing this was to lay down those principles on which at all
times the government of a great nation, such as England,
should be based. I claim that the principles he formulated
were sound, and that both the application which has been
made of them since he wrote and our continued need of
them at the present day justify us in according to him the
high status which he coveted but never ventured to claim
for himself, that of a builder.

XIII. JEREMY BENTHAM[1]

I

In one of his best-known perorations R. L. Stevenson, ending a plea for dangerous living, asks his readers' admiration for the death which catches people 'like an open pitfall, and in mid-career, laying out vast projects and planning monstrous foundations, flushed with hope, and their mouths full of boastful language'. To be so 'tripped up and silenced' is, he contends, a 'brave and spirited' end. 'Does not life', he asks, 'go down with a better grace, foaming in full body over a precipice, than miserably straggling to an end in sandy deltas?' The death of Jeremy Bentham on 6 June, 1832, the centenary of which we commemorate, fits neither of these descriptions at all precisely. He was a third of the way through his eighty-fifth year. He had lost the sense of taste and his other senses were weakening. He had some other physical infirmities, including a tendency to dribble at the mouth; but of all these he made a jest. Towards the very end his memory had shown signs of failing. Yet death caught him 'in mid-career, laying out vast projects and planning monstrous foundations, his mouth full of boastful language', only the more conscious for the near approach of death of how much there was to do and how little time to do it in. His quiet end, with its characteristic rally in the last minutes, directed to minimizing the pain—the pain to others, which his death might cause—can hardly be likened to the rush of a torrent over a precipice. In its long course his life and his work had grown from small beginnings gradually and without a break, like the waters of a great river, and his end was like the end of such a river, merging insensibly in the sea.

In less poetical, but perhaps more accurate, language

---

[1] All references otherwise unspecified are to volume and page of J. Bowring's *Works of Jeremy Bentham* (11 vols., 1843).

Bentham's life is one which, followed from end to end, may be seen to have yielded continually increasing returns; and it is this more than anything else that accounts for the radiant happiness which, according to all who came into close contact with him, was so unmistakable a characteristic of his later years. A precocious and unusual boy, of poor physique and doubtful health, with little liking or aptitude for sport and games, is not likely to be very happy at school. It is not surprising that the young Jeremy found Westminster 'a wretched place for instruction' and its fagging 'a horrid despotism'. At Oxford he may have been unlucky in his college and associates, and his precocity undoubtedly led to his being sent there too young, but it is difficult to find any man of mark of those days who did not speak of the place, as he did, with asperity. He had the advantages of a comfortable home, a good supply of books, a great variety of mixed company, and long country holidays in which he was left a good deal to his own devices. But on the other hand his mother, of whom he was very fond, died before his eleventh birthday, and after her death his affections, naturally strong, were somewhat starved. With his father he was never on easy terms: 'a very affectionate father but a very troublesome one' he called him mildly, looking back, later in life.[1] The father was inordinately proud of his precocious son; he tended to force his precocity (as James Mill did later with his eldest son), seeing in him from a very early age a future occupant of the woolsack; he caused the sensitive and retiring boy perpetual uneasiness by repeated attempts to show him off in company. Meanwhile, though well endowed financially, he kept his son so short of money that at Westminster and Oxford Jeremy was ashamed of his poverty and of his mean appearance, and was constantly in debt. Another depressing factor for Jeremy Bentham as

---

[1] x. 64: cf. also letter to Samuel Bentham of 23 May 1775—'at present we are all the best friends imaginable. He certainly does love you and me next to his money' (cited by Everett, *A Comment on the Commentaries*, p. 6).

a boy was the inadequacy of his physique. He says he was a 'dwarf' at Westminster, the smallest boy, except one, in the school. This contributed to give him a sense of his own insignificance, which he had difficulty in throwing off. Bowring, whose acquaintance with Bentham began in 1820 (x. 516), says in the first chapter of the life that he 'often said' something like this: 'I have done nothing; but I could do something—I am of some value—there are materials in me, if anybody would but find it out. As it is, I am ashamed of an unrecognized existence. I feel like a cat or a dog that is used to be beaten by everybody it meets' (x. 26).

If Bentham really used such words as these after he made Bowring's acquaintance, it can hardly have been without conscious irony. For by that time his genius had received a fuller and wider recognition than has ever been accorded to any Englishman, not a man of action, with the possible exception of Isaac Newton, during his lifetime. But probably the words represent the report of friends of earlier date. In his youth his gifts were by no means wholly unrecognized. His father, as I have already said, was but too conscious of them. At school he earned the nickname of 'the philosopher', and had a great reputation for his Greek and Latin verses. This reputation he maintained at Oxford; and a copy of alcaics, which he composed, as a freshman of the ripe age of twelve years nine months, in honour of the accession of George III, was described by the great Dr. Johnson himself as 'a very pretty performance for a young man'. 'A mediocre performance', said Bentham, 'on a trumpery subject, written by a miserable child' (x. 41). Whatever he thought at the age of twelve, he soon came to have a low opinion both of classical studies and of Dr. Johnson. The study of the classics, apart from its undoubted utility in certain learned professions, he came to think waste of time; and Dr. Johnson was 'the gloomy moralist' (x. 13), 'the pompous vamper of common-place morality—of phrases often trite without being true' (x. 142). Besides that, by the age of twenty, in reading

Helvetius, it had come to him that *genius* was derived from *gigno*, and that genius in English, true to its derivation, meant production or invention. 'Have I a *genius* for anything?' he asked himself: 'What can *I* produce?' 'What is of all earthly pursuits the most important?' he went on to ask; in Helvetius he found the answer, legislation. Then 'Have I a genius for legislation?' he asked, and after much hesitation, 'I gave myself the answer, fearfully and tremblingly—Yes!' (x. 27).

Bentham succeeded, with difficulty and to the great disappointment of his father, in evading the career at the Bar for which he was destined, while obtaining the legal training which he wanted. He travelled, and formed a special attachment to France. He began to conquer his diffidence in company and to know his way about the world. But for some years the projected career of invention showed little sign of materializing. He did in fact begin what turned out to be his life's work—the work of clarifying and reforming the laws—as early as 1772 (*æt.* 24); but these labours were slow in producing even literary fruits. His first published work, the slashing attack on Blackstone which is known as the *Fragment on Government*, came out anonymously in 1776, and made something of a sensation, until the vanity of the author's father made its authorship known. But Bentham himself was already set on bigger things; and to him this was a mere parergon.

Indirectly, however, the book was a decisive influence on Bentham's life; for because of it five years later (1781) Lord Shelburne sought him out in his chambers at Lincoln's Inn, and for the next few years Bowood became his second home. He spoke always afterwards of Lord Shelburne (who became the first Marquis of Lansdowne in 1784) with the deepest affection and gratitude, though his descriptions are infected with a characteristic irony. It is clear that he valued very highly the opportunities opened to him by his visits to Bowood of getting an insight into the ways of 'Whig Lords' and influential politicians. His letters from Bowood are full of high spirits; they testify to a natural pleasure in finding himself in the company of the great: but on the whole he was not impressed. His judgements are severe, especially on William Pitt. At the age of seventy (approx.) he entered the following note in his Memorandum Book (x. 511)—'*J. B.'s Knowledge of the World, Whig Lords, &c.*—Those who live with them and, by describing their doings and looking at their titles, pretend to know what they are—know only what they say. I, who might have lived with them, and would not live with them—and who neither know nor care what they say—know, and without living with them, what they think.' But in respect of this knowledge Bentham would probably have admitted, if questioned, that he owed much to his visits to Bowood; and he is reported by Bowring as having said to him of Lord Lansdowne: 'He raised me from the bottomless pit of humiliation—he made me feel I was something' (x. 115).

This increased self-confidence quickly bore fruit in *The Principles of Morals and Legislation*, which was not published till 1789, but was circulated in draft as early as 1782 (x. 124). The only thing that needs to be said about this book now is that Bentham's conception of it is correctly indicated by its title: it is an attempt to lay the foundations for that legislative activity to which he had already devoted his life. This practical and productive orientation differentiates it sharply from any other treatise reckoned ethical known to me. The book was not a digression like the *Fragment on Government*. It was central enough, but it was essentially an introduction, preliminary work upon the foundations.

Before the *Principles* actually appeared Bentham had settled in England again after an absence of two and a half years (August 1785 to February 1788). Against the advice of Lord Lansdowne and other friends, he resolved to join his younger brother Samuel (b. 1757) at Crichoff in the Ukraine. Samuel was an ingenious young engineer and inventor, who had gone to Russia some years before, and had been taken by Catherine's favourite, Prince

Potemkin, into his service. The Prince gave him the rank
of lieutenant-colonel, made him superintendent of a ship-
building yard, and general supervisor of his costly and
chaotic schemes of westernization—'Jack of all trades',
wrote Jeremy from Crichoff, 'building ships, like Harle-
quin, of odds and ends—a rope-maker, a sail-maker, a
distiller, brewer, maltster, tanner, glassman, glass-grinder,
potter, hemp-spinner, smith, and copper-smith' (x. 147).
Of the two and a half years about a year is accounted for
by the two journeys—out, by Smyrna and Constantinople;
back, by Warsaw, Berlin, Hanover, The Hague. But Bentham got through a lot of work in the eighteen months or
so that remained. It was at Crichoff that he wrote his
Defence of Usury, which had immediate success on its publication (during his absence, in 1787), and shocked even
some supporters of *laisser-faire* by its uncompromising
advocacy of that principle.[1] It was here also that, with
the help of brother Samuel, he worked out his Panopticon
scheme, which came out as a substantial volume in 1791,
and in the end claimed more time with less result than any
other venture of his life. And all the time he was digging
deep in his chosen field of law, piling up the manuscripts
which Dumont was later to edit.

But what drew Bentham originally to Russia was undoubtedly his 'passion for improvement', as he called it
(x. 79): he thought he saw an opportunity of getting something done: and from that point of view the visit was not
a success. Russia was evidently not, at least not from the
Potemkin angle, the fruitful field for which he had hoped.
It may be doubted whether the influence of brother Samuel
was altogether good for Jeremy. One of his chief charms
was his tendency 'to be interested in every passing event'
(x. 552), and Samuel turned him to material inventions,
which were not his true field. Apart from the costly

---

[1] 'The request which agriculture, manufactures, and commerce present
to governments, is modest and reasonable as that which Diogenes made
to Alexander: *Stand out of my sunshine*. We have no need of favour—
we require only a secure and open path' (iii. 35: from the *Manual of
Political Economy*, 1793).

Panopticon project, which constituted a major preoccupation for some sixteen years of his life, he worked during
the same period at a frigidarium (refrigerator) for preserving fruit and vegetables, at a machine to serve as a silent
monitor of order in the House of Commons, and other
ingenuities. M. Halévy detects a pause in Bentham's
development in the period succeeding the visit to Russia,
and there are clear signs of a certain unsettlement at this
time, for which the Russian expedition and the French
Revolution are probably jointly responsible. Bentham was
not swept off his feet by the Revolution as most of those
who shared his passion for improvement were. One of his
favourite maxims was the saying of Helvetius: 'If you are
to love men you must expect little of them'—'this sentence', he says, 'has been a real treasure to me' (x. 587).
With this deflationary habit of mind, and a deep-seated
distrust of such Whig nonsense as the Social Contract and
the Rights of Man, he could scarcely participate in the
orgy of faith and hope which overcame his younger contemporaries. His colder, more practical vision saw, however, a great opportunity for action, and he set to work
with excitement and enthusiasm to take advantage of it.
His visits to France had given him the lowest opinion of
French government, so that he was not unprepared for
revolution there; they had also secured him a number of
friends and correspondents in Paris. These connexions
were strengthened during the early stages of the Revolution by the fact that Dumont was working for Mirabeau.
Dumont had not yet become Bentham's editor, but was
already his admirer. The two had met for the first time at
Lord Lansdowne's house in 1788; but before that Dumont
had been struck by some of Bentham's writings, shown to
him by Romilly. Thus the Lansdowne circle, and especially
Romilly and Bentham, were able, as Halévy says, to 'set
themselves up as advisers to the Constituent Assembly'.
First Romilly, with the aid of Trail and Bentham, drew
up a Digest of Parliamentary Procedure for the States-
General. Later Bentham sent the National Assembly a

more ambitious and comprehensive study of the same order called *An Essay on Political Tactics*. In 1790 he sent the same body his *Draught of a Code of Judicial Organization*. In 1791 he sent it his *Panopticon*, offering himself to go to France and conduct a prison constructed after his model. In 1793 he sent to France through Talleyrand his tract *Emancipate Your Colonies*, expounding a conviction of some standing with him, that the connexion between colonies and their mother-countries is of benefit to neither party. Then (as once again in 1830) he addressed the French as 'fellow citizens'; for in 1792, in company with Joseph Priestley, Thomas Paine, William Wilberforce, Thomas Clarkson, James Mackintosh, George Washington, and others, he had been accorded the title of French Citizen.[1]

His hopes for France, like those of most of her friends, scarcely outlived the year 1793; but as the exaltation with him had been less marked, so the depression, when it came, was less serious. In 1789 he had been taken to task by Lord Lansdowne for his leaning to republicanism (x. 195). By the middle of 1791 his opinion of the National Assembly had declined owing to its attacks on property (x. 262). Early in 1793 Romilly (who had been far more enthusiastic for the Revolution than ever he was) advised against the publication of *Truth vs. Ashhurst* on the ground of 'the praise given to the French' (x. 288). By October of that year we find Bentham fearing that 'Jacobinism ... has taken too strong root in France to be exterminated' (x. 296). The hostile examination of the rights of man, called *Anarchical Fallacies*, which was put together finally

---

[1] Among the works of this period is a remarkable tract entitled *A Plan for an Universal and Perpetual Peace* (iv. 546–60). The only information given as to its date by the editor is that it belongs to a group of papers bearing dates 1786 to 1789. Universal peace is to be based on complete surrender of all colonies, freedom of trade, absence of alliances, a fixed quota of armaments, open diplomacy. Formally it will involve a general and permanent treaty between the European countries, establishing a common court of law, but not attempting to back common decisions by force. The only other common organ will be a general congress or diet of the contracting powers, which shall meet and discuss in public. Kant's more speculative venture under a similar title came out in 1795.

in 1795, speaks of the 'degradation and degeneration' of France (ii. 524). As to the effect on his general political outlook, in May 1793 he wrote to Dundas, sending him some of his tracts, and says incidentally—'Some of them might lead you to take me for a Republican—if I were, I would not dissemble it: the fact is, that I am writing even against *Parliamentary Reform*, and that without any change of sentiment' (x. 293). Through it all his friendship for France remained. In 1796 he wrote to Wilberforce suggesting that they should make use together of their privilege of French citizenship to go to France and arrange terms of peace (x. 315).

Bentham would have been less than human if the shattering events of the French Revolution had not somewhat diverted him from his appointed path. To such major perturbations each man reacts after his kind, and Bentham's reactions were entirely in keeping with his character and opinions. It is, however, very strange to find him in 1790 covering sheets of paper with draft addresses to electors and writing to Lord Lansdowne to complain that he had not carried out his promise of finding him a seat in Parliament.[1] Now, like many others who have received favours from the great, Bentham was always very careful to maintain his independence in his relations with Lord Lansdowne. Here is his own description of an incident between them, not dated, but belonging presumably to the early days of their connexion. 'He asked me what he could do for me—I told him, "nothing"; and he found this so different to the universal spirit of those about him, as to endear me to him' (x. 116). This past incident makes the present letter the more strange. It is not, of course, the letter of a humble suitor. The favour is one for which he never asked, for which he would never have asked: it was Lord Lansdowne's spontaneous offer. All this at length, mixed up with passages of childish

---

[1] x. 229, 245. He seems to have spoken previously of going into Parliament in a letter to his brother of 1776, but jestingly and contingently on 'marrying £30,000' (*A Comment on the Commentaries*, p. 10).

vanity and fulsome self-praise, at times directly insulting to Lord Lansdowne, and spread over no less than sixty-one pages of manuscript. Lord Lansdowne's reply was a masterpiece, firm, friendly, and polite: he disclaimed the promise, but undertook to do what he could. Nothing shows better Bentham's mercurial, affectionate ways and his freedom from false pride than the letter with which he at once replied, ending the matter.

'My dear, dear Lord,—Since you will neither be subdued nor terrified, will you be embraced? . . . So Parliament may go to the devil, and I will take your Birmingham halfpence, and make a low bow, and put them gravely in my pocket, though they are worse than I threw away before. . . . Offer?—why no, to be sure it was not—why didn't I tell you I only called it so for shortness? More shame for you that you never made me any. . . . It was using me very ill, that it was, to get upon stilts as you did, and resolve not to be angry with me, after all the pains I had taken to make you so . . .'

and he goes on to suggest a visit to Bowood (x. 243). The relations of the two were re-established; but they did not continue for long on the old footing. It seems that Bentham did not visit Bowood again after 1792, though correspondence continued for a time and he was occasionally a guest at Lord Lansdowne's table. In that year by the death of his father, he came into a considerable property, and his whole way of life was altered. This may have contributed as much as a coolness over the Panopticon to the end of the Bowood visits.

No part of Bentham's life is poorer in novelties or surprises than the fifteen years following the French Terror. He had lost the intimacies of the Lansdowne circle and for a long time he formed no new circle of his own to take its place. For much of this time he must have been a rather solitary worker, going to and fro between his farm at Hendon and his house in Queen's Square Place. He was as full as ever of schemes of improvement, now directed to England and for some years mainly economic in character; and he was still reduced to tears at times by the shabby

treatment meted out to the Panopticon project (Wilberforce, x. 390 n.: 'I have seen the tears run down the cheeks
of that strong-minded man through vexation. . . . He was
quite soured by it; and I have no doubt that many of his
harsh opinions afterwards, were the fruit of this ill-treat-
ment'). Further, he was still at work on the grand scale
on the laws and the administration of justice. But of all
this work little or nothing reached the general public; and
with the governments of that time of confusion and reaction
it was hardly to be expected that his schemes would carry
much weight. Yet his reputation was growing. Halévy
is no doubt right in saying that even as late as 1808, when
he reached the age of sixty, Bentham was still for the wider
English public 'principally and almost exclusively the
man who wrote the *Panopticon* . . . one of the "men of one
idea" who were at that time so numerous in England'.[1]
But Dumont was at work on his manuscripts, and brought
out in 1802 at Paris the three volumes of the *Traités de
Législation*. By 1808 he was widely known on the Continent, and the flood of foreign correspondence, which was
so marked a feature of his later years, had already begun.
Even in England his writings were subjected to criticism
as early as 1804 in the *Edinburgh Review*. Still the early
years of the nineteenth century form perhaps the nearest
approach to slack water that is to be found in the flood
of Bentham's life. Whether loneliness or disappointment
had anything to do with the proposal of marriage[2] which
he made unsuccessfully in 1805 I do not know; but it is
difficult to believe that the project of moving his residence
to the highlands of Mexico, formed and canvassed with
characteristic thoroughness in 1808, had no other grounds
than those of health on which it was advanced.[3]

---

[1] *Growth of Philosophic Radicalism*, p. 251.

[2] x. 419. Professor Everett has recently published his discovery of
an earlier love affair. In 1775 Bentham fell in love with a Miss Dunkly,
a 'penniless beauty' of seventeen. Lack of means and his father's
opposition led to the surrender of the project of marriage (*A Comment on
the Commentaries*, p. 5).

[3] x. 439. As late as 1810, however, when Mexico was finally given

But now that he was sixty, when he might have seemed
to contemporaries to have shot his bolt, the last and greatest
chapter of his life was just about to begin. In 1808 he
made friends with the clever young Scottish journalist,
James Mill; and in a short space of time from the association of these two was born the sect of the Benthamites and
Utilitarianism as a political force. The crowded story of
these last years defies brief analysis. As Bentham grew
older and more conscious of the approach of his end, he
threw off more and more whatever remnants of caution he
had retained. His attacks on abuses have a new impetus
and venom; and they are given to the public instead of
being confided to correspondents or hoarded in his study
drawers. In a letter of sympathy to an unknown corre-
spondent, who had been accused of libel, he wrote in 1830
—'I am myself the most egregious and offensive libeller
men in power in this country ever saw' (xi. 43). That is
probably true of these last years. The attack on Lord
Eldon which he published in 1825 was described as 'the
most daring production that has ever appeared'. Within
a year of the beginning of his association with Mill he was
writing in favour of radical reform of Parliament and very
soon he came out publicly in support of the movement.
By 1810 he is in touch with Cobbett, and the rising star
of Brougham has been drawn into his orbit. In 1813 he
becomes a partner with Robert Owen in the New Lanark
Mills. In 1815 he enters the controversial field of popular
education with his proposals for a Chrestomathic school.
(In July of that year he expresses the fear lest Waterloo
has meant 'the death of all hopes of a free government in
France' (x. 485).) In 1817 Francis Place is his guest at
Ford Abbey. In 1818 reform resolutions drafted by Bentham are moved in the House of Commons by Sir Francis
Burdett. In the twenties Benthamite educational efforts
at length found concrete expression in the Mechanics

up, he considered the possibility of going to Venezuela to legislate for
that country; and by that time he boasts that he is famous all over the
world (x. 457, 458).

Institute and University College. By this time Bentham
is the revered 'father of reform', and Daniel O'Connell is
his 'humble disciple' (x. 597). There are two simultaneous
developments in all this, both mainly due to Mill: first,
Bentham's alliance for the first time in his life with other
independent workers for reform; secondly, the development of a strictly Benthamite group or school, a possibility
of which Bentham dreamed as early as 1790 (x. 246). Mill
early brought into the group David Ricardo, who became
its official economist, and Ricardo brought in later the
young banker, George Grote, who was to be the leader of
the Philosophic Radicals in the reformed Parliament. By
1823 the Benthamites were strong and compact enough
to come forward publicly as a group of like-thinking people,
and they launched their own quarterly, the *Westminster
Review*.

Through all these years the controversy and correspondence incidental to these domestic pre-occupations is
crossed and complicated by grandiose schemes for foreign
countries. His offer to codify for any country stood open;
and on this and other subjects he was in correspondence
with the United States, Spain, the Spanish-American
colonies, Portugal, Greece, Russia, and Bavaria. Lord
William Bentinck, appointed Governor-General of India
in 1827, invited him to think that he would be the real
governor of India; but Bentham, though pleased by the
compliment, evidently thought that Bentinck was neither
clever nor well informed enough to arrange that. In 1828
Bentham even engaged the Duke of Wellington in correspondence; and he seemed to take it as final proof that he
counted for something after all, when the Duke returned
courteous and considerate replies to his letters.

All these interests continued in full vigour to the end.
Within a year of his death he was working hard at two
projects which came to nothing—the project of a daily
paper to be called the *Universalist* and the project of a
Parliamentary Candidate Society. The Benthamites lost
their leader two days before they got their Reform Bill;

but they had their marching orders. They knew that Bentham was not yet finished with, and that the Reform of Parliament was not an end but a beginning.

II

In the manifold activities which constituted the mature life of Jeremy Bentham one may see a central line of development, which starts from propositions so general that they are commonly reckoned philosophical, and ends in projects of action so detailed and so closely related to changes actually effected that they accept more naturally the measures of action than the measures of thought. Not that projects of action are wanting in the earlier stages, or that principles fail at the end. He was always full of schemes of improvement, great and small. But the essential development being, as I have said, from the general to the particular—from theory to practice, from end to means —it follows that the passage of time tends to bring increased integration to Bentham's activities. The schemes he advocates come into closer and more vital relation with the principles he professes. They have less the mark of the capricious ingenuity of an inventor, and more the appearance of a considered attempt in the light of certain principles to meet the needs of a given situation. Another way of putting this would be to say that Bentham became practical for the first time in his old age. He once wrote in early middle life to a friend that he was idle, and partly, he added, on principle.[1] This deliberate idleness may be interpreted as a conscious resistance against all temptations to a premature descent to earth. It has sometimes been said or suggested that before the period of his association with James Mill, Bentham was not interested in politics. Such a view is absurd; for his whole life is the expression of a fundamental devotion to that and nothing else. Further, at no time in his life had he any interest in the small change of English politics. He was never prepared to accept an issue as important because parties and politicians were

[1] Letter to Wilson (1781: x. 93).

quarrelling about it. A citizen of the world by adoption, he disowned all national prejudices. He had his own measures of importance; among the chief, the degree of influence on the happiness of future generations. In this sense, at all times in his life, wherever important and far-reaching political decisions were afoot, he was interested and, to the extent of his opportunity, active. That he should be more easily and more frequently involved in the detail of political action at the end of his life is accounted for, without reference to external events, by the fact that from the beginning the appointed terminus of his thought was action. The opportunity came at length, disappointingly late in his life; but he grasped it with both hands and used it so that the better part of his achievement should accrue to generations which had not known him.

The full assessment of Bentham's life and work has never yet, I think, been attempted. For Elie Halévy's great book on *The Growth of Philosophic Radicalism*, though it covers in its luminous survey practically everything else, does not pretend to do justice to Bentham's contributions to the science of law. Clearly it would be foolish, even if I had the competence for it, to attempt a general assessment here. In fact I propose, in concluding this tribute to Bentham's memory, to touch what I have described as the central line of his development only at its two ends. I will say something first of his most general principles, of his philosophy; and secondly, of his projects of action, his impact on politics.

First, then, as to his philosophy. To be quite frank I must begin by saying that in Bentham the speculative motive is so secondary that strictly he can hardly be reckoned a philosopher at all. If his name were to be entirely cut out of our histories of philosophy no significant link would be found to be missing. The ethical utilitarianism, from which the *Principles of Morals and Legislation* starts, was a doctrine gradually built up by a succession of thinkers during the eighteenth century. There was no novelty of principle in Bentham's brief formulation of it.

Such originalities as are to be detected in his handling are, characteristically, of two kinds: first, in the direction of simplification: the principle is stated at its most trenchant and with a minimum of qualification: secondly, in the direction of application; i.e. of a forward march from the principle, taken as true. Both points testify to the predominance of the practical over the theoretical interest in Bentham's make-up.

It was only at the beginning and end of his life that Bentham was actually at work in fields that are commonly called philosophical; first, during what may be called the Bowood period, before his departure for Russia, when his interest was ethical; and again after 1810, when his work on the theory and practice of legislation drove him into the field of logic. In between those two periods he seems to have felt no need of raising philosophical questions; and in his writings and memoranda between those dates philosophy hardly receives even passing mention. Possibly he was influenced by the general contempt into which 'philosophy' fell in the reaction which followed the French Terror. But his attitude to philosophy in the last period is of a piece with his attitude in the first. It is regarded as the source of the most general propositions on which action depends. That this is his conception of Ethics hardly needs proof; and that Logic is conceived similarly is expressly avowed in the definition which he set at the beginning of the short treatise on the subject which he composed in his last years. He defines Logic as 'the art which has for its object or end in view the giving to the best advantage direction to the human mind, and thence to the human frame, in its pursuit of any object or purpose, to the attainment of which it is capable of being applied' (viii. 219). Holding such a view of philosophy, he is of course a believer in its value: he is ready to defend it against current detraction. Here is a note of 1818–19 (x. 510): '"I hate metaphysics," quoth Edmund Burke, in his pamphlet on the French Revolution. He may safely be believed. He had good cause to hate it. The power he trusted to was *oratory*

—*rhetoric*—the art of misrepresentation—the art of mis-
directing the judgement by agitating and inflaming the
passions.' Similarly, discussing metaphysics in his *Logic*,
he writes: 'Religionists, lawyers, fashionable sentimental-
ists, and poets have under the name of metaphysics found
something which has appeared to them to thwart their
views, opinions, interests, or prejudices, and against which
they have accordingly used their endeavours to cover it
with reproach and bring it into disrepute' (viii. 221). Thus
he is in favour of philosophy because he believes in knowing what one is doing and why. Philosophy is an examination of the principles of action, and thus potentially a
valuable agent of reform.

The predominance of the practical interest leads, however, to a certain impatience with the refinements of
speculation. The memorandum which contains the rebuke
to Edmund Burke, which I have just quoted, asserts also
that the value of metaphysics depends on the importance
of the ideas to which it applies itself. In 1789 he was sent
by his friend George Wilson the copy of a book by a certain
Dr. Gregory on Liberty and Necessity. In reply Bentham
regretted that 'a practical professional man should stand
forth as an author on subjects so purely speculative'.
'*Entre nous*', he said, 'I don't care two straws about liberty
and necessity at any time. I do not expect any new truths
on the subject: and were I to see any lying at my feet, I
should hardly think it worth while to stoop to pick them
up' (x. 216). A rather different line of objection to metaphysical speculation is contained in his letter to Brissot of
the same year deprecating the proposed Declaration of
Rights in France. 'It is a metaphysical work', he wrote,
'—the *ne plus ultra* of metaphysics. . . . Political science is
not far enough advanced for such a declaration' (x. 214).
But in this case he had, of course, already convinced himself that rights are the children of law, and that abstract
rights are dangerous and misleading fictions.

We are brought here to an element in Bentham's general
outlook which unites him closely to the central English

philosophical tradition on a side of it to which perhaps too little attention has been paid in the histories of philosophy. I refer to his deep preoccupation with words and their relation to things—a problem which became acute for him owing to his revolt against the concept of legal fiction as used by English lawyers. In different forms this problem obsessed Hobbes, Locke, Berkeley, and even Hume—for his celebrated question, ' From what impression is this idea derived ? ' is only a variant of the theme. Bentham's most genuinely speculative writings are late papers devoted to such problems under the headings Logic, Language, and Ontology. Mr. Ogden has recently brought together a number of these in a single volume with the general title *Bentham's Theory of Fictions*. The papers in question have hitherto received little attention from philosophers, and Mr. Ogden may be right in thinking that this neglect is unjust. On this point I am not yet convinced. The most obvious philosophical tendencies which they show are a nominalism akin to that of Berkeley and a common-sense metaphysic, reminding one rather of Hobbes, based on the notion of material substance. The chief novelty they contain is one which finds expression in Bentham's later memoranda on other subjects—an extended use of the term fiction to apply to all nouns substantive which are not names of bodies. So taken, fictions are no longer mere fancies or falsehoods: on the contrary they are indispensable to thought. And when Bentham gives, as examples of fictions, ' common law, mind, soul, virtue, vice ' (as he does in a memorandum of 1831 (xi. 73)), that does not imply that the use of these terms is illegitimate; at most, that it is dangerous. They must not be mistaken for names of ' real entities ' (bodies), and they are only correctly used when their relation to real entities is determined.

Among the many things which Bentham wished to reform was Language; and the curious will find in these papers the explanation of the ' unintelligible style ' (Hazlitt), the ' extraordinary language ' (Macaulay) of which critics complained in his later works. They will also find here some explanation of that narrowness of outlook of which they also with justice complained—of his total rejection of poetry, of religion, in short, of all aspects of human experience impervious to ratiocination. He was essentially a positivist;[1] and what Hazlitt said of him in his lifetime is true: 'he has not allowed for the wind': 'he has not looked enough abroad into universality' (*Spirit of the Age*, 1825).

In the field of political action Bentham applied his ethical principles mainly in two ways. First, he insisted that the one and only proper test of the adequacy of any law or institution is the quantity of the happiness which it produces. 'The sole object of government ought to be the greatest happiness of the greatest possible number of the community' (i. 301). This is what Bentham called the principle of utility or (more commonly in his later years) the greatest happiness principle, as applied to politics. Secondly, he held firmly to the interpretation of all human action as directed fundamentally to securing increase of pleasure or diminution of pain to the agent. This interpretation does not of course exclude the possibility of devotion to the good of others: some are so constituted or so situated that in the service of others they find their chief delight. I may quote once more his oft-quoted remark about himself. 'I am a selfish man, as selfish as any man can be. But in me, somehow or other, so it happens, selfishness has taken the shape of benevolence' (xi. 95). It will be noticed that the phraseology implies that he regards his case as exceptional. His biographer, John Bowring, tells us that in practice he had 'an exalted opinion' of human nature (xi. 77). This was no doubt true of him in a sense, especially in his old age, when Bowring knew him; but I have already quoted his approval of Helvetius's advice to expect little of men, and the following sentence from the

---

[1] I use this term with no special reference to the later speculations of Auguste Comte, but as a name for the type of philosophy which takes the given in experience as its basis, and in building on this attaches almost exclusive weight to the natural sciences.

Constitutional Code represents his standing estimate of human nature for political and legislative purposes. 'Whatsoever evil it is possible for man to do for the advancement of his own private and personal interest at the expense of the public interest—that evil sooner or later he will do, unless by some means or other, intentional or otherwise, he be prevented from doing it' (ix. 192).

I turn now, lastly, to Bentham's politics. In my account of his life I have tried to make clear by implication how I understand his development; but there is something more to be said about it. The impression is sometimes given that the radicalism of Bentham's old age was the result of a conversion, or substantial change of front, due to pique or disappointment at the reception of his schemes in the aristocratic circles in which he had formerly moved and on which he had set his hopes. Words used by Bentham himself in reminiscence, looking back on his life, lend some colour to this view. Speaking of Wilkes, with reference to his early twenties, he said: 'I was a determined aristocrat in his time—a prodigious admirer of Lord Mansfield, and of the King' (x. 66). 'Bewitched by Lord Mansfield's grimgibber' (x. 45) is another phrase used, worth preserving for its own sake. But even there he adds: 'I was however a great reformist; but never suspected that the people in power were against reform. I supposed that they only wanted to know what was good in order to embrace it' (x. 66). Similarly he tells us that in the dispute with the American colonies his judgement was on the government side; but he gives as his reason for this his objection to the theory on which the Americans based their action—that of natural rights (x. 57). It should be noted that both these references are to a very early period of his life, before the writing of the *Fragment on Government*. Against these reminiscences I would set one piece of contemporary evidence. A memorandum of 1773 or 1774, falling within this period, runs thus: 'The people is my Cæsar: I appeal from the present Cæsar to Cæsar better informed' (x. 73). Generally I should maintain that Bentham in his mature life was always at heart a radical. The change of the last years was a change of tactics, not of principles.

Bentham's father was a City of London Tory. His whole family was Tory, and some of them had been Jacobites. But it is a mistake to suppose that to be a Tory in the eighteenth century was to have a prejudice in favour of aristocracy; if anything, the opposite was the case. In the middle of the century it was the Whigs who were the 'Court Party': the Tories were the 'Country Party'. It was the Tories who at that time pressed the delegate theory of representation, which was later to be taken up by the advocates of Parliamentary Reform. It is impossible, as a matter of fact, to find in Bentham's early writings any sign of a leaning to aristocracy or of a dutiful trust in its wisdom. When Bentham welcomed the French Revolution, in spite of its borrowings of natural rights from America, it was the dethronement of the aristocracy that seemed to him the chief gain. 'Happy France! where aristocratical tyranny is laid low; while in England it is striking fresh root every day' (March, 1790: iv. 321). Bentham's Toryism was probably no great obstacle here. And though the 'passion for improvement' which possessed him was not exactly a Tory characteristic, yet Bentham's lifelong suspicion of the holders of power has more in common with the fractiousness of the eighteenth-century Tory, who was habitually against the government, than with contemporary Whig confidence in the 'matchless constitution'.

The programme which Bentham advocated in his last period was on the face of it a programme of unqualified democracy, but the reasons by which he backed it gave his democracy a cynical flavour, typical of a time of disillusionment. His reforms included the abolition of the monarchy and of the House of Lords. The single-chamber parliament was to be elected by ballot on the basis of adult suffrage (the enfranchisement of women was a reform to which he failed to convert James Mill) for one year only. Members of Parliament were to be paid for their services. Such a

programme could only spring, one might suppose, from a
profound belief in the wisdom and virtue of the ordinary
man; but in Bentham it springs rather from a deep distrust of the wisdom and virtue of their rulers. He was as
resolute in rejecting the 'imposture of collective wisdom'
as ever Godwin was. 'What then shall we say of that
system of government of which the professed object is to
call upon the untaught and unlettered multitude (whose
existence depends on their devoting their whole time to the
acquisition of the means of supporting it) to occupy themselves without ceasing upon all questions of government?'
(*Anarchical Fallacies*, 1795: i. 522). This was written in
1795 or a little earlier. The passage starts with a comparison between the trash put out by the French in politics
and the pure gold of their work in chemistry. The suggestion is that invention, in politics as in chemistry, comes
always from the gifted few. There is no evidence that
Bentham ever withdrew from this position. In his later
years he can be found arguing that the rich are less moral
than the poor (e.g. x. 519) and that reason has less obstacles
to its reception in a democratic organization than elsewhere (ibid.), but never that the 'people' is a repository of
constructive wisdom. 'Place the chief care of each man in
any other breast or breasts than his own (the case of infancy and other cases of intrinsic helplessness excepted),
a few years, not to say a few months or weeks, would suffice
to sweep the whole species from the earth' (1822: x. 80).
That is for Bentham the irrefutable basis of democracy.

A note jotted down in Bentham's memorandum book
before the visit to Russia may be said to sum up at that
early date in nine words the essentials of the position which
Bentham took up on the constitutional question at the end
of his life. 'The eye of the public makes the statesman
virtuous' (x. 145). Representative Government is merely
a kind of inverted Panopticon. That was described by him
to Brissot as 'a mill for grinding rogues honest, and idle
men industrious' (x. 226). The parliamentary mill was
not different in its intention: it had the similar task of

grinding private interest into public service. But whereas
that secured its end by keeping the many inmates at the
periphery under the continuous observation of a director
posted at the centre, this secures it by keeping the authoritative centre under the continuous observation of the surrounding many.

But both were means, not end; and in politics the end
was set for Bentham by that passion for improvement
which was the centre of his life. In 1829 the young Macaulay
of the *Edinburgh Review* taunted the Benthamites with
believing 'that the sole hope of the human race is a rule of
three sum and a ballot box' (*Essays*, i. 429). In the heat
of the Reform Bill struggle it was only natural that the
importance of the constitutional issue should be magnified.
But this was never Bentham's belief; or at least, if so, only
in the harmless sense that Radical Parliamentary Reform
was the one necessary first step before those 'great plans
of national reform, of which there is such abundant need'
(1790: iv. 321) could be set on foot. Because the Reform
Bill was a means, and not an end, Bentham's influence did
not end with his death, in the hour of victory of that cause.
The reform of the law, which had already begun during
Bentham's lifetime, was continued and completed by the
Reformed Parliament after his death. A generation later,
Sir Henry Maine said that he did not know 'a single law
reform effected since Bentham's day which cannot be traced
to his influence'.[1] Within a few years of his death the
editor of his collected works, John Hill Burton, enumerates
some two dozen major reforms already carried through as
directly due to him, and adds another dozen (most of which
have in fact since been executed), as awaiting execution
(i. 3 n.). These lists could easily be extended. They constitute a record of practical productivity probably without
parallel in this or any other country. There is a tendency
to think of these reforms as mainly negative in character,
as consisting in the removal of harmful restraints and inherited abuses. John Stuart Mill's fine essay on Bentham

[1] *Early History of Institutions* (1875).

encouraged this view, describing him as 'the great subversive or . . . critical thinker of his age and country'.
There is, of course, much truth in this. He was bound to
deal with the political problems more or less in the form
in which his time set them to him. But constructive
elements are not wanting. His contributions to the Census,
to Municipal Reform, to the development of the Poor Laws,
the Civil Service, and the Post Office, to the foundation of
a system of inspection and registration in a variety of
fields, show a strong constructive bent in a direction which
we are better able to appreciate than Mill was. Few things
are more significant of this bent than his emphasis on the
need in every department of government of full and accurate statistics. We shall not go far wrong if we regard
him on his more positive side as the founder of the modern
science of administration.

Perhaps there is a moral to this story, of immediate
application. This man, whose memory we honour to-day,
worked in almost complete detachment from the routine
of politics and from its controversies. No man has ever
operated powerfully on events at so great a distance from
them. If the same distance and detachment could be
secured, together with something of the same passion for
improvement, might not, even to-day, something similar
be achieved? It would be too much to look for another
Bentham: nature no doubt has long ago broken the mould.
But a University department of administration, well led
and suitably organized, might do some similar service in
its day and generation, with the additional advantage that
its life would not be limited even to Bentham's eighty-five
years. The aspiration of such a department would be fitly
summarized in Talleyrand's beautiful tribute to Bentham:
pillé de tout le monde, il est toujours riche—'robbed by every
one, he remains rich'.

XIV. THE EMPIRICISM OF J. S. MILL[1]

I

Mill's View of his own Historical Position

FROM the beginning to the end of his career Mill saw himself philosophically as a member of a rather unpopular minority. He conceived himself to be living in a time of strong reaction against eighteenth-century philosophy. In this reaction the leaders were the Germans, and their influence dominated thought both in France and in England. He was in his own view the champion, before a hostile public, of an older and sounder method than the fashionable mysticism and obscurantism. This diagnosis holds equally for the *System of Logic* (1843) and for the *Examination of Sir William Hamilton* (1865).

The ruling influences in the reaction, as Mill conceived it, were Thomas Reid for England, and for the Continent Immanuel Kant. But the roots of their doctrines lay farther back, ultimately in Descartes, continuing through Spinoza and Leibniz to Kant, Schelling, and Hegel. The 'older and sounder' tradition is to be found in Bacon, Hobbes, Locke, Hume, and Hartley. In his own day and country it was represented by Bentham, James Mill, and, later, Alexander Bain, opposed by Coleridge and Hamilton.

Mill formulates this opposition so often, and in such various contexts, that there is an embarrassing wealth of material to draw upon in describing it.[2] Perhaps the best statement is that contained in the essay of 1840 on Coleridge, if it is remembered that this was written at a period

---

[1] From the *Proceedings of the VIIth International Congress of Philosophy*.
[2] See *Autobiography* (World's Classics, ed. Laski), especially pp. 151, 190, 230, 232. Further *Dissertations and Discussions*, i, Essays on Sedgwick (1835) and Coleridge (1840); ii, on Bailey (1842) and Whewell (1852); *Logic* (1843), Introd. and Bk. VI, ch. iv; *Letters*, i, pp. 113 (1839), 116 (1840), 146 (1849); Letter (1841) in *Journals of Caroline Fox*, ii. 325; *Auguste Comte and Positivism* (1865), pp. 71, 119; *Examination of Sir. W. Hamilton's Philosophy* (1865), especially chapters i, ii, viii, ix.

of maximum estrangement from Benthamism and with an evident desire to make out the best possible case for the other side. What follows here is merely a summary of that statement.

Mill starts his account from what he calls 'their highest philosophical generalizations', i.e. from their account of the sources of human knowledge and their possible development. The prevailing theory of the eighteenth century was, he says, that of Locke, commonly attributed to Aristotle, that all knowledge consists of generalizations from experience. This involves the denial of the *a priori* and of truths 'cognizable by the mind's inward light and grounded on intuitive evidence'. 'Sensation and the mind's consciousness of its own acts are not only the exclusive sources but the sole materials of our knowledge.' From this view Coleridge, with the Germans since Kant and most of the English since Reid, strongly dissents. They claim that the mind has a capacity within certain limits of perceiving the nature and properties of Things in-Themselves. Above Understanding is Reason, a power which by direct intuition perceives things and recognizes truths not cognizable by the senses. These truths are not perhaps innate; but they are at most suggested by experience. As examples of such *a priori* truths and knowledge they cite the fundamental doctrines of religion and morals, the principles of mathematics, and the ultimate laws even of physical nature.

Even in the Coleridge essay Mill avows himself on this general issue an unqualified supporter of 'the school of Locke and Bentham'. Things-in-Themselves, 'the hidden causes of the phenomena which are the objects of experience', are radically inaccessible. 'We see no ground for believing that anything can be the object of our knowledge except our experience and what can be inferred from our experience by the analogies of experience itself; nor that there is any idea, feeling, or power in the human mind which, in order to account for it, requires that its origin should be referred to any other source.'

Even here, however, in what Mill calls the pure science

P

of mind, 'Coleridge and the Germans' have not lived in vain.
The Locke school needed rejuvenation. It had fallen low,
into the 'shallow ideology' of Condillac and his followers.
In pure metaphysics (which for Mill often seems to approximate to psychology) the only advance since Locke is that
made by Hartley. Even in this field, then, their protest was
timely and salutary. But this is the least valuable part of
their philosophical contribution. Their services are better
seen in 'practical philosophy'.

In this department of thought the end of the eighteenth
century found England differently situated from the Continent. On the Continent philosophy was master, and tradition was beaten off the field: in England compromise
reigned. Hence opposed types of error: 'On the Continent
the extravagances of new opinions; in England the corrup-
tion of old ones.' The *philosophes* aimed only at destruction.
If superstition, priestcraft, prejudice, and the like were once
destroyed, all the virtues and graces must, they thought,
spontaneously appear. In this they were wrong, mistaking
the familiar for something universal and natural. They
failed to detect the manifold civilizing and restraining
influences on which the social order they knew depended.
The time was in fact one at which destruction was needed;
but they encouraged their contemporaries to throw away
the shell without preserving the kernel.

This gave the school to which Coleridge belonged its
great opportunity. It was able to meet a philosophy which
blindly anathematized the past with a philosophy which
was 'at once a severe critic of the new tendencies of society
and an impassioned vindicator of what was good in the
past'. It succeeded in achieving a genuine philosophical
detachment which removed all suspicion of mere Tory
partisanship. Looking far beyond all immediate and tem-
porary controversies, this school 'has done exactly what we
blame the eighteenth-century philosophers for not doing'.

Mill characterizes the new contribution to practical philosophy in the following sentences:

'They were the first, except a solitary thinker here and there,

who inquired with any comprehensiveness or depth into the
inductive laws of the existence and growth of human society ...
who pursued, philosophically and in the spirit of Baconian investigation, not only this inquiry, but others ulterior and
collateral to it. They thus produced, not a piece of party
advocacy, but a philosophy of society, in the only form in which
it is yet possible, that of a philosophy of history ; not a defence
of particular ethical or religious doctrines, but a contribution,
the largest made by any class of thinkers, towards the philosophy of human culture. . . .

'Hence that series of great writers and thinkers from Herder
to Michelet, by whom history, which was till then "a tale told
by an idiot, full of sound and fury, signifying nothing", has
been made a science of causes and effects; who, by making the
facts and events of the past have a meaning and an intelligible
place in the gradual evolution of humanity, have at once
given history, even to the imagination, an interest like romance,
and afforded the only means of predicting and guiding the
future, by unfolding the agencies which have produced and
still maintain the present.'[1]

One final quotation. At the beginning of the discussion
summarized above, Mill states the general opposition between the two schools of thought in the following terms:

'The Germano-Coleridgian doctrine expresses the revolt of
the human mind against the philosophy of the eighteenth
century. It is ontological because that was experimental;
conservative because that was innovative; religious because
so much of that was infidel; concrete and historical because
that was abstract and metaphysical; poetical because that
was matter-of-fact and prosaic.'

II
Mill's Diagnosis Examined

The most interesting feature of Mill's account of this
phase in the history of European thought is that the conflict, as he sees it, is one in which each side represents a
combination of opposites. The German school are ontolo-

---

[1] Mill clearly thinks that this more valuable side of the reaction has
hardly penetrated England. He complains in a footnote of Cimmerian
darkness still prevailing wherever 'recent foreign literature or the
speculations of the Coleridgians have not penetrated'.

gists or metaphysicians, believers in *a priori* knowledge and in intuitive or self-evident principles. But they are also pioneers in the concrete historical method: in the social field at least, it is they, and not the heirs of Bacon, who are the experts in Baconian and inductive investigation. The school of Locke, on the other hand, is experimental, maintaining that there is no innate or intuitive knowledge and that all truth is derived from experience; but in the social field it champions an abstract and 'metaphysical' method.

At the time when Mill wrote the article on Coleridge he was engaged upon the Sixth Book of his *Logic* ('On the Logic of the Moral Sciences'), and the aspect of the opposition which most interested him was the contrast of methods in Social Science. This question had been in his mind for ten years and more. His attention had been violently called to it in 1829 by the *Edinburgh Review*'s bitter attack on his father. The young Macaulay clinched his assault with the challenge: 'Our opposition is fundamental: we believe that it is utterly impossible to deduce the science of government from the science of human nature.' When Macaulay's two articles appeared, Mill was already sitting very loose to the Utilitarian creed. It is indeed doubtful whether in 1829 he would have consented to call himself a Benthamite or Utilitarian at all. The *Autobiography* (pp. 132–6) tells the story in detail, and in the main accurately, though perhaps it slightly under-estimates the strength and duration of this anti-utilitarian reaction. Full weight is given here to Macaulay's articles, but only as bringing to a head a development already in progress, and the reader is referred to the Sixth Book of the *Logic* for Mill's solution of the problems raised.

What Mill, *more suo*, offers us in the *Logic* is a compromise or middle position. The Utilitarians, he says in effect, were wrong, as Hobbes was wrong, in believing in the possibility of a social science modelled after deductive geometry. On the other hand, Macaulay and the opponents of the Utilitarians were equally wrong in calling for a purely inductive method. 'In social phenomena the composition of causes

is the universal law.' The complexity of the facts makes
the experimental methods inapplicable. The right method
is what he calls the physical or concrete deductive method,
which begins by determining the laws of the separate agencies at work and ends in general theorems as to the effects
of legislative measures and forms of government.

In this Sixth Book we find Comte superimposed upon
Bentham. (Comte began to publish his *Philosophie Positive*
in 1830, but Mill made its acquaintance first in 1837.) Bentham was right in believing, as against Montesquieu and his
followers, that a universal science of politics was possible;
he was right again in thinking that the possibility of such
a science depends on there being discoverable 'tendencies
common to all mankind'. But Comte was right in his theory
of the *consensus* of social phenomena. Hence Mill sketches
his plan for an Ethology, which shall determine the laws of
the formation of character in individuals and in nations,
but at the same time refuses to claim for the *a priori* argument any independent or absolute value. 'An amount of
knowledge quite insufficient for prediction may be most
valuable for guidance.'

In Mill's view this compromise seemed a decisive departure from political utilitarianism, and it must be remembered that in the first half of the nineteenth century
utilitarianism was a political label. He seems to have felt
that it was only in metaphysics that he remained a member of the school in which his father had brought him up. As
early as 1833 he wrote to Carlyle[1] that his opinions 'except
in mere metaphysics are quite as unlike theirs as yours are'.
Again in the following year[2] he says he has scarcely one of
his 'secondary premises' in common with them. It is significant that the work of his father's which he edited was
the *Analysis of the Human Mind*. Towards the end of his
life he adopted the name of utilitarianism for his ethical
views, but by that time the Utilitarian Radicals had left the
political scene.

The formula for Mill's development is complicated by the

---

[1] *Letters*, i. 85.   [2] Ibid., 91.

powerful influence of Comte—in whom perhaps for a time
he saw the merits of the German movement without its
defects, though later he found plenty of false mysticism in
Comte—but, putting Comte aside, it is probably true to say
that Mill felt himself, and in the main rightly, as compro-
mising on the opposition from which we started. Between
religion and infidelity his compromise was expounded, to
the scandal of many of his followers, in the posthumous
Essays on Religion. For the rest, he retained his preference
for the experimental as against the ontological, for innovation as against conservatism; but he deserted the abstract
and metaphysical for the concrete historical method, and
the first article of his political creed became a belief in those
individual differences which the abstract method over-
looked. What is strange is that he does not claim for the
resulting position that it is a more consequential empiricism
than that in which he was brought up.

III

Empiricism?

This brings us to the question, What is Empiricism? Or,
in the particular case, What is Mill's Empiricism?

Starting from the latter question, we find in Mill two main
motives, which are to some extent at odds with one another.
(1) It is an essential part of his empiricism to champion the
ideals and methods of natural science. He is deeply concerned to prove the applicability of these ideals and methods
to human life and society. But the ideal of science is deductive; and only so far as this ideal is realized is universality
achieved and prediction made possible. For human life,
then, he wants a science as much deductive and as little
observational as possible. It would be best of all if the
geometrical parallel would fit. In fact it does not, and he
accepts a second best. But matters from which deduction
is wholly excluded are regarded as left in the darkness of
'mere empiricism'.[1]

But (2) Mill's experience of life convinced him of the

[1] *Logic*, vi. i and x.

sovereign importance of individual originality, as the one spring and source of fruitful advance. That here science is baffled he will not admit. He seeks desperately for a science that will reveal its secret. Hence these poor abortive ghosts of an individual and social ethology, which long haunted him, but never came to life. In the historical thought of the idealist reaction he caught a glimpse of what he was seeking, and wrongly ascribed to it a Baconian and inductive method. But the reaction was really in revolt against the abstractions of science, continuing Berkeley's protest against the corpuscularian philosophy. It sought the concrete fact, and particularly in history, which is the antithesis of science. In virtue of his experience, but not of his empiricism, Mill reacted sympathetically to this development.

It may perhaps be suggested that Mill was no true empiricist; and it is certainly true that most recent empiricism, e.g. that of Bergson or of William James, is of a different cast. But this devotion to the scientific ideal, with its consequent inability to digest history until it is falsified into science, is part of the tradition of the European school of experience. This is the form of rationalism, it seems, into which empiricists readily fall. Historically, hedonism has consistently accompanied a sensationalist or empiricist theory of knowledge; and hedonism is the most scientific and rationalist of all theories of conduct. Hedonists claim to present a science of action, exaggerating more than any other ethical school the power of man to determine by reasoning the course of his life. In England the school of experience looked to Hobbes and Locke as their founders. But Hobbes claimed to be the Galileo of Civil Philosophy, who made it scientific and deductive by determining once for all the laws of human motion; and Locke argued that in morals and politics the deductive and demonstrative method was at home. Thus, whatever may be thought of Mill's attitude to the idealist philosophy of history—as to which, indeed, the tradition gave no clear lead—his conception of the place of science in human affairs was true to the empirical tradition as he knew it.

The explanation of this must be sought by an attempt to answer the more general question, What is empiricism? What is the vital centre of the movement of thought on which the people we call empiricists are carried? The school of experience has revolutionized itself since Mill's day, and the leaders in this revolution, like Bergson in France and William James in America, have reflected much and fruitfully on the meaning of this term, which James at least was proud to claim for his own doctrine. (For James, see particularly R. B. Perry's preface to the posthumous *Essays in Radical Empiricism*, with the references there given. For Bergson, see the opening pages of his Oxford lectures entitled, *La Perception du Changement*.) The essential difference between the new empiricism and the old is briefly indicated in James's principle that a true empiricism must base itself on every kind of experience, with its implied criticism of the older empiricism as unduly sensationalist. But this development does not of itself affect the position of thought or science. James and Bergson agree that thought is only a second best, forced upon us by the limitations of our senses. Bergson likens thought to paper money. James asserts that 'the deeper features of reality are found only in perceptual experience'. From this starting-point it is natural to conceive thought, as Mill conceived it, with science for its characteristic expression, as a convenient device which by abstraction and generalization enables us to determine the outlines of that which we are unfortunately not in a position to perceive.

Now experience is in fact confined within narrow limits, even when every kind of experience is taken into account. By it alone man cannot hope, in Hume's phrase, to 'people the world'. Hence the emphasis on the sovereign value of direct experience, the denial of all originality to '*reason*', tends to have the rather paradoxical-seeming effect of bringing into exaggerated relief the importance of *reasoning*. It is the art of thought to make a little experience go a long way, as paper money builds a vast credit system on a small accumulation of specie. In this way the empiricist falls naturally into a conviction of the supreme value of scientific abstraction and an ardent desire to extend its beneficent work.

I claim that it is possible on these lines to show that the combinations of apparent opposites, which we noted as marking Mill's description of the rival schools of thought in his time, represent no internal contradiction on either side, but a natural development from the starting-point of each. I have confined my discussion to Mill's own side of the issue. Of the others it is perhaps sufficient to say here that, as those who depreciate reason tend to over-estimate reasoning, so they, in vindicating reason, in claiming for thought freedom and originality, may legitimately aim at reducing reasoning to strict subordination.

XV. IS A SCIENCE OF THEOLOGY POSSIBLE? [1]

ANY difficulty there may be in regarding a particular inquiry as actually or potentially scientific is likely to have its ground either in the subject-matter with which the inquiry is concerned, or in the aim governing the treatment of it, or in both. The question of the method used probably needs no separate consideration. For method is an independent variable, i.e. a science can use different methods at different times without changing its name, and no particular method seems to be included in the description 'scientific'. Further, a method is conceived by those who operate it as dictated by the nature of the subject-matter and the aim of the inquiry. In addition to these intrinsic determinants, there may at any given place and time be external factors, such as the attitude of the political power or the state of public opinion, which make the prosecution of a given science difficult or impossible. Thus a really scientific treatment of the problem of race is hardly possible in present-day Germany, and at all times economic and social speculation is somewhat hampered by the passionate explosions which it is always in danger of arousing. I consider, then, that the question whether a scientific theology is possible may be subdivided into the three questions: whether there is anything in (*a*) the aim of theology, or (*b*) its subject-matter, or (*c*) the external conditions of its prosecution, which precludes it from treading 'the sure path of a science'.

I

Aim

A science, it is generally agreed, aims at knowledge. It continually checks and extends what we have of certainties and probabilities within a defined region. With so much in the world that is unknown, one often wonders how the

[1] Aristotelian Society, *Supplementary Volume XIV*.

scientist decides what is worth investigating; but he is helped in this by a powerful and well-organized tradition which largely dictates its own continuation; and there is also the pull of practical need and interest affecting the distribution of scientific labour at any place and time and partly determining the order of priority among scientific problems. Since knowing and the search for knowledge occur within a world which includes also much else, it is evident that these activities are not ultimately sufficient to themselves: they will inevitably be in intimate and continuous relation with other activities (e.g. practical and artistic activities), united with them in the common service of human life. Consequently, though the scientist *qua* scientist wants knowledge and nothing else, he does not resent it that a problem should be set to him by a practical need. He would, however, complain if he were forbidden to follow the argument out to its end, on the ground that its continuation was of no practical importance; and he would feel that his scientific life was threatened if he were ordered to conceal or contradict scientifically important results of his researches, on the ground that practical interests made their publication inexpedient or their disavowal imperatively necessary. But it is worst of all when the interference arises from an impurity in the scientist's own motive, when, with no consciousness of guilt, he announces as scientifically proved or verified only those things which he desires himself to believe or is pressed by external influences to support. Then we may say with Plato that the lie is in his own heart. 'Knowledge for the sake of knowledge', like 'art for art's sake', is a sound and necessary principle if it is addressed to the scientist as a demand for purity of motive in his work.

In this matter of aim or purity of motive it is clear, I think, that the theologian is often an object of suspicion, and we have to find out what justification this suspicion has. Now probably every theologian would say that his aim was knowledge, that he was working whole-heartedly for such approximation as was possible to a knowledge of

God and His ways. On the other hand, most of them would probably assert this with qualifications and additions, which at least give a handle to the suspicion that the theological search for truth is not fully autonomous, but is in subordination to some other activity. The signs of this are various and different in different writers. Among them are the following: They tend to show a confidence in their assertions about God not proportionate to the strength of the arguments offered; and they are often sceptical as to the possibility of obtaining knowledge by the theological road at all. In a purely scientific inquiry such scepticism would surely be felt as disabling: if it is not so felt in theology, theology cannot be truly scientific. When the scientist compares his efforts with those of the theologian, he is apt to notice that the theologian comes to his inquiry equipped with certainties to which, scientifically, he has no right. He treats things as certain which he does not even assert to be known. Such certainties impose external limits to questioning, which a science cannot tolerate; for where the aim of knowledge is supreme, questioning is stilled only by the answer which is known to be true. So the scientist asks whether the theologian is not, perhaps, more like a barrister, whose search for truth is limited by his brief. The limits are, of course, much less narrow than those of any conceivable brief, but the position, he might claim, is analogous in that the theologian has a case to expound and defend, and therefore, however pure his devotion to truth may in fact be, his activity is not an expression of that devotion (therefore, not essentially a scientific activity), but subserves some further end, e.g. (in the case of the theologian) the service of the Church and the strengthening of religious faith.

These points may be conveniently illustrated and developed with the assistance of Archbishop Temple's recent Gifford lectures, *Nature, Man and God*. Theology, in his view, is 'the science of religion'. It 'formulates the deliverances of the religious experience'. It 'starts from the Supreme Spirit and explains the world by reference to

Him'.[1] Theology, like all science (including, it seems, philosophy), is an exercise in conceptual thinking, which is valuable, but has been seriously over-valued by 'Greek and scholastic and Cartesian philosophers'. Such thinking is never an 'apprehension of reality'. It is rather 'an *interim* procedure', corresponding 'to the analytical study of the score between two occasions of hearing great music'. The part played by theologians is that of 'musical critics, analysing and summarizing; but they too will return from theology to worship, as St. Thomas passed from the *Summa Theologiae* to the *Lauda, Sion, Salvatorem*'.[2] It will be noticed that here Dr. Temple represents the limitations of theology as common to all conceptual thought, i.e. to all science; but most of you will probably feel with me that the parallel is, to say the least, imperfect between St. Thomas's passage from theology to worship and, say, Newton's surrender of theoretical physics for the administration of the Mint. (The comparison is, of course, mine, not Dr. Temple's.)

Dr. Temple fully recognizes that there is imperfect identity of aim between most of what is called theology and science. But the gap, if there is one, may possibly be bridged by the old conception of natural theology. This conception is actually the basis of the Gifford foundation, and is discussed a good deal in Dr. Temple's lectures. Those who introduced the term certainly meant by it a theology which is given a purely scientific character by being made independent of revelation and all other extraneous control. 'Natural religion', said Charles Blount (1693), 'is the belief we have of an eternal intellectual Being, and of the duty which we owe him, manifested to us by our reason, without revelation or positive law.' The systematic exposition of such a belief might well be called a scientific theology. The extra-scientific factors above mentioned seem to be excluded by definition, and can only come in so far as it is untrue to its name. Dr. Temple's

[1] *Nature, Man, and God*, pp. 44, 45.
[2] Ibid., pp. 316, 317.

treatment of this conception is very interesting. He understands natural theology as 'the scientific study of Religion, as it exists among men, in relation to the general interpretation of man's experience as a whole within which religion is a part'. He adds that one of its functions is to investigate the validity of the claim made by religion 'to be not only one part along with others, but the dominant element, exercising over all the rest a certain judgement and control'. To admit that claim without criticism would be 'to go over to the other method with which natural theology is contrasted', i.e. to theology proper.[1] Thus natural theology is conceived as subjecting to critical examination that religious experience which theology or 'theological philosophy'[2] takes as its unquestioned point of departure. It is evident that natural theology, as conceived by Dr. Temple, has a far more concrete and empirical character than Charles Blount intended. But to his conception also the qualification 'scientific' could hardly be refused.

II

Subject-matter

What are the constitutive conditions of science on the side of subject-matter? It is difficult to give a very definite answer. In the general sense which I take 'science' in our question to bear, it is equivalent to the German *Wissenschaft*, and includes, for instance, mathematics, chemistry and all the natural sciences, history of all kinds, and philosophy—every field, in short, in which the aim of knowledge is systematically prosecuted. The boundaries between science and science are not always perfectly clear, and therefore it would be difficult to refuse the name scientific

[1] *Nature, Man, and God*, pp. 18, 19.
[2] Ibid., p. 44. I believe that Dr. Temple does not intend these terms to be precisely identical, but means the second to be taken as including the first; i.e. a true theology might be one section of a theocentric philosophy, viz. that section which is specially devoted to the 'deliverances of religious experience'.

to an inquiry because of a doubt which science had a right to it. If some one argued for classifying Darwin's *Origin of Species* as history I do not know that he could be refuted. Even if by dissection of the world we could specify a different process or entity for each departmental science as its subject-matter, history would cross our principle of division by taking all process for its province and philosophy by claiming the whole world. But if we think of scientific projects which have failed to establish themselves, we shall find that their difficulties often arose from their choice of subject-matter. The field selected was, or was thought to be, unsuitable owing to the fact that its contents were insufficiently unified or insufficiently self-contained. 'Sociology', as conceived by Comte, was criticized on the former ground, and J. S. Mill's project of an individual and social 'ethology' could probably be attacked effectively on the latter ground.

No such ground as this seems tenable for an objection to the claim of theology to be scientific; but there are undoubtedly peculiarities in its subject-matter, the most obvious of which is this, that the reality is disputed of the Being of which it purports to give an account. Most sciences are defined with reference to what may be called *prima facie* existents, admitted features of ordinary experience. In these they find their starting-point, and to these they appeal in verification of such theoretical constructions as they may undertake. This alleged science is named, it seems, after some theoretical interpretation of reality; otherwise, how can there be the possibility of dispute?

This objection certainly reveals a peculiarity in the position of the theologian, which makes him unique among inquirers claiming the name of scientist. But is this peculiarity such as to invalidate his claim to the name? The parallel with other sciences can to some extent be restored if theology is defined as the systematic study of religious experience; for religious practice and belief falls, obviously, within the class of *prima facie* existents. God will be included in the initial statement of the theological problem only because reference to God is so central in the records of religious experience that religion and belief in God have come to be taken as identical. On this view, God for the theologian is not (as the objector supposes) a ready-made interpretation of reality, to be defended against attack, but a half-defined implication of religious experience, to be further defined on the evidence of that experience and in the light of what otherwise is known or conjectured about the world.

Theology, so conceived, would not be committed as such to any particular view of this central religious postulate. The finding of the inquiry might be that religion contributed nothing whatever to a sane view of the world. Theology, in a word, would as little imply a belief in God as demonology implies a belief in demons. But though this implication is, I think, irresistible, it is, in fact, rather academic and unimportant. It might be more proper, nevertheless, to confine the term theology to positive and constructive expositions of the Divine Nature, and such restriction for two reasons would not seriously prejudice the claim of the inquiry to the name of science: first, because the Divine has, in fact, been conceived so variously that the acceptance of its objectivity as basis leaves ample room for free speculation; secondly, because, by a right instinct, purely negative and destructive studies in any field are felt to be unwarranted intruders. There are probably persons who take the view that aesthetic values are quite insignificant and unsubstantial; but the exposition of such a view in detail would be somewhat oddly entitled an essay in aesthetic. There must be a positive basis to such a negative argument; and the book is properly named after the positive affirmations on which it rests. Thus, an attack on the foundations of art or religion might be history, or psychology, or economics, or philosophy, and would be more properly so named than aesthetic or theology. I conclude, then, that theology may reasonably be construed as involving belief in God without sacrifice of its claim to be scientific.

But there is a further point. The discussion of subject-matter has brought me again to the conception of Natural Theology or Science of Religion, to which the discussion of aim also led. The question is whether there is any real distinction between this science and philosophy, whether it is not identical with the philosophy of religion, and thus at least as integral to philosophy as ethics or aesthetics. Clearly, a given philosopher may find no cosmic significance in religion, and in his scheme the philosophy of religion will play no part; but those who do find religion significant will need to exhibit its significance, and will not this chapter of their philosophy constitute the only scientific theology which their system allows? For reasons which I have given more fully elsewhere,[1] I am disposed to answer this question in the affirmative. The main reason is this: that in my view the belief in God, which is the central affirmation of religion, is essentially a philosophic judgement and can only be fully presented in a philosophic argument.

Summarizing the whole argument, then, we get the result that a theology can only become scientific by becoming a philosophy. While it remains distinct from philosophy, it is precluded precisely by what distinguishes it from philosophy from being purely scientific.

III

External Conditions

Under this head I mean to include every factor affecting the inquiry or its prosecution which cannot be regarded as following directly from the character of the inquiry. I have put this question last, and I propose to deal with it very briefly, not because it is unimportant, but because it might be held to be not strictly relevant. The pressure of public opinion, always strong in matters of religion, is perhaps a secondary phenomenon, which needs no particular discussion. The issue which, I think, ought to be

[1] *The Nature and Grounds of Religious Belief* (Riddell Memorial Lectures), Clarendon Press, 1934. (See *supra*, pp. 31 sq.)

raised under this head is the question as to the true nature and limits of religious authority with special reference to the study of theology. Archbishop Temple in his Lectures discusses at some length the place of authority in religion, but without that special reference.[1] 'Authority', he says, 'is an indispensable element in all vital religion', and he clearly thinks that within certain limits, which he does not try to define, a Church ought to determine authoritatively a theological orthodoxy. 'Heresy', he says, 'may be compatible in the individual with deep religion which as a whole is sound; but the Church is bound to regard heresy as for its purposes a more serious evil than some abberations which in the individual would be more pernicious.' It seems to be implied here that the Church is justified in imposing some kind of ban on doctrine judged heretical; and we know that in fact this has commonly been done.

What is important for our discussion is the consequences of such an attitude for the practice of theology. I think it is evident that the influence of the notions 'orthodoxy' and 'heresy', authoritatively defined and supported by powerful religious communities, considerably diminishes the possibility of a scientific theology. It may be replied that natural theology remains untouched by such restrictions, but in practice this is not the case. For a study of religious experience is not likely to be most fruitfully pursued by those who have none; the practitioners will, in fact, be members of Churches, and each Church will be on its guard to protect its own orthodoxy. Therefore, in actual fact the limits within which a scientific theology is attainable must be judged to be a good deal narrower at the present time than the preceding theoretical discussion suggested. The fear of heresy may be well founded, but to the extent to which it operates it cannot but preclude that freedom of speculation which is of the essence of the scientific spirit.

[1] *Nature, Man, and God*, pp. 328 ff.

XVI. WILL AND ACTION IN ETHICS[1]

I

ETHICS or Moral Philosophy investigates the application of the terms 'good' and 'bad'. We constantly use these predicates, and Ethics is an inquiry into our use of them. But this pair of terms is used over a very wide field and no one inquiry could cover it all. A ship or a tea or a house may be called good; and the investigation of such judgements would require a knowledge of ships, teas, or houses. Moral Philosophy does not pretend to cover the whole field or to investigate every use of the terms: it is concerned only with the moral use, or more explicitly with the use of the terms in reference to human conduct. And even this limitation may not be sufficient. Anything sought or desired by man may be said to be thought good in the moment in which it is sought or desired: we talk sometimes of a good stroke of business: we also speak of good actions, good characters, good men. All these three uses have reference to human conduct; but it may be doubted whether the meaning of good is not different in each use. But there is no doubt that the last is the use with which Moral Philosophy is chiefly concerned and from which the inquiry must start.

There are two obvious questions which may be asked concerning any predicates, and therefore concerning the predicates 'good' and 'bad':

(1) What do the terms themselves mean?

(2) To what subjects are they properly applied? i.e. what is the proper subject of the predicate in question?

The first of these questions would naturally be interpreted as a request for a definition. But it is an obvious

[1] This fragment was found among Professor Stocks's papers, and may be part of an intended book on ethics. It is clearly not in the final form in which he would have published it, but readers may be glad to consider it here in relation to some of his other work. It appeared also in *Philosophy*, July 1938 and October 1938, and is reproduced by courtesy of the Editor.

fact that not all terms are capable of definition. There must be a stopping-place somewhere to the process of explaining one term by another. We must be brought in the end to simple unanalysable notions in regard to which the method of definition breaks down. Now philosophy is concerned with these ultimate notions, and therefore definition is of little use to it. We should not be surprised to find that 'good' like 'being', 'beauty', or 'truth' is a simple indefinable notion, not capable of derivation from any more comprehensive notion. It is often questioned whether the method of definition has any great value in other spheres, but in philosophy certainly it has very little. A definition of good (in any sense) is therefore not our aim.

But there are ways of deepening and 'precising' our understanding of a term even though it is incapable of definition. We have, of course, to assume that the term is in use and is understood already. But on that assumption it is still possible and may be profitable to ask the second question mentioned above—what is its proper application? This question is not meant to imply that the customary application is wrong—or it would seem to contradict the above assumption. It is, in fact, necessary to assume that in the main it is right. If the upshot of the philosophical inquiry were to be expressed in such statements as: 'This which you call good is bad'; 'That which you call bad is good', philosophy would simply be giving a rival answer to a question asked and answered well or ill in ordinary life in the course of ordinary practical reflection. But though practical men are by fits and starts philosophers in some degree, philosophy would have no claim to a special place in the world of mind unless it had a question of its own to which it desired an answer. In the sphere of Ethics I say that the philosophical question is the one formulated above in the words: 'What is the proper subject of the predicates "good" and "bad"?'

To ask such a question is necessarily to embark on a *criticism* though not (except incidentally and by accident) upon a *correction* of current applications of the terms.

The terms, of course, are used erroneously. The same thing is called by one man good and by another bad, and each man thinks himself right and the other wrong: they do not think that both may be right. Hence there is actual error in regard to these terms. But even if all uses of the terms were correct and there were no such errors, the philosophic criticism of the terms would still be useful and valuable. It would take the common attributions as data from which to start, and would sift and test them in the sense that it would attempt to understand them better. It could not find terms simpler than good and bad for the predicates; but it could attempt to discover the general and essential nature of the subjects to which the predicates were applied. Every such attribution is particular (that action was a good one) or at most general (stealing is bad): it might seek for a universal and in finding it would arrive at a clear discrimination of the essential and the accidental in the things called good and bad. It is clear that the more adequate and consistent the customary attributions are the more chance is there that the philosophic question will find an answer, while, on the other hand, if the ordinary uses are utterly haphazard and confused, the search for an answer to the philosophic question is a search for a will-o'-the-wisp. In this sense moral philosophy presupposes the substantial rightness of the customary uses of the terms good and bad. But however right ordinary speech is, the philosophic question must humanly remain a separate question which requires a separate answer. Human intelligence does not find universals without taking the trouble to look for them, and it is only so far as the ordinary man, not conscious of being a philosopher, seeks and formulates some kind of universal by the way that he is a philosopher.

The discrimination of the essential and accidental and the effort to find a universal is usually regarded as a work of abstraction. Taken literally, that implies that the universal is a part of the particular, a part common to all the particulars which fall under the one universal, and the universal can therefore be formed by removing in thought the other parts of the particular wholes. This gives a simple recipe for finding the universal. Take a number of particulars which are suspected to belong together: analyse their constituents and discover which are constant and which vary from particular to particular: the sum of those which are constant will be the universal, i.e. the universal is the H.C.F. of the particulars. This is highly misleading. Any part of a particular is particular and not universal. The universal is not in that sense in the particulars at all. If the question is asked whether the universal is inside or outside the particulars, it is safer to answer outside than inside. For by particular is meant not the thing, but the thing as grasped by perceptual thought, and perceptual thought does not grasp the universal. This shows that it is wrong to think of a universal as a common element in all the many particulars. No part of a particular is universal: the universal is therefore not a part of the particular.

Yet the universal is to be found by abstraction, and philosophy is generally described as abstract thought. It is abstract from the point of view of common sense and ordinary experience in which we are all at home: the epithet is earned by the fact that the effort of the philosopher is to remove himself from that point of view, and in that experience his results have no currency. 'Abstract' is a negative description of philosophy, implying that much is left behind when thought passes to what is not perceived or experienced. The word contains a suggestion of depreciation: the abstract is thin, cold, unreal: what is, is concrete. But the philosopher is sure that his is the real world, and sometimes stigmatizes the world of perception as abstract and comparatively unreal. Which, then, is the real or concrete goodness—the goodness you experience in a friend or the universal which philosophy reveals? The question need not be answered. It is enough to see that philosophy in seeking the universal is seeking something which perception does not find and the perceived does not contain, and that nevertheless it finds its data in the world of perception and is somehow relevant to it.

Philosophy, then, seeks a better understanding of the terms good and bad, not by attempting to define those terms, but by seeking for the universal nature of that of which they are properly predicated. If its procedure is abstract, that word must be taken as only a provisional description, not as committing us to any view of the relative adequacy and inadequacy of philosophy and common sense or of the relative reality and unreality of their objects.

What is the proper subject of the predicate good? One and one only said the Stoics, and Kant following them— viz. the human will. The human will, when good, is not the best of many good things: it is the only good thing. The will is good or bad: all other things, without exception, fail to exhibit this distinction—are ἀδιάφορα ('indifferent').

'Good', says Zeno,[1] 'are wisdom, temperance, justice, courage, and everything which is or partakes of virtue. Bad are unwisdom, profligacy, injustice, cowardice, and everything which is or partakes of vice. Indifferent are life and death, repute and disrepute, pain and pleasure, riches and poverty, sickness and health, and the like.'

That is, in the sense in which virtue is good and vice bad, nothing else is either good or bad. Virtue must be considered an attribute of will, and all Greek philosophers regard wisdom (some with qualifications, some without) as an attribute of will and hence deserving the name virtue. The Greeks not having in their vocabulary a word precisely corresponding to our 'will', use as a rule the notion of action instead. Zeno's doctrine confines the application of good and bad to action.

The opening paragraph of Kant's *Fundamental Principles of the Metaphysic of Morals* puts the matter rather differently. He makes distinctions which the Stoics did not make, but on the main point his view is the Stoic view:

'Nothing can possibly be conceived in the world, or even out of it, which can be called good without qualification except a good will.'

[1] Cf. Ritter and Preller, *Historia Philosophiae Graecae*, 516.

He goes on to mention certain things which are called and are in a sense good, but are not good in this unqualified sense.

(1) 'Talents of the mind' such as intelligence, wit, judgement (cf. 'wisdom', above). 'These gifts of nature', he says, 'may also become extremely bad and mischievous if the will which is to make use of them, and which therefore constitutes what is called character, is not good.'

(2) 'Gifts of fortune' such as power, riches, honour, health, happiness. It is the same with these. They 'inspire pride and often presumption if there is not a good will to correct the influence of these upon the mind, and with this also to rectify the whole principle of acting and adapt it to its end'.

The goodness of which these two classes of things used by the will are capable is utility or usefulness, and in certain cases, when misused, they become unuseful or mischievous. What is unconditionally good cannot become bad.

'Thus', he says, 'a good will appears to constitute the indispensable condition even of being worthy of happiness.'

He goes on to a third class of conditional goods.

(3) Qualities serviceable to the good will itself, facilitating its action, yet having no intrinsic unconditional value. They are said *always to presuppose a good will*. The instances given are moderation in the affections and passions, self-control, and calm deliberation. These, he says, 'are not only good in many respects, but even seem to constitute part of the intrinsic worth of the person.' They are not, however, unconditionally good, 'though they have been so unconditionally praised by the ancients. For without the principles of a good will, they may become extremely bad; and the coolness of a villain not only makes him far more dangerous, but also directly makes him more abominable in our eyes than he would have been without it.'

The third class of conditional goods raises problems which we shall have to deal with later. Kant's words about 'the ancients' show that he intends here to criticize the Greek identification of the moral good with virtue. A *prima facie* contradiction may be noticed in his statement. If these qualities always presuppose a good will, how can they be compatible with a bad will? If they really constitute, even in part, the intrinsic worth of the person, how can their presence in the bad man make him worse? We may also observe that Kant identifies will with character, and that virtue is commonly regarded as pertaining to character. It is difficult to think of character or action except as marked by whatever of temperance, moderation, calm judgement, and self-control a man may possess. It therefore seems paradoxical to say that will is good or bad unconditionally, while these qualities are not. To these problems we must return: they are only mentioned here to show the divergence of the two views, which are nevertheless at bottom one and the same.

Essentially the two views are the same, since both assert that the moral good differs not in degree but in kind from other so-called goods. These other things have no right to the name good at all, says the Stoic. Kant says they may have it if some condition or qualification is attached to the term good. That condition is the presence in the man who has or uses them of a good will. Both views deny that the moral good is the best of good things: each says instead that it is the only good. Both views find this good in good conduct, but while one describes the source or principle of such conduct as virtue the other finds it in will.

A thing which is conditionally good fails to be good whenever the condition in question is not satisfied. The same thing therefore may be at one time and under one set of circumstances good and at another time and in other circumstances bad, if the good and bad are conditional. (So Kant argues from the fact that certain good things are also bad that they are only conditionally good.) The unconditional good, on the other hand, is always good. It may be unprofitable to itself or to others, but it is always good. Now there are some philosophies which make moral good, goodness of character or conduct, a conditional good. Good character or conduct, for example, may be said to be that character or conduct which profits its owner or which brings him happiness—or which profits the community and brings it happiness. The conduct is valuable for a result which it brings. It is hard to show that good conduct always is profitable (in either sense) or that profitable conduct is always good—i.e. the current applications of good and bad to conduct do not lend themselves easily to this interpretation. And such a theory really deprives the moral good of all meaning. Good is said to mean useful, and the word useful refers us to that by which the thing is used and the purpose for which it is used. But a man cannot be said to use his will; for to use is to will. Therefore the good will cannot be useful to the agent. Anyhow, the notion of profit or utility drives us away from conduct to something else for which conduct is profitable, and we should have to study that and determine its nature before we could discover what conduct is good and what bad.

Plato makes a triple classification of goods: (1) things good in themselves, (2) things good for their results, (3) things good for both reasons; and hopes to show that 'virtue' or 'justice' falls in the third class. But when men try to prove that goodness has good results, they usually beg the question. They show not that the conduct which we recognize as good is always good in its results, but that being good it is by that alone proved useful. But the utility of goodness is one thing and goodness of utility another. Conduct is, in fact, neither good because it is useful nor useful because it is good. Goodness is one thing and utility another, and we must be content to have the two ideas separate. It is best to content yourself with the class of things good in themselves, and avoid special pleading to show that honesty is the best policy.

Anyhow, the view which we have adopted from Kant and the Stoics is the diametrical opposite of any view which attempts to derive goodness from utility. The will is good and it alone is good: it is good in itself, as a picture is beautiful in itself, and not because it lends itself to any purpose or end of its own or any other being's creation.

We have now to consider what the good will is and what are the conditions of its realization.

In order to understand more clearly the meaning of the assertion that the will alone is good let us consider some common applications of the word good. A *man* is good, a *character* is good, an *action* is good. But since a man's goodness and goodness of character is shown in action, let us take the last assertion for our starting-point. The assertion that an action is good depends upon a conjectural account of the psychology of the agent, i.e. as we usually say, of the motive of the act, and is reducible to the assertion that the will embodied in the act is good. One man saves another from death by drowning or by other men's violence. Such an act would be presumably called good. But if it were discovered in some way that the man saved was the debtor of his saviour, and that the saviour's only motive was the wish to recover a debt which he could not recover in the event of death, the epithet good would be withdrawn. If again it were discovered that the man saved was the enemy of his saviour and that the saviour had worse things than death in store for him, perhaps the epithet bad would be substituted for that of good. This shows that if action is taken to stand only for the more external side of the transaction—for what is roughly within the reach of observation—actions are neither good nor bad. In the sense in which it is the subject of these predicates action is an activity of the spirit. What is called the motive of the action is either an intrinsic part of the action in this sense or the action itself. It cannot be separated from it. Common language calls actions good and also says that the goodness of an action depends upon its motive: from these two statements we can only conclude that the motive is an element in action, when action is made the subject of moral approbation and disapprobation.

When we talk of the results of an action, on the other hand, we use (or may use) action in a far more external way. For the most part it is true that the results are the same whatever the spirit in which or the motive with which the act is done. When the bullet is once shot the results are beyond the agent's control. The act is done, its results may be startling and unexpected: anyhow, the agent's intention in shooting will not affect them for good or evil. In this double use of the word action we have the seed of an ambiguity which has given birth to some fallacious arguments. The word must be used cautiously, always remembering that action sometimes includes and sometimes excludes motive: it includes motive when it is the subject of moral predicates and excludes it when considered in the light of its consequences and results.

The contention of those who say that the will, and it alone, is good and bad is that, when an action is called good, what is really meant is that an agent's will expressed in action is seen to be good. We have seen that the term 'action' is not unambiguous, and that its precise relation to 'motive' is obscure. What precisely motive is and how it can be discovered we shall have to discuss later; but if we put will instead of action we shall get rid of all ambiguity for the moment. What, then, is will? All action is an expression of will, and all will expresses itself in action. The will is the man *qua* active or agent. To act or do is to make some alteration in an existing situation. In order to know what the agent's will was, what you have to know is (1) the situation before action, (2) the situation after action, (3) what the situation before action appeared to him to be. Given complete information on these three points (which is difficult if not impossible to get) you have complete data upon which to judge the moral value of the action; you know what the agent's will was.

It may be objected to the above statement that there is will not expressed in deed and that there is will faultily expressed in deed. Besides the agent's knowledge of existing fact and the actual changes effected by his agency there is, the critic would say, his will—a third thing, not to be inferred from the other two. It may be that it is the will, conjecturally estimated, which is judged good and bad: but we cannot discover what that will was from what was effected or what was known by the agent, either or both together. A man may have the best will in the world to help and yet find no occasion for helping, and no opportunity for expressing that will in any way whatever. Or instead of helping he may, in the very attempt to help, hinder. So that the will may be either totally unexpressed in deed or totally misrepresented by the deed.

If this criticism were sound we might ask how will is ever known at all, how we are ever able to pass a moral judgement at all. On any theory, however, it is fairly certain that we are very seldom justified fully by the evidence in our moral praise and blame. And the critic would reply that in the whole and in the long run the will generally fulfils itself in deed—so that if we wait a little, withholding judgement, we shall discover the truth. That reply gives little handle to criticism.

The true answer to the criticism is one which we can all verify in our own experience—viz. that no man knows what his own will is except from his own acts, and that in inferring his neighbour's will from his neighbour's acts he is doing precisely what he does in his own case. A man may have a conviction, which seems like certainty, that in a given situation he will act in a certain way and have every 'intention' of so acting, yet when the time comes he may act in precisely the opposite way. The will is not, as we sometimes fancy, made up in advance: it is up to date and no more and readapts itself to each fresh element in the situation as it appears. It is only so far as the situation is (or is thought to be) made up beforehand that the will can be made up beforehand, and the act, as it were, done in advance. The difficulty in inferring another man's will from the effects he is seen to produce is not due to the obscurity of his will—for one's own will is equally obscure and unpredictable—but rather to the difficulty of discovering precisely what he knew.

By a true instinct the criminal lawyers have evolved a principle that the only thing which excuses a man from the penalty of the law is ignorance of the circumstances —one circumstance only excepted, viz. the terms of the law itself. (The exception is necessary because the act is made punishable at law because it is thought bad; it is not bad because it is punishable at law. We are, of course, only dealing with punishable acts which are also morally condemned.) Thus if the plea of good intentions is to hold good in the criminal courts, it must be reduced to the form of a plea of ignorance of some relevant circumstance or circumstances. Now I believe it to be a fact that 'good intentions', when it would be upheld as a valid excuse by a moral judge, can always be reduced to ignorance of this kind. A wife poisons her sick husband. How does she prove her good intentions? By proving that for some reason she was ignorant of the character of the drug she gave, so that she could reasonably expect to assist the cure by the action which in fact hastened death. If it could be proved against her that she was blinded by no such ignorance, her plea of good intentions automatically collapses. Thus if we hear of a will not fulfilled in deed or falsified in the deed and wish for more precise information, we should expect to get it in the form of an account of some ignorance or of judgement relevant to the matter in question.

But, you may say, there is another possibility, lack of opportunity. This is not a real possibility unless the will can be made up beforehand. The only real opportunity is in present circumstances, and such opportunities the will takes according to its lights from moment to moment throughout life. A plan devised beforehand and not relevant to opportunity in this sense is a mere day-dream and has no part in will at all. I may wish to be a member of Parliament, but that wish is only part of my will so far as it is already influencing my action, and it can influence my action only when it is in my power to take steps which will bring the achievement of my ambition—in some degree, however small—nearer. We do not will what is impossible, and lack of opportunity means in the end impossibility.

The unrealized will is a day-dream of disappointment—a theory of what we should have willed if circumstances had been different. Such dreams are more and less solid: such theories contain more and less of truth: anyway, there is no way of testing them. They are mere theory, and hardly more likely to be well founded when they concern oneself than when they concern somebody else.

The objection, then, may be ruled out. The will never expressed in deed is a dream, and the will faultily expressed is a fact mis-stated. The will always expresses itself, but sometimes through ignorance it alters events in a fashion which it regrets. As we are always insufficiently informed as to the circumstances in which we act—every action being therefore to some extent a leap in the dark—there is plenty of room for excuse and much need of charity of judgement here. 'They know not what they do.' It is the only excuse for failure, and it is the best rebuke to the pride of success.

It is implied in what has been said that the will cannot be put into words. When it has come into existence (i.e. *after* action) it can be described, like any other individual thing, but like other individuals never completely or exhaustively. Before it exists, too, it can be predicted, but only with the insecurity that clings to all predictions even when the prophet is he who knows the possibilities most fully, viz. the agent himself. It is important to remember that an assertion about a man's will is very often a prediction, i.e. a guess: a statement of what he will or would do under certain conditions. When will is used in the present with reference to future contingencies (e.g. will to help) or with reference to a man's state just before action, we are apt to think of the will as a simple proposition or proposal adopted by him; but in so thinking we delude ourselves. What happens is that a man, continually exercising his senses and his intelligence upon his surroundings, reacts continually to the information which senses and intelligence provide, and his reaction is that positive interference with circumstances which we call action. The simplest

actions are called by psychologists reactions or reflexes—
e.g. the shutting of the eye when some visible object, say
a fly, moves straight upon it—but they are actions, only
actions of a simple and inferior type. They are in principle
the same as actions of the most developed strategy. They
may be called simple and inferior because the element in
experience to which they respond is simple and inferior in
importance. The power of the developed will is largely
that of withholding response to the superficial features of
a revealed situation and responding instead to its deeper
and more permanent features. The soldier withholds
response to the whistle of a bullet by the simple and
obvious device of running away, and builds himself bullet-
proof fortifications. So as we gain experience of life we
learn to disregard little annoyances and disappointments,
and to deal instead with the more permanent current of
events.

Will, then, is a response to an apprehended situation.
We respond inevitably to the whole of what we apprehend.
If we have little intelligence and rely chiefly on our senses,
like children, what we apprehend is varied, rapidly changing, somewhat fragmentary: the natural consequence is
that the actions of children are vivid, changeable, and
disjointed. As the intelligence becomes more and more
competent to see through the kaleidoscope of sense to the
relatively slow-moving strata of experience, action naturally and inevitably becomes more sedate, more precise,
methodical, and consecutive. It is not unnatural that men
who believe that behind the puzzling variety of sense
experience is an eternal unchanging reality have been
tempted to believe that if men's minds could only reach
to that and concentrate their thoughts upon it, their wills,
without losing touch with the actual or relevance to its
demands, might acquire a like constancy and immutability
—so that their action while preserving like the world an
appearance of change and variety might express a will
which was always the same. Such a knowledge would be
like the sight of the Pole-star which, being alone unmoved

relatively to the earth, is a safe guide to the way over the earth. Without either adopting or criticizing such a theory, we may take it as an expression of the inevitable and easily verified relation of thought in all its varieties to action. The function of sense and thought is not (primarily at any rate) to forecast the unknown future or resuscitate the dead past, it is to give us information as to the actual present situation in which we find ourselves, and upon that information we act. The philosophers who believe, like Plato, in the knowledge of the eternal as the only safe guide in life do not promise us that we shall be able to deduce from such a knowledge by any intellectual process a sovereign plan for unravelling all practical difficulties or that we shall be able in virtue of that knowledge to predict the future. The world, they say, is eternal; we shall know the world; and to that knowledge our action will be inevitably responsive. Our will also will be in a sense not temporal but eternal, by the same law which governs the simplest sense-reflexes of a child or an animal.

Will, then, is a reaction to a situation as apprehended, and consequently power to apprehend what is is of the greatest moment to it. In such a reaction let us consider what place should be allotted to the notion of motive, a notion on which our moral judgements are often said to turn. Motives may be said in general to be named after a result which an action is intended to produce. ('Intended' is perhaps obscure since intention has not yet been discussed.) The reference to a result is sometimes direct, as when we say 'his motive was the desire to help a friend', sometimes indirect, as when we talk of motives of economy, avarice, &c. In these last two cases the sparing and hoarding of money are easily specified as the 'ends' or results-to-be-produced in question. Sometimes, e.g. when we speak of motives of affection or resentment, the reference is as much backward into the past as forward into the future. Generally any desire, affection, emotion, or propensity may be alleged as motive; and it is fairly obvious that the desire or emotion specified is intended to account

R

for and corresponds to the direction or tendency of the action, i.e. of the intended interference with circumstances. Sometimes quite nakedly as in the first case ('desire to help') the attribution of a motive consists simply in alleging in the agent a more or less constant tendency to move in the general direction instanced in the act. But in the end this is always the meaning of motives. They are something in the man rather more permanent than the individual will and on the other hand rather less permanent than the individual character which finds expression at a particular moment in a particular action.

Now if will is a man's power to react to circumstances by altering them and motive is a disposition to alter them in a certain direction, motive is will and will is motive. The only difficulty in such an identification is that the will has hitherto been considered as an individual manifestation in a single act while the motive appears to be something more general—so we might regard the will as the motive individualized in the particular situation and the motive as the will generalized into a constant tendency. But consider the facts rather more closely. What do we mean by the 'direction' of an action? All actions are necessarily selective: one thing only can be done at a time: always certain elements in the complex whole which we call the situation are altered in preference to others equally alterable. Such dispositions or desires as have been mentioned would betray themselves in this business of *selection*. In virtue of avarice, e.g. a man would be ready to alter any circumstance which obstructed access to money and reluctant to alter any circumstance which served as a protection to his hoarded wealth. Similarly in virtue of cowardice a man would be reluctant to alter any fact which safeguarded his person and ready to alter any that endangered it. But antecedent to selection is the observation which discovers what the situation is, and in regard to *observation* also the dispositions and desires would play their part. An avaricious man would perceive quickly any factor advantageous or disadvantageous to his special interest of hoarding and a coward would notice immediately the factors which made for and against safety. In the same way a selfish man shows his selfishness not merely in not acting so as to help others, but also constantly in not observing the effects which his action has upon the interests of his associates: he tends to ignore that element in the situation altogether and to see only what directly concerns himself.

Now the field of will is necessarily limited by the field of observation. Much of what is observed is in a greater or less degree irrelevant to the response in action; but it is quite certain that will or action cannot be a response (even if it is accidentally relevant) to what is not observed. (Accidental relevance is what we call a fluke.) The relation of observation to will is complicated by the fact above noticed that will (in the form of desire) to some extent determines our selective observation; but, confining ourselves for the moment to the single act, we may say that the limits of observation determine the limits within which will operates. A statesmanlike view of things is a necessary pre-condition of statesmanlike action, and narrow or one-sided observation creates a like character in a man's conduct.

It follows from all this that when we attribute a motive to action we implicitly assert an unverifiable hypothesis that a certain factor in the situation was especially prominent in the eye of the agent taking stock of his position before action, and that, of the multitude of consequences that any alteration has, one set of consequences was specially in his mind. The hypothesis is clearly unverifiable because we cannot get inside his mind and see what he saw, and even if we saw what he saw we should still have doubts because of the multitude of irrelevant detail which must cloud even the narrowest and most specialized observation. If a man acts so as at the same time to benefit both himself and a friend, who shall say that the one or the other consequence preponderated? There is no reason why he should know himself; but, of course, he may know,

since the one profit or the other may have been entirely
unforeseen or even the opposite of what he expected. The
important thing is that the attribution of motive seems to
involve, at least in the instances given, the theory of a one-
sidedness in the judgement of the agent and consequently
in his action; and since such a limitation seems to be a
defect in practical wisdom, it looks as if the good will
would be altogether free from motive in this sense—good
action would be unmotived action.

In short, motive is a desire which limits observation and
through observation limits action. But such limitation
cannot be a good thing. Therefore the good will must be
free from such desires. This argument is probably sound
in the main, but it will perhaps need some qualification
before it can be finally accepted. (But there may be good
or useful prejudices as well as bad, and to be without prejudices (in this sense) means that you are overwhelmed
by the press of detail. Selection, however risky, is a practical necessity.)[1]

II

We may look at the relation of will and motive from
another side as follows. Will, we have said, is an individual
response to an individual situation. Like the situation
itself, it is not a fixed thing persisting through change, but
involved in a continuous flow of change, readapting itself
constantly in one respect or another to recognized changes
of circumstance. It can have no more immutability than
circumstance, and if it is not to be left behind in the march
of events and become old-fashioned it should have the
capacity for the same rapidity of change. Now motives also
change, but in a different way. First one motive operates,
then another, as circumstance stimulates different inclina-
tions or dispositions: now fear, now curiosity, now love,
now hate are aroused separately and together. Thus
motives, as influences on action, come and go; but in

[1] This sentence appears as a pencilled parenthesis at the bottom of
the manuscript page.

themselves they seem more stable. Cowardice, avarice, generosity, personal love and hatred are at least deep-rooted tendencies capable of infinite repetition in action; and it is to such tendencies that we most often appeal in alleging a motive for an action. They are all tendencies to act in certain ways and therefore they are tendencies of will. If an avaricious man is to act generously or a coward to act bravely we think of him as having first to overcome something in himself which drives him in the contrary direction. There is postulated a discord and rebellion in the will itself, a struggle between two wills—or we may say the will is trying to overcome its own bad habits. Now such tendencies and habits of will are all summed up (and perhaps more besides) in the word character. What the avaricious man or coward has to overcome in such a case is nothing less than his own character. And character is thought of as something capable of change and development indeed, but also as constant and compelling, and often as forming with circumstance the determining cause of human action.

Looked at in this way motive and character seem to determine action and to deprive the will of power to deal with circumstance as may seem best. Action is determined by will, will is determined by motive, and motive is determined by character. There is thus no power of origination in will—even the growth or development postulated seems to spring only from new circumstances—and as the man is so will he show himself in action: will is the slave of character.

The only way to freedom suggested is that will, when good, is free from motive. Good action is alone free since it alone depends on no pre-existing disposition or desire. But what is this way of escape worth if, as we have said, motives are summed up in character? To be free of motive is to be free of character; and the good action which is unmotived will be characterless. But character is the personality itself, and if character is to go, with it will go all opportunity for love or friendship, all humanity even. We therefore have to choose between two horns of a dilemma: either all will is enslaved to character, or good action and the good man are colourless abstractions. That is the logical consequence of the doctrine that character in the form of a motive determines the will.

The position just sketched is a familiar one: much plausible but fallacious reasoning has been based upon it; and it is important to determine the outlines of an answer to it. Take first the general proposition that character determines the motive which determines the will. (Co-operation of circumstance, of course, assumed.)

This doctrine is an expression of our general tendency to explain the present by the past, i.e. of the conception of causation expressed in J. S. Mill's inductive logic by the formula 'the cause is the invariable unconditional ante-cedent'. Character is that in which the effects of past actions and circumstances are stored up in the individual ready to be brought to bear on new actions and situations. Through character, past action and circumstance deter-mines the response in action to present circumstance. The immediate antecedent which is the cause of action is the motive, but a motive like any other fact of experience has antecedents in past action which account for it.

Much of the apparent strength of the position vanishes if we reflect that motive and character (regarded as the assemblage of possible motives) are not separate and dis-tinct pre-existent entities of which the will shown in the action can be regarded as the consequent effect. It is the character and motive exhibited *in* the act which is judged good or bad, and what is exhibited in the act is not strictly speaking the same as anything that existed before the act. If, therefore, we are to talk of the present as determined by the past we shall have a present character-motive-act combination determined by a past character-motive-act combination, not a pre-existent character giving birth to a posterior motive, which in its turn gives birth finally to an act. The assertion will be, therefore, that past character determines present character and past action present action. The only other interpretation would make present character determine present action, but that does not square with a theory of causation which requires the determining cause to be antecedent to its effect. As re-interpreted, then, the doctrine is not that will is enslaved to motive and character, but that will, motive, and character are all alike creatures of the past history of the individual in whom they are seen.

But so interpreted the doctrine ceases to bear upon the relation of motive to will from which we started. It raises instead the metaphysical problems of the relation of present and past and of the freedom of the human will, and the problem of the continuity of human personality through all growth, change, and development. To these problems we must return later: for the present we must confine ourselves to the relation of motive to will.

Avarice, generosity, and other dispositions which serve to supply motives are not to be inferred from a single action. We rely on a series of actions which exhibit a common tendency. The motive specifies directly or indirectly, as we saw, the result to be achieved in action, and in thinking of the motive as repeatable and repeated we think of a general end which the agent keeps constantly in mind. A man's actions do undoubtedly hang together in some such way as this: the will has a tendency to repeat itself as far as circumstances permit. There is thus good inductive ground for assuming that the will forms habits; and it is as habits of will that avarice, generosity, &c., are best thought of. A tendency to habit means that repetition is easier than variation. If, therefore, there are habits of will, decision in any emergency will not be unbiased; it will be weighted in certain ways: and since such bias is a creation of a man's past history, in this form the past will at least to some extent mould the present. In this form the question of the value of motive again arises. Are such habits conducive to goodness of will? Are they not rather a limitation to its power and range? Mere absence of habits of this kind could not, of course, constitute either goodness or badness of will: but if they exist they must be of importance, and until we know their value we do not even know what a will really is.

The upshot is that we must for the present qualify our description of the activity of will by recognizing that a man comes to any situation that may confront him not equally free to originate change in every direction: besides the limitations imposed by circumstance, there are limitations provided by the lines of habitual response: to some extent, therefore, he comes to any emergency already compromised and committed. The question before us is the question as to the power, value, and extent of these limitations. But we have seen at least this—that it is wrong to think of such habits as limitations imposed by some external entity upon will: they are in will, habits of it: to it, therefore, they should appear (though perhaps they do not always) as freedom, not as slavery, as choice, not as limitations upon choice. It is only when we look at the man from without, and ask what prevents him from doing what is obviously demanded by the situation, that we see these habits as limitations and restrictions to the freedom of his choice.

Reflection on these lines inevitably brings us to the notion of virtue. The Stoics, as we have seen, described the moral good as virtue, and the moral bad as vice, and they were criticized by Kant for so doing. It is what the will is, he said, which is judged good and bad; but virtue and vice are properly qualities which the will employs. We have followed Kant in asserting that will alone is good or bad and that will is an individual response to an individual situation. But no philosopher would maintain that virtue was any such response or resolution. Virtue is always considered to be something more than a particular determination of will: it is regarded rather as something behind such determinations, controlling and as it were inspiring them, giving some guarantee of the agent's capacity to produce a similar response to any similar situation. Without such a guarantee of repeatability the act is held to fall short of goodness. Aristotle, for instance, realized that the moral good had its being only in action; but he held that mere inspection of the act unsupported by knowledge of the agent's character could not justify the conviction that the moral ideal was achieved in it. It was necessary, he thought, to know not merely that the act was as it should be, but also that it was the manifestation (1) of knowledge, (2) of purpose (disinterested), (3) of a firm and irreversible attitude. The first two requirements may be passed over: they are necessary only because Aristotle here takes action in the external sense.[1] When we say the subject of the moral judgement is will, we necessarily make it a judgement upon a purpose or resolution, and a purpose is formed in response to information received, and must be judged (as we have seen) in relation to that information. For by knowledge Aristotle means knowledge of the situation—of the circumstances of the act. It is the third requirement which introduces virtue. The externals of an act may be satisfactory, even though by chance or in obedience to command; but in those cases the act is no true act—no evidence of will. But further we are told, even when there is no question of chance-success or external origination, the act may be perfectly adequate and yet imperfect: there may be a tremor and inconstancy in the will which, while not obstructing the *external* perfection, should preclude us from asserting *internal* perfection. The steadfast and constant will is the proof of virtue, and when a man has it he has achieved the moral good. Good actions do not prove a man good, but they go to make him good. For goodness is a habit acquired, like other habits, by practice. If for some length of time we see that our actions conform in every detail we can control to those of goodness we shall in the end acquire the habit of goodness ourselves. Thus the greatest stress is laid by Aristotle on repeatability as a mark of the completely good act, and virtue (without which the completely good act is impossible) is a habit formed by repetition. As good actions produce good habits,

[1] Cf. above, p. 235.

so bad actions produce bad habits: the good habits are virtues and the bad habits are vices. As good acts do not prove a man good, so bad acts do not prove a man bad: before badness is asserted we must be sure of a firmness and constancy of purpose, accompanying the act, which is vice and, as it were, guarantees repetition.

The influence of this, as of other Aristotelian doctrines, has been enormous: it has moulded the language used on these subjects in modern Europe and still dominates our thought more than we know. It seems commonplace and common sense, because by the time we first meet it face to face we have long been familiar with its terms and features. We find it disappointing like the original picture seen after many years' familiarity with cheap reproductions of it. But in truth it is neither commonplace nor common sense: the doctrine of the *Ethics* is not even reasonably coherent. The emphasis laid on habit seems inconsistent with the autonomy of the will, and the whole doctrine suggests a distribution of moral praise and blame differing considerably from that which is customary in everyday life. The point from which we must approach the doctrine is settled by the preceding discussion. We were inclined to suppose that a habit is a handicap and limitation to will, and that a will which is to show its full power either for good or for evil must be free from such limitations. But we are now told that will, whether for good or evil, finds its realization in something of the nature of habit. Here is a plain contradiction which must be cleared up.

First, about habit. No one, so far as I know, has ever attempted to maintain that the habitual, as such, attracts a higher degree of moral praise or blame than the non-habitual. On the contrary we are apt to think of the growth of habit as involving in its own region a recession and diminution of will and attention, and an approximation to the automatic, which threatens in the end to remove it from the sphere of moral valuations altogether. In other words we recognize will as the subject of the moral judgement, and regard will as antithetic to habit: the more will the less habit, and the more habit the less will. It is therefore *prima facie* highly paradoxical to find the moral ideal in the exercise of a kind of habit. When the habit is fully formed, one would think rather that the time for speaking of moral good or evil was past. What is claimed for habit is rather that both directly and indirectly it makes for efficiency. Its direct value is seen in all forms of skill. If you think of the process of learning to play an instrument or shoot a gun or take photographs, &c., you see at once how large a part habit plays. Movements which at first needed effort and attention come to achieve themselves automatically and when they reach that stage they are not only more rapid but also more accurate than they were in the early stages. This is the direct value—increased rapidity and accuracy of movement. The indirect value is no less obvious. When attention and effort are no longer required they are not simply superseded. They are set free for other tasks. We can only attend to one thing at a time; but thanks to habit we can do several quite difficult things at once. The infant requires all its attention for the difficult matter of walking and, if it tries to talk as well, probably falls over; but we can walk and talk at the same time without difficulty. An accomplished knitter finds knitting so easy that she can combine knitting with practically any activity which does not require rapid motion or the use of the hands. It would be tedious to multiply instances. Indirectly the value claimed for habit is that it sets the attention free for other things. Under both heads the minimization of will and attention are admitted: these indeed constitute the value of habit as an economizer of human effort.

Now assuming that it is will which sets habit in motion— i.e. which *starts* the knitting, walking, &c.—it is obvious that habits of this kind do not diminish but actually increase the range and power of the will. A man with a number of spheres of action firmly held by such habits can do more things more accurately than one who lacks them. The number of possible occupations open to him at any given moment is made larger, not smaller, by his habits.

That is obviously true in these cases, but a difference and a difficulty is seen when we turn to the habits which are virtues and vices, or to those habits which are alleged as motives. These are habits *of* the will itself—i.e. they are comparable not to the automatic action of the hands with the knitting needles or piano notes, but to a habit (e.g.) to knit from five to six or to play the piano from nine to ten. Habits of the last kind obviously do tend to limit the agent's freedom of choice. We must therefore turn to habits of will and consider whether there are such things, what they are, and what their value is (positive or negative) to the human will. Do they make either for efficiency or for goodness?

When it is said that 'to form habits is to fail in life' or that 'the only habit a child should form is the habit of forming none' it is habits of this last kind which the writers had in view. They think of habit and will as essentially antagonistic, so that a habit of will means an inactivity of will. Will is considered as a capacity of free adaptation to the requirements of life and habit as a tendency to the repetition of the same manœuvre. They recognize in humanity this tendency to stereotyped reactions and regard it as a danger. The man who saves himself from it preserves his powers free and untrammelled. If in a novel situation the old oft-repeated manœuvres failed, the man of habit would be at a loss what to do; but the man of no habits would be free to act as seemed best. The novelty of the emergency would very likely discover gaps in his mechanical equipment, but on the internal side he would be free to improvise and to use what equipment he had to the best advantage. He would combine the freshness and power of youth with the ripe experience of age, and escape the dilemma expressed in the proverb—*si la jeunesse savait, si la vieillesse pouvait!* This view, then, gives as an ideal of efficiency an opportunism which excludes habits of will. To form a habit is to sell your freedom, to forsake the path of improvisation which shows an active will and brings success in life.

Writers, on the other hand, who extol habit and represent it as constitutive of the moral good, show a tendency to interpret habit rather in the other way as an acquired skill. But habit, taken in this sense, is not will; it is a gift or talent used by the will; and our moral judgements praise or blame men not for their talents but for their use of them. Habit in this application is not an originator of action; its function is that of so co-ordinating the parts of our procedure that one effort of will will do what twenty did before: it affects the internal machinery of action and makes it doubtless more efficient; but it is thoroughly within the will's control. The skill of the pianist enables him with one glance at a piece of music to execute a whole bar on the instrument, but his playing of the bar is as free and voluntary an act as the blundering piecemeal performance of the novice—more so, in fact, for he succeeds in doing what he intended better than the novice does. Thus the increased range brought by habit in this sense is not purchased at any cost to the originative freedom and adaptability of the will. But such habits, again, are acquired gifts which are employed by will; and the moral good must lie not in the gift but in the will which uses it. If, therefore, virtue is such a gift, virtue is not the moral good.

From these general considerations it would appear that habit cannot in either use be either wholly or partly identified with the moral good. In the one sense habit is the enemy, in the other the servant, of will. But before registering this conclusion let us consider virtue and the virtues and see how far habit in either sense is involved in them.

If courage is a habit, what kind of a habit is it? Courage requires for its exercise a situation in which a specific element known as danger is present: it requires secondly knowledge on the part of the agent of the presence of danger: courageous conduct is that of the man who does what is right in spite of the known presence of danger.

Knowledge of danger tends to produce in men a specific emotion, fear: and under the influence of fear a man's first movement is in the direction of diminishing danger by such simple means as running away. But the courageous man does not run away: he may feel the emotion of fear, but he is master of it to the extent of refusing the action to which it prompts: indeed, if right and duty point that way, he is seen doing the very opposite, increasing the danger which is the stimulus to fear without giving any sign of wavering in his resolve to do the right. Defined, then, with reference to the situation courage is right behaviour in face of danger; defined with reference to the emotion it is a capacity for conquering fear so as to do the very opposite of that which fear prompts. In terms of habit courage might be called the habit of facing danger or the habit of conquering fear. Its opposite, cowardice, would be the habit of retreat before danger or the habit of being worsted by fear. There is postulated a battle between the will and the emotion. Courage means the customary victory of will, cowardice the customary victory of the emotion.

If, then, other virtues are like courage, virtue is a capacity to persist in a course of action in spite of the presence of a disturbing emotion: the emotion disturbs because it tends to arouse a will to do otherwise: two rival wills (actual or potential) are thus postulated; and the victory over emotion is a victory over a 'lower' by a 'higher' will. ('Higher' and 'lower' are not meant to signify a moral difference or to beg any moral question. The higher will is the more general and permanent responding to a general and comprehensive view of the facts, the lower is the more momentary and transient relevant to a more partial apprehension: the will induced by fear, as we have seen, has reference only to that element in the situation which is called danger.) Virtue, then, might justly be called self-control or strength of will. Further, if virtue is a habit, that can only be because this victory over the lower self or will comes to be achieved more easily and completely with repetition. This, in fact, we are always told is the case, and some writers even point as an ideal to the state in which the disturbing emotions will have no disturbing influence at all. In such a state of complete virtue will, of course, would not be automatic: it would still be necessary, as before, to scan the situation and act carefully with due regard to it, and action would involve effort: but the control of the higher over the lower will would be automatic in the sense that the wayward movements of emotion would be stifled at birth with no conscious effort on the part of the agent. He would not be aware of his self-control any more than he is aware of the constant checking of tendencies to overbalance which occurs when a man stands upright.

It is hardly worth while here to test this account of virtue, drawn from the single instance of courage, by an exhaustive examination of other virtues. The traditional list of virtues is a muddle, and it may be doubted whether most of them have any real existence for modern popular thought. Even Plato's cardinal virtues—wisdom, justice, temperance, courage—are hard to co-ordinate under a single notion. Wisdom is at least a bad name for an attribute of will, and Aristotle himself found a difficulty in incorporating justice with the other virtues of character. Justice certainly deserves special treatment. But for our present purpose we may safely assume that courage and temperance are the only two virtues which are of importance, and that if we can bring them together we shall have little difficulty in dealing with other claimants to the name.

Temperance falls fairly easily under the same formula as courage. It is true that there is a *prima facie* difference in the fact that the enemy of temperance is not described as an emotion but as an appetite or desire. We have seen, however, that the disturbing power of emotion rests upon its arousing a will at variance with *the* will; and an appetite or desire is just such a tentative movement of will responding to some easily specified element in the situation, even if its direction is opposite and it is associated rather with pleasure than with pain. Anyhow, it is beyond dispute that in temperance also we find self-control, the victory of the higher over the lower will, the ability to persist in a course of action in spite of inducements to desert it; and here also we are told that practice makes perfect, self-control becoming easier with repetition, and are recommended an ideal of a state in which the tendency to pluck flowers by the wayside shall be so under control that the wayfarer will not be aware of it at all.

Virtue, then, we may conclude, is a habit of control: its enemies are emotion and appetite: it claims the name of habit since it becomes easier and stronger with repetition, and because it exhibits that approximation to the automatic which is the mark of habit. It can hardly be doubted that such a habit is a habit of will; but at the same time it is difficult to say that such a habit in any way lessens or restricts that capacity of free adaptation which is asserted to be the essence of will. The habit which is virtue, therefore, does not seem quite to fall into either of our two classes of habit. Courage and temperance are not the servants of will in the sense in which the skill of the pianist is: but neither are they the enemies of will as habits of routine are. It remains to discover their relation to these two classes of habit and their precise value to the efficiency and moral value of the will.[1]

[1] Here the manuscript breaks off.

INDEX

PRINTED IN
GREAT BRITAIN
AT THE
UNIVERSITY PRESS
OXFORD
BY
JOHN JOHNSON
PRINTER
TO THE
UNIVERSITY